# Wild & Wacky Weddings

D1623004

pil
Publications International, Ltd.

**Contributors:** Laurie L. Dove, Mary Fons-Misetic, Mary Kidwell, Erika Cornstuble Koff, Nina Konrad, Sue Sveum, Kelly Wingard, Kelly Wittmann

**Factual Verification:** Kathryn Holcomb

**Front Cover Art:** Adrian Chesterman

**Back Cover Art:** Shutterstock

**Interior Illustrations:** Art Explosion, Linda Howard Bittner, Dover Publications, Getty Images, Shutterstock

Louis Weber, CEO
Publications International, Ltd.
7373 North Cicero Avenue
Lincolnwood, Illinois 60712

ISBN-13: 978-1-60553-910-2
ISBN-10: 1-60553-910-4

Manufactured in USA.

8 7 6 5 4 3 2 1

# Contents

# Here Comes the Bride!

The official union between a man and a woman takes place in cultures around the world, from the top to the bottom of the globe. These marriages are cause for celebration: Two people are committing to live their lives together, from this day forward, 'til death do them part. So why not have a party to mark the occasion?

Because wedding celebrations are so prevalant and have been happening for so long, there's an entire culture surrounding them. In this book, we tried to gather as much interesting, weird, hilarious, and just plain fun wedding information as we possibly could. Here's some of what you'll find within these pages:

- Tattooed wedding bands: What's up with that?

- The story of Darva Conger, the emergency room nurse who won the 2000 reality TV show *Who Wants to Marry a Multi-Millionaire?*, only to file for an annulment immediately after the honeymoon.

- How *not* to shop for a wedding dress.

- A closer look at elopement. It's the perfect solution for some couples—could it be for you?

- Tips on how to manage your wedding when your maid of honor is…a guy.

- Plenty of stories about real-life "bridezillas" who managed to make their special day a total disaster.

- The unbelievable tale of the woman who married a fair ground ride. (Seriously!)

- Two words: Pet weddings!

This book is chock-full of quizzes, fast facts, and in-depth articles that will deepen your knowledge of the business of weddings, both today and in the past. Enjoy!

# Outlandish Marriage Laws

*Unromantic as it may sound, a marriage is a legally binding contract. Depending on where you live, the fine print may reveal some illogical or zany stipulations.*

## Faking It, Making It, and Breaking It in North Carolina

It's a Class 2 misdemeanor in North Carolina for a man and woman who are not legally wed to pose as a married couple when registering at a hotel.

If you are actually married, a North Carolina union can be nullified if it is not consummated due to inability to "perform." No pressure! Another unique North Carolina law allows a home-wrecking third party to be sued for "alienation of affection." In a 2010 case, scorned wife Cynthia Shackelford hauled her husband's mistress to court for breaking up her marriage and was awarded $9 million! That's a lot of affection.

## Will You Marry Me?...Psych!

In South Carolina, the Offenses Against Morality and Decency law includes a clause that prohibits males age 16 and older from falsely proposing marriage as means of seduction. So those prom night promises better be legit, or he could get thrown behind bars. However, there is a disclaimer that lets the guy off the hook if he can prove the female acted in a manner that was "lewd and unchaste."

## Absentee Wedding

One can become legally married in Montana without being physically present. A "double proxy wedding" allows stand-ins to recite vows before a judge and even sign the marriage license on behalf of a real bride and groom who are unable to attend (often due to military deployment or perhaps serious illness or injury). Way to represent!

# Offbeat Wedding Customs

*Around the world, different cultures celebrate
the bride and groom in some pretty unusual ways.*

## Tying

"Handfasting" is a tying ritual practiced in one way or another throughout the world. In some African tribes, it involves tying together the wrists of the bride and groom with cloth or braided grass during the wedding ceremony. For Hindus, a string is used, and for the ancient Celts, handfasting *was* the complete wedding ceremony: A year and a day after the tying ritual, the couple was legally married.

Among the *fellahin* in northern Egypt, the priest conducts the handfasting ceremony by tying silk cord over the groom's right shoulder and under his left arm; then he says a prayer and unties him. Next, the priest ties the wedding rings together with the same cord, and after questioning the bride and groom about their intentions, he unties the rings and places them on the couple's fingers.

Though they don't call it "handfasting," Thai couples link their hands together for the wedding ceremony with a chain of flowers, while Laotians use a simple white cotton string. But why just tie the couple's hands together when you can tie up their whole bodies? Guatemalan couples are "lassoed" together with a silver rope; Mexican couples with a white rope or rosary. In a traditional Scottish wedding, the bride and groom tie strips of their wedding tartans together to symbolize the union of their two clans.

## Breaking

Shattering crockery for good luck is a "smash hit" in a number of cultures. Russians throw their champagne glasses on the ground, as do the Greeks (along with their plates). Jewish weddings end with the breaking of a wine glass to symbolize one of three things: the destruction of the ancient Temple of Jerusalem, the end of the bride and groom's past lives, or that the couple will share as many years as there are shards of glass.

Italian couples also count the shards from a broken glass or vase to see how many years they'll be happily married. Gypsy fathers-in-law count to see how many grandchildren they can expect, and Czechoslovakians just say the more pieces of the plate on the floor, the better the marriage.

Ukrainians follow a tradition called *Vatana,* breaking dishes with silver dollars to symbolize future prosperity, while the German custom is to host a pre-wedding dish-smashing party, called the *Polterabend,* during which family and friends shatter china (because glass is considered bad luck) for the engaged couple to clean up—the first of many messes they'll have to deal with as husband and wife. Bulgarian brides raise the stakes by filling the dish with food—wheat, corns, and raw egg—before tossing it over their heads; an English bride might drop a plate of wedding cake from her roof.

Other cultures skip the dish and just break the food. Hungarian brides smash eggs to ensure the health of their future children, and Sudanese ceremonies are marked by the breaking of an egg outside the couple's new home to symbolize the groom's role as master of the house. Many Middle Eastern cultures observe a pre-wedding "grinding" ritual in which the unmarried girls drape a cloth over the heads of the bride and groom and one of the girls—the "grinding girl"—grinds two lumps of sugar over them to repel evil spirits. The Iranian twist on this ceremony involves shaving crumbs from two decorated sugar cones over the heads of the newlyweds for luck.

## Circling

This custom may seem a little "loopy," but it's practiced the world over. Hindu couples finalize their union by taking seven steps around a ceremonial fire. Seven is also the magic number for Jewish couples. Traditionally, after stepping under the *chuppah,* or wedding canopy, the bride circles the groom seven times to represent the seven wedding blessings and seven days of Creation—and also to demonstrate her subservience to the groom. (In modern ceremonies, the bride and groom will often circle each other to show equality.)

For other cultures, three is the lucky number for circles. In the Eastern Orthodox tradition, a priest leads the couple in their first steps as husband and wife three times around the altar—to signify the dance around the Ark of the Covenant—while the choir sings three ceremonial hymns. Croatian wedding guests circle a well three times in honor of the holy Trinity and toss apples into it to ensure the couple's fertility. Moroccan brides circle their new home three times before entering it and officially assuming the role of wife.

## Kidnapping

Likely a holdover from days of yore when women were stolen by rival tribesmen and forced into marriage, kidnapping is today a lighthearted custom practiced around the world. In a number of small German villages, the couple's friends kidnap the bride days before the wedding and hide her somewhere for the groom to find. The groom typically begins his search in a local pub, where he buys drinks for his friends to persuade them to help. In Latvia, the bride is often kidnapped by the groomsmen during the wedding reception, and the groom must pay a ransom (like buying drinks or singing a song) to get her back.

In some cultures, the bride and groom voluntarily leave. Danish grooms disappear during part of the reception so single men can kiss the bride; then the bride leaves so single girls can have a go at the groom. In the African nation of Burkina Faso, Fulani brides and grooms take turns hiding from each other—the bride before the wedding, the groom after. In both cases, it's up to the groom's friends to lead the search.

In Scotland, the groom isn't so much kidnapped by his friends as he is embarrassed. On "stag night," his buddies dress him up in drag, parade him to local pubs, and occasionally at the end of the night, strip him of his clothes and tie him to a tree in front of his house.

# Getting Spliced and Other Slang for Saying "I Do"

*Why just "get married" when there are so many better ways to say it?*

## Start-up Slang

**Tying the knot** is probably the oldest way to say you're getting married. It's so old, it's said to date back to a time when zippers hadn't been invented and buttons were rare—so people tied on their clothes. On the wedding night, the groom had the pleasure of untying the knots in his wife's clothing and undergarments.

The phrase may also be a reference to the ancient practice of "handfasting," or tying the hands of the bride and groom together during the wedding ceremony to symbolize their union. **Getting hitched** also comes from handfasting—even if "hitching" does also refer to a rope-making process used for tying up horses!

## The Sailor Way

If you want to be nautical, say you're **getting spliced.** After battle, sailors often repaired broken ropes by "splicing"—winding two pieces together to form a single line—and eventually used the phrase to refer to the marriage of one of their mates. **Knitting** may be another term sailors brought to shore: Knitting was slang for girls, derived from the perception of knitting as women's work. More obvious options are **dropping anchor, landing,** or **getting hooked.**

## Plain and Simple

If you want to go the literal route, you can say you're **middle-aisling it, wedding-belling it, settling down,** or **merging.** And if you're not so happy about spending your life with someone, tell people you're **putting the clamps on, snapping on the ol' ball and chain,** or **getting tied down.**

# Happy Meals and Happy Guests

*Forget $100 a plate sit-down dinners or lukewarm rubber chicken. Here's a look at some wedding couples that chose to go with Value Meals for their receptions. Literally.*

## Fast Food Fix

In the popular television sitcom *How I Met Your Mother,* Lily and Marshall ended their wedding day at a fast food joint after being denied food at every turn during their reception. In this case, there was indeed a traditional sit-down dinner, but waiters took away their plates and well-wishers interrupted them—resulting in their only food being champagne-soaked strawberries.

## They're Lovin' It

For some wedding couples, however, fast food is the real deal. One Madison, Wisconsin, bride and groom had a very logical reason for serving burgers at their wedding reception: The groom was the local Ronald McDonald! The popular clown and his kindergarten-teacher bride had a normal wedding followed by a reception at the community center—featuring burgers and fries from McDonald's.

## Over One Billion (Wedding Guests) Served

McDonald's has been the food of choice for quite a few wedding couples around the country.

- In Scottsdale, Arizona, one McD's was the site of a vintage car rally every Saturday night. The bride and groom both showed cars there on a regular basis, so when they decided to get married, the logical choice for the party was McDonald's.

- Trisha and Tyree Henderson held their reception at a Fairborn, Ohio, McDonald's. The pair met there three years earlier when they both worked in the restaurant's drive-thru lane. McDonald's might not scream "romance" to you or me, but the Hendersons fell in love under the golden arches. What could be more romantic than that?

- Cost was the main factor for a young New York couple that chose McDonald's for their reception. After buying a house, they were short on cash, so they were looking for a low-cost alternative to the traditional reception. Fifty guests enjoyed cheeseburgers, fish filets, 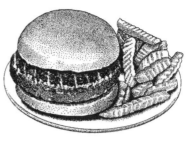 and Chicken McNuggets at a Long Island McDonald's. The meal was topped off with a Ronald McDonald cake and hot fudge sundaes—all for about $250.

## Think Outside the Church

Of course, McDonald's isn't the only game in town when it comes to fast food wedding receptions. Paul Brooks, of Normal, Illinois, rang in the New Year by proposing to his girlfriend, Caragh Brooks. The couple (who met on an Internet dating site) found they had many interests in common, including the food at Taco Bell. In fact, they liked the fast food eatery so much that they held not only their reception there, but the ceremony as well. Several dozen guests ate "Mexican" food amidst streamers and balloons, while the regular customers looked on. The bride's $15 pink dress brought the total cost of the wedding up to about $200.

## Something Different

If wedding cake is a priority, you might want to think Dairy Queen. It's not traditional buttercream or fondant, but a DQ ice cream cake is pretty darn good. Friends of Dairy Queen assistant manager James Manzano and his bride, Toni Walker, tested the ice cream wedding cake firsthand when the two became the first couple ever to wed at a DQ franchise. Twenty-four guests and a handful of customers watched the ceremony and stayed to munch on chicken fingers and fries. One eight-year-old spectator said she thought it was romantic to get married someplace where you don't usually get married—a place "where you can get ice cream." Out of the mouths of babes.

# "I Do" to Extravagance

*From enormous diamond engagement rings
to sumptuous get-away rides, we uncover a "who's who"
of outrageous luxury items.*

Weddings are once-in-a-lifetime events, so it's no wonder a little luxury is involved. For some wedding parties, however, there's nothing "little" about their festivities—or their outrageous expenses. We tip our hat (and our wallets) to couples in the following categories:

## Massive Guest List

When Sheikh Mohammed bin Rashid Al Maktoum, ruler of Dubai, married a real-life princess in 1981, the weeklong event cost millions. Of course, the tally doesn't even count the custom-built stadium that served as a backdrop for the wedding vows—and accommodated a whopping 20,000 guests.

## Best Scenery

In 2007, when Larry Page of Google billionaire fame married a Stanford grad student, even Google Earth may have run into trouble attempting to pinpoint the remote locale—an exclusive, private Caribbean island. And, as if the scenic locale wasn't enough, Page

rented neighboring island Virgin Gorde to offer the couple's 600 A-list guests plenty of elbowroom. Wondering about the massive price tag required to stage such a mass occupation? Yep, we Googled it, too: An estimated $2 million or more.

# Most Ostentatious Bauble

Pop star Christina Aguilera received a five-carat diamond engagement ring in 2005 from future husband and music executive Jordan Bratman. At the time, the heavyweight bauble was valued at about $100,000. Still, it wasn't as pricey—or as large—as the $2 million, ten-carat diamond engagement ring actor Michael Douglas offered to Catherine Zeta-Jones.

Both rings may be impressive, but they pale in comparison to the diamond engagement ring presented to actress Liz Taylor by Richard Burton. The ring featured a 69.42-carat, pear-shaped diamond. The attention-getting stone was mined in 1966 and originally weighed more than 240 carats; then it was purchased by famed jeweler Harry Winston and divided in two. After selling at an auction for more than $1 million, a significant portion of the diamond ended up on Taylor's ring finger. The diamond ring was so large and valuable, that in 1978, when Taylor sold it, it fetched enough to fund a hospital in Botswana.

## Unique Getaway Car

Rather than the predictable limousine, United Kingdom millionaires Barry Drewitt and Tony Barlow took a more whimsical approach to their send-off. A glass carriage, shaped like a pumpkin and pulled by six plumed white horses (à la *Cinderella*), transported the couple. Don't have room to stable all those horses in your garage? There are still plenty of expensive options. If you're 21 or older, have a valid license, lots of insurance coverage, and plenty of cash, you can book a luxury car for your big day. Whether it's an Aston Martin V8 Vantage Roadster or a Rolls Royce Phantom, you'll leave your wedding—and your life savings—in style.

## Over-the-top Gown

In 2009, just as the wedding season got under way, the Wedding Culture Expo revealed a truly over-the-top wedding dress. Located in China's Jiangsu Province, the expo's show-stopping wedding gown featured a design so unusual that it cost would-be buyers nearly $1.5 million dollars. Why? The gown featured multiple jade stones—and was covered entirely in showy peacock feathers.

## The Lady Wore...

*Before 1840, brides in the Western world were married in many colors.*

### Setting the Trend

Yes, sometimes brides were married in white, but just as often, they chose other hues—even black. Their gowns might be dresses they'd worn before and would usually wear again. After 1840, however, white became the color almost every woman wanted to be married in and many demanded a "special" dress that would be worn on their wedding day and that day only.

So what happened in 1840 to change wedding style so dramatically? Young Queen Victoria of England. At just 20 years old, she married her cousin, Albert of Saxe-Coburg and Gotha, a handsome German prince. And she wore a white wedding dress. Unlike many royal engagements, this marriage was not all about power or politics, though it would certainly be advantageous in those areas. Victoria and Albert were truly in love, and their love would change not only how brides dressed but people's attitudes toward courtship and marriage.

### Love and Marriage Finally Mix

When we think of "the Victorian age" now, we imagine a time of prudery and repression, led by an old widow in black. But when Victoria ascended the throne at age 18, she was fresh, youthful, and full of energy, if not beautiful. Her marriage to Albert was a good example of a larger trend that was taking place in the 19th century. Men didn't want to marry any ol' woman who could give them children, and women wanted to be seen as more than just housekeepers and breeding partners. Suitable companionship was no longer enough; people wanted to marry for love. And Victoria and Albert became the perfect role models. It was obvious to all that the queen had made a happy marriage that was, ahem, very active. Though Victoria loathed pregnancy and childbirth, the nine children she had with Albert makes it pretty obvious that she was unable to keep her hands off her husband!

## Nice Day for a White Wedding

When Victoria chose white for her wedding dress, it had nothing to do with morality, purity, or virginity. It was simply a fashion statement: She wanted to use a white lace called "Honiton lace" on the dress, but she couldn't find a suitable color to pair with it. Finally, she just decided to do white on white, and the Honiton lace was sewn onto a white silk dress. Of course, once brides began imitating the queen—which they immediately did—the color white came to represent the virginity a bride was "giving" to her new husband. Purity wasn't the only perceived characteristic of a white wedding dress, however. A white dress worn for one day only was also a sign of social status. Many people simply could not afford such luxury, so those who could enjoyed showing it off and even flaunting it in the faces of those less fortunate.

Throughout the Victorian era, of course, wedding dresses were long, but starting in the Edwardian era (around the turn of the century) dresses were cut in whatever styles were popular at the time. Everything old is new again, though, and this trend reversed itself in the 1930s. Since that time, the vast majority of wedding dresses, especially those for first-time brides, have been long and white. While it is highly doubtful that Queen Victoria would appreciate, say, a strapless, mermaid-style wedding dress, she might be pleased to know that she still has at least some influence on wedding style 170 years later.

# Real-life Wedding Crashers

*Sure, 2005's* Wedding Crashers, *starring Owen Wilson and Vince Vaughn, was a hit. In real life, however, the premise is not quite as funny.*

## Crash Like No Other

In September 2007, a reception hall in quiet Idaho Falls, Idaho, was home to one of the most audacious attempts to crash a wedding ever recorded. Throughout the evening, one of the female guests dined, danced, and snatched a bite of wedding cake before the bride and groom even had a chance to cut the first piece. The woman signed the guest book, chatted with the wedding party, posed for photographs, and helped decorate the couple's getaway car.

But, as newlyweds Sciara and Charles Dougherty would later discover, Kimberly Cooper was not on the guest list. Cooper, with her 12-year-old daughter in tow, stole hundreds of dollars in wedding gifts. When police discovered several wedding presents and gift cards from the wedding in Cooper's home, she blamed her daughter for the crime.

Cooper was also accused of crashing another wedding, just hours after the Doughertys' reception ended. Newlyweds Courtney

and Josh Van Tress became suspicious after gift cards went missing, and no one seemed to be able to explain Cooper's presence as a "mystery guest." When the couple saw Cooper the next day during a chance encounter at a local Target store, they confronted her—as she was busy paying for purchases with gift cards from their wedding.

# Dress the Part . . . or Not

Unfortunately, there are a number of accounts of wedding crashers helping themselves to more than prime rib and cake. In August 2007, Anthony and Jennifer Smith of Garden Grove, California, returned from their honeymoon to discover a guest stole money-filled envelopes from their cache of wedding gifts. The well-dressed guest wore blue and burgundy clothing—just like the rest of the wedding party—and made off with about $1,500 in cash.

But not every crasher blends in as seamlessly. In September 2009, police in Seymour, Indiana, reported that a man wearing a baseball cap and T-shirt appeared uninvited at Aaron and Margaret Thompson Brown's wedding, where he swiped a large wire birdcage filled with checks, gift cards, and cash worth about $5,000.

# When Crashing is Expected

For Angus MacLane and Tashana Landray, crashing a 2001 wedding made for a memorable second date. When MacLane and Landray married four years later, they invited others to do the same. Among the invitations was one addressed to the couple whose wedding they'd attended uninvited in 2001.

MacLane and Landray offered additional meals at their reception dinner, using place cards reading "Wedding Crasher No. 1" and "Wedding Crasher No. 2." Although no one laid claim to the name cards, a few wedding crashers did attend. One of them danced with the bride's stepmother!

# Celebrity Crashers

In September 2009, talk show host Rush Limbaugh admitted he crashed the wedding of Rick Yost and Heather King. When band members hired to play at the couple's wedding reception took a break and retired to the hotel restaurant, they recognized Limbaugh as one of their fellow diners and invited him to the reception. And Limbaugh's appearance didn't go unnoticed—a band member announced his arrival into the microphone. Guests looked perplexed, but the good-humored bride and groom asked Limbaugh to pose for a few photographs. He was reportedly relieved his stint as a wedding crasher had a happy ending.

# Say "Yes!" to the World's Most Romantic Places to Propose

*Proposals can pack a serious punch of romance.*
*So when it comes to popping the question, atmosphere is key.*
*Below are some of the best spots the world has to offer.*

**The Pont Neuf (Paris, France):** *Ay, me. Say amour.* Paris, France: the city of lights, the city of love, and most importantly the city of *ahhh*mazing proposals. An effervescent cheerleader for lovers everywhere, Paris is the epicenter for idyllic romance, so there is no surprise that its iconic structures follow suit. Pont Neuf, ironically meaning "new bridge," has now become the oldest bridge in France, making it a magical composition of old world charm and new age love. Available at all hours and completely void of any expense to roam, this distinctive destination overlooks the Seine River and is most striking at sunset when the city takes on an amber glow.

**Overlooking the Pitons (St. Lucia):** Every guy wants his proposal to be perfect. After all, it will be the story his bride will retell over and over again to anyone who will listen—at least until it is topped by the actual big day. So if the future groom wants to give his girl a ga-ga gorgeous proposal, he needn't look any further than the ga-ga gorgeous Gros and Petit Pitons in St. Lucia. Creating a picturesque backdrop of serenity, these volcanic wonders skyrocket over 3,000 feet from the admirably saturated blue waters below. Definitely a more costly alternative, this proposal spot can feature everything from a helicopter ride to a dip in the therapeutic Sulphur Springs.

**Hot-Air Balloon Ride over the Masai Mara (Kenya, Africa):** Hands down, one of the most well-known, well-loved adventures to experience, the calming nature of a hot-air balloon ride is undeniable, and when it's combined with the unmatched tranquility surrounding Africa's Masai Mara, there is no question of its magic. Sure, this kind of proposal can be rather expensive to accomplish, but when the outcome is a priceless result, it's impossible to compare.

**A Sunset Sail in Bora Bora (Tahiti):** Her timbers will surely shiver when you set sail at sunset in beautiful Bora Bora. The Le Meridien Bora Bora specializes in such proposals and can easily help any lovesick pup create a perfect memory. The epitome of Polynesian perfection, these sunset sails have all the ingredients for one outrageously quixotic "Will you marry me?" session: crystal clear waters, tropical breezes, sparkling champagne, and lovers at sunset. Bora Bora truly does offer more-a more-a!

**Central Park (New York, New York):** Central Park has been the mecca for romantic comedies the world over. From Carrie and Big (*Sex and the City*) to Ross and Rachel (*Friends*), film and TV watchers really connect with New York–based love affairs, making Central Park a no-brainer for proposal settings. Unlike most seemingly romantic spots, Central Park doesn't have to be warm to be beautiful. It is just as magnificent—if not more so—when it's cold . . . just one more perk to this already incredible park. And for a true man with a plan (and a little extra dough), the Per Se restaurant in NYC is ideal. Overlooking the entire park, the splurge-worthy dinner for two needs to be booked at least two months in advance but provides a nine-course menu, as well as personal service, to create a one-of-a-kind environment.

**Vertigo Restaurant (Bangkok, Thailand):** One of Thailand's most appetizing treasures, the Vertigo Restaurant—part of the Banyan Tree Hotel—provides the utmost in exotic atmosphere, but its striking appeal is only the beginning. Where this killer of cuisine really dazzles is in its efforts to keep every proposal personal. The concierge will work with every Prince Charming to provide sentimental touches, such as her favorite flowers or top-choice wine. Set 61 floors above the bustling city of Bangkok, this delectable dining experience makes a statement all on its own, but once it is accompanied by a beau down on one knee, the results are nothing short of electric.

# Birds Do It

*Mate for life, that is. And so do these monogamous breeds.*

- **Prairie Voles:** The male of this rodent breed prefers to stay with the female he loses his virginity to and will even attack other females.

- **Bald Eagles:** Like all raptors, including the golden eagle, hawk, and condor, bald eagles remain faithful until their mate dies.

- **Wolves:** Wolves and penguins practice serial monogamy. This means they have several mates throughout their lives but only one at a time. Penguins usually switch it up each mating season.

- **Anglerfish:** Like a parasite, the male bites into the female, fusing his mouth to her skin. Their bloodstreams merge together, and the male hangs there, slowly degenerating until he becomes nothing more than a source of sperm for the female. (Sound like any bad marriages you know?)

- **Black Vultures:** Gossip gets around—just ask a vulture. If one of them gets caught mating with a bird that's not its partner, it gets harassed not only by its "spouse" but also by all the other vultures in the area.

- **Gibbon Apes:** These monkeys make a close-knit family unit, with mom, dad, and babies even traveling together as a group.

- **Red-Backed Salamanders:** Males of these species are the jealous type, physically and sexually harassing their female mates if they suspect infidelity or even see them associating with another male. Yikes.

- **Termites:** Termites can mate for life (that's about five years) and raise a family together—but they often leave each other within the first two hours of mating if something better comes along.

# Fast Facts

- In Switzerland, newlyweds traditionally make a wish and break a pretzel in the same way people in other cultures break a wishbone or a glass. The Swiss still incorporate the lucky pretzel in wedding ceremonies.

- Pennies got their reputation as being lucky from the Victorian wedding saying "Something old, something new, something borrowed, something blue, and a silver sixpence in your shoe." In the United States, the penny replaced the sixpence as a guard against want for the newlywed couple.

- Jane Seymour, third wife of Henry VIII, picked out her wedding dress on the day her predecessor, Anne Boleyn, was executed.

- Egyptian pharaohs often married their siblings because it was believed that pharaohs were gods on Earth and thus could marry only other gods.

- The wedding of King Henri III of France was delayed by several hours when Henri insisted on dressing his bride's hair himself. He also designed her wedding gown and a number of her other dresses.

- During New Year celebrations in Germany, people tell fortunes by dropping molten lead into cold water. The lead takes a shape, and each shape represents something different. A heart or circle indicates an impending wedding.

- The first bachelor to become president was James Buchanan. He had been engaged 37 years earlier but backed out of the wedding. His fiancée, Ann Coleman, overdosed on medication soon after.

- For couples who last this long, the traditional gift for a 70th wedding anniversary is platinum.

# "I Do" YouTube

❧ ❧ ❧ ❧ ❧

*Weddings provide a natural center-of-attention context that unleashes everyone's inner superstar, and YouTube.com has become the go-to forum for sharing personal wedding videos. Some of these videos have surpassed the friends and family rounds and become mass email-forward fodder.*

## Now that's Entertainment

Kevin Heinz and Jill Peterson didn't wait for the reception to kick up their heels. Their ceremonial processional was a Bollywood-style dance sequence. To the catchy tune of Chris Brown's "Forever," bridesmaids and groomsmen sport sunglasses and shimmy, shake it, or even do The Worm down the church aisle. The groom somersaults in; then the entire wedding party, in a mostly synchronized routine, promenades back down the aisle to get the crowd pumped for the bride's entrance. The video was posted on YouTube in July 2009 and racked up a million and a half hits within months. The couple even scored an appearance on *The Today Show*. The routine was planned, but they didn't practice until an hour and a half before the wedding!

## The Psych-Out Surprise

By far, the biggest YouTube wedding trend is for the bride and groom to begin their first dance traditionally, but then abruptly break song to showcase a more upbeat house-bumping number. Sound effects such as a record scratching or skipping help facilitate the transition.

Alessandro and Jonelle begin slow dancing very appropriately to Edwin McCain's "I Could Not Ask for More" during their monumental first dance. However, to everyone's surprise, schmaltz tapers off midway through, and Jonelle suddenly struts her stuff to Michael Jackson's "The Way You Make Me Feel." And Alessandro has the moves, too! One might suspect he moonlights as an MJ impersonator for a cruise line.

Likewise, another couple cuts off "Endless Love" to bust a move to C + C Music Factory's "Gonna Make You Sweat" and other songs uncannily reminiscent of a 1991 "party mix" tape.

"Mr. Roboto" gets a lot of play. Soldja Boy's "Crank That" is also a YouTube wedding phenom, including a Father/Daughter dance where Pops tries his best to keep up. At least he has the "Superman" move down.

## Glitter Glove Optional

Many couples have turned to the King of Pop to liven up their weddings. "Billie Jean" and "Beat It" are YouTube wedding mainstays. There is even a cult of competing wedding dances to Michael Jackson's "Thriller." In one, the bride, looking like she took the whole bottle instead of just one pill, lethargically goes through the choreographed motions surrounded by several ladies.

However, the breakout "Thriller" hit was posted by cbu377. At first, the five groomsmen just walk around limply, like zombies, and perhaps people assumed they had been over-served at the open bar. But then the recognizable "Thriller" chords chime in. The men form a geeselike V and reenact the video's memorable dance number. The delighted crowd revels in their own little mob flash experience. As of 2009, the cbu377 YouTube video has attracted more than four million views, including 4,000-plus comments, and it averages the coveted five star rating.

## Not What Darwin Had in Mind

One of YouTube's biggest wedding hits has to be "Brian and Katie's Evolution in Wedding Dance." Part entertainment, part music history lesson, first, Brian gyrates to "Hound Dog," then Katie shakes her tail feathers to Chubby Checker's "The Twist." In rapid-fire pace, they zip through every cliché wedding song (think "The Hokey

Pokey," "The Chicken Dance," even "The Macarena"), as well as every song frequently heard on a karaoke stage, including "Ice Ice Baby," "Greased Lightnin'," and, yes, "Thriller." Brian and Katie have racked up more than ten million views and an impressive 8,500 comments.

## Wedding Bloopers

Everybody wants their wedding day to be unforgettable. Was it your scrumptious wedding cake that people will remember? Your heartfelt vows? Your gorgeous dress? Usually it is the unscripted moments that stick out in people's minds. And YouTube has plenty of unexpected "caught on video" wedding bloopers.

In one popular YouTube sensation, the best man steps up to hand over the rings. He trips, plows face-first into the bride's shins, and she falls backwards into the scenic pool behind—taking the priest down with her! The shenanigan has some viral viewers crying, "Fake!" Either way, people falling is almost always funny, and YouTube boasts an album's worth of wedding day pratfalls: A groom carrying his bride down a snowy trail slips on the ice, and they both wipe out; a flower girl missing the step and belly-flopping forward into the ring bearer; a groomsman fainting.

One video depicts the bride and groom making a sprinting getaway out of the reception hall amidst a shower of tossed rice. Maybe the groom got some rice in his eye, because he smacks into a glass door and hits the floor hard. The caption reads: "1 concussion + 10 stitches = 1 missed honeymoon."

## Burnt Toast

YouTube is also chock-full of recorded wedding toasts. Some are posted because they are legitimately hilarious or touching. Others are posted for cringe factor. And the beauty of YouTube is that every captured moment streams indefinitely. Forever. A lot like marriage.

- *In 1934, Lyndon B. Johnson and his wife, Lady Bird, were married with a $2.50 wedding ring bought at Sears the day after he proposed to her.*

# Need a Friend? How About Two?

*Wait . . . a wedding filled with guests that the bride and groom don't know? Is this the result of the biggest wedding-crasher convention ever, or did this couple simply hire people to show up? Well, thanks to Ryuichi Ichinokawa, they very well could have!*

## Rent-a-Friend

According to *USA Today,* Ryuichi Ichinokawa of Japan started renting himself out nearly four years ago and based it on "spare(ing) clients' blushes at social functions such as weddings and funerals." Seems useful enough in theory, but wouldn't the blush be even bigger if everyone found out a guest was rented? Talk about awkward.

As claimed by Ichinokawa, however, in all of the years he's been working the scene, he has never been discovered. Ichinokawa is a self-proclaimed master of faux best-man speeches and can be all yours for the low cost of $150. Wedding toasts and karaoke performances are extra. (For real, people, the truth is stranger than fiction.)

## The Booming Friend Business

Ichinokawa's business now houses 30 agents, which means the super-desperate can rent a best man, but they can also throw in a maid of honor, crazy uncle, "oldest, dearest" friend, and weird neighbor—basically the staples at every wedding celebration. Ichinokawa insists that his business is very gratifying. He's providing a service for the otherwise unserviceable, and after all the time-consuming prep work is done—it's showtime.

Showtime indeed, as Ichinokawa's company is merely the tip of the iceberg. There are ten other social agencies in Japan providing the same rent-a-friend services for all occasions. And while most brides- and grooms-to-be still choose to invite their guests the old-fashioned way, there is something to be said for a company of people who brave what, apparently, no one else could or would!

Weddings Through the Years

# Sing Me a Song...
# About Marriage

*Everyone knows the popular songs featured in weddings and receptions. But what about those songs about marriage and weddings?*

## 1900s

- At the turn of the century, the American economy was booming, and young people were optimistic about love and marriage. That optimism was reflected in the *fin de siècle* hit "When We are Married," by Harry MacDonough and Grace Spencer.

- "Under the Bamboo Tree," written by John Rosamond Johnson, Bob Cole, and James Weldon Johnson for the 1902 musical *Sally in Our Alley,* was a fun and silly way to say, "I love you."

- The 1907 "Wedding of Uncle Josh and Aunt Nancy," by monologist Cal Stewart, wasn't so much a song as a story, but that didn't stop it from hitting number 3 on the American *Billboard* charts!

## 1910s

- "I Want a Girl (Just Like the Girl That Married Dear Old Dad)," a 1911 smash hit with lyrics by William Dillon and music by Harry Von Tilzer, is still a sentimental favorite for many senior citizens today.

- "I Love You Truly," composed by Carrie Jacobs-Bond, went all the way to number 1 in 1912. It remained popular over the years when it was featured prominently in the film *It's a Wonderful Life* and the TV show *All In the Family* (who can forget Edith Bunker's, er, *interesting* rendition?).

- "On the Level, You're a Little Devil (But I'll Soon Make an Angel of You)," by Joe Young and Jean Schwartz, was the naughty way to propose in 1918.

## 1920s

- The '20s were pretty wild, and the sexual revolution had begun, but in 1925, Irving Berlin's "Always" was a pledge to remain faithful to one's best gal.

- "I Married the Bootlegger's Daughter," written and recorded by Frank Crumit in 1925, captured the zany spirit of Prohibition days.

- "The Wedding of the Painted Doll," a rather strange and almost creepy song by Arthur Freed and Nacio Herb Brown, was included in the popular 1929 film *The Broadway Melody.*

## 1930s

- So little is known about mysterious blues legend Robert Johnson that we cannot be sure what year his "Honeymoon Blues" was written, but we do know it was sometime in the Depression Era.

- By 1933, things had gotten so bad that singing star Dick Powell had to reassure a prospective mate, "I'm Young and Healthy" in the 1933 film *42nd Street.*

- Al Dubin and Harry Warren also wrote "With Plenty of Money and You" (also sung by Powell in *Gold Diggers of 1937*) about the frustration of having to put off married life because of the hard economic times.

## 1940s

- Loneliness and longing were the order of the day as American men went off to war and their fiancées and wives waited for them back home, as reflected in such radio hits as the Andrews Sisters' "I'll Be With You In Apple Blossom Time" in 1940 and Dinah Shore's "You'd Be So Nice to Come Home To" in 1943, which was written by Cole Porter.

- After the war, exhausted Yanks were ready to unwind, and lighter songs like Irving Berlin's "The Girl That I Marry," from the 1946 Broadway show *Annie Get Your Gun,* became popular again.

## 1950s

- Frank Sinatra's "Love and Marriage," with lyrics by Sammy Cahn and music by Jimmy Van Heusen, was a big hit in 1955, but it perhaps gained its widest audience as the theme song of the TV show *Married . . . With Children* more than three decades later.

- "Peggy Sue Got Married," by Buddy Holly and released on a compilation album after he died in 1959, was later the inspiration for the 1986 film starring Kathleen Turner and Nicolas Cage.

- Though "Hawaiian Wedding Song" was written in 1926, it didn't become a hit until Andy Williams released his version, which went to number 11 on the *Billboard* charts in 1959.

## 1960s

- Written by Jeff Barry, Ellie Greenwich, and Phil Spector, "Chapel of Love" was recorded by The Dixie Cups in 1964 and spent three weeks at the number 1 spot on the *Billboard* charts.

- Beach Boy genius Brian Wilson expressed his longing for domestic tranquility in "Wouldn't It Be Nice," a 1966 song cowritten by Tony Asher. (Fellow Beach Boy Mike Love would later sue for—and win—songwriting credit on this *Pet Sounds* track.)

- Stunning new talent Barbra Streisand belted out "Sadie, Sadie, Married Lady," with lyrics by Bob Merrill and music by Jule Stein, first in the 1964 Broadway musical *Funny Girl* and later in the blockbuster film version.

## 1970s

- When Richard Carpenter heard "We've Only Just Begun," which Paul Williams (lyrics) and Roger Nichols (music) wrote for a bank commercial, he knew his sister Karen could make it a huge hit in 1970 (and it is still one of the most popular songs for weddings to date).

- Paul Stookey's "The Wedding Song (There Is Love)" charted in 1971 after he first performed it at the wedding of bandmate Peter Yarrow.

- In The Fifth Dimension's recording of Laura Nyro's "Wedding Bell Blues," which became a hit on the cusp of the '70s, vocalist Marilyn McCoo begs fictional boyfriend "Bill" to finally pop the question.

## 1980s

- Oh, those cynical '80s! Billy Idol's nasty "White Wedding," an international smash in 1982, was quite a departure from the sickly sweet cheese of the '70s.

- "Kiss the Bride," Elton John's 1983 hit, was backed by a video of Elton pining after a biker bride (long before most of us realized he'd probably prefer the company of the leather-clad, Harley-riding groom).

- Finally, it was back to sweetness and sincerity with Foreigner's heart-tugging 1988 offering, "I Don't Want to Live Without You," which peaked at number 5 on the *Billboard* charts.

## 1990s

- Paula Abdul squeaked "Will You Marry Me?" on her 1992 hit, which was helped by the publicity surrounding her marriage to Emilio Estevez.

- In 1995's "Only Wanna Be With You," by Hootie & the Blowfish, frontman Darius Rucker expressed ambivalence about his girlfriend's desire to "wear my ring."

- Country star Clint Black and actress wife Lisa Hartman had a 1999 hit with the duet "When I Said I Do."

# Trash the Dress

*Wedding dresses have gotten more and more expensive over the years—some easily reaching the cost of a decent used car. So what do brides do with these priceless gowns after the big day? Trash 'em!*

## Trashing Trend

Well, maybe not *every* bride trashes her dress. Some brides sell them or donate them. Most probably still have them cleaned and wrap them up in the hopes of passing them down to their daughters. But there is a new trend that's appealing to today's brides. It's called "Trash the Dress." Now, this doesn't mean the wedding—or marriage—was a disaster. It has nothing to do with trashing the groom. Actually, it's art.

The idea was the brainchild of photographer John Michael Cooper, who says the concept has nothing to do with being destructive but rather going out and creating some art. The interesting element is the contrast between the pure, untouchable bride, and that same bride having fun—wild, messy, dirty fun.

Artist Lynn Michelle Renken, another photographer who has been capturing Trash the Dress moments on film since the early 2000s, believes the whole idea is for the bride to come up with a more creative way to express herself. It's a chance to do something she, obviously, can't do on her wedding day.

## Photography One Step Further

The wedding day photos are all about the couple, the purity, and the sheer perfection of the moment. Sure, they're having fun. There's joy. There are smiles. But there's something solemn on that day as well. It's sacred.

So after all that hard work of choosing just the right dress, having photos taken, and striving to keep the dress clean all night long, there is something fun about using that same dress to get a little crazy. And capture it all in a very different type of photograph.

Renken says she tailors these types of photo sessions to each individual bride or couple. People have really done a lot of creative things for their "trashy" photo shoot, but ultimately, it depends on what the bride's interests are—and how comfortable she is with mussing her dress. The gowns are rarely completely destroyed, but they probably won't be able to be worn again either.

## Trash It!

Some brides choose to go it alone for their Trash the Dress photos. Others include the groom. Some share the experience with other brides—everyone dressed up in their bridal finery.

One bride, who trashed her dress along with three close friends, was in it for the fun. The group hopped on four-wheelers and rode through mud puddles, producing photos that reflected pure delight.

Shana Dahan had her Trash the Dress pictures taken in the Las Vegas desert. Her parents had to ask: Was she sure this is what she wanted to do? She was. And the photos of a beautiful bride in a beautiful dress leaping through the blowing sand are striking. Dahan called it exhilarating.

Jessica and Samuel Goulet decided to act out a part of their wedding vows for Trash the Dress—"'til death do us part." The pair dug themselves a shallow hole in the sand, lay down in their wedding clothes, and scattered dirt on top of themselves. A bit macabre, perhaps, but the photo was certainly one to remember.

## Rock the Dress

While open to the idea, some brides are a little leery of the phrase, "Trash the Dress." Some photographers have started calling it "Rock the Dress" to put a more positive spin on it. They've moved past the mud to include photos of the couple rocking out in activities they enjoy—all dressed up. Scuba diving, horseback riding, and nature walks with the dog have all been captured in digital glory.

One bride got together with her new husband, her wedding dress, his tux, some paint, and a couple of brushes. Smiling and laughing, the pair shook colorful droplets all over each other. Now *that's* art.

# Tallest, Shortest, Longest, Oldest

*Of course every bride and groom are special—
but there are some who make world history.*

- **Tallest married couple:** *Guinness World Records* reports this honor goes to 7'5½" bride Anna Hanen Swan, who married 7'2½" groom Martin Van Buren Bates in London on June 17, 1871. But the tallest *living* married couple is none other than Wilco and Keisha Van Kleef of the United Kingdom, who stand at a towering 7' and 6'5", respectively.

- **Shortest married couple:** This title likely goes to Chinese groom Li Tangyong, who is a little over 3'7" and his bride, Chen Guilan, who is just shy of 2'4". They were wed in October 2007.

- **Shortest marriage:** In April 2008, Greek groom Mihailis Kutsakiozis and his Turkish bride Sevel Kelebik called it quits after just 30 minutes. But that doesn't beat the Saudi Arabian who ended his marriage immediately following the ceremony, after the bride's brother attempted to take a picture of the happy couple—against the groom's wishes. Rather than start a family quarrel, the groom simply divorced his wife (which he could do just by saying "I divorce thee" three times).

- **Shortest celebrity marriage:** As for Hollywood marriages, no one has yet to beat Britney Spears's 55-hour-long union to Jason Allen Alexander in January 2004—not even Rudolph Valentino and Jean Acker, who separated after six hours in November 1919: Their divorce wasn't finalized until 1923.

- **Longest marriage:** North Carolina couple Herbert and Zelmyra Fisher claimed the title when they celebrated their 85th wedding anniversary on May 13, 2009. At ages 104 and 101, the couple can also claim the award for oldest living married couple.

- **Longest engagement:** Octavio Guillen and Adriana Martinez got engaged in 1902 in Mexico at the age of 15—and finally made it down the aisle 67 years later at the age of 82!

- **Oldest bride and groom:** Blushing bride Minnie Munro was 102 when she married her 83-year-old groom, Dudley Reid, in Point Clare, Australia, on May 31, 1991. With a similar 19-year age difference, 103-year-old Harry Stevens married his 84-year-old bride, Thelma Lucas, at the Caravilla Retirement Home in Beloit, Wisconsin, on December 3, 1984.

- **Longest wedding ceremony:** Talk about growing old! Imagine attending the several months' long wedding ceremony of Qatr Al-Nada, the daughter of ninth-century Egyptian ruler Khumarawayh Ibn Ahmad Ibn Tulun. Apparently the event exhausted the resources of the Tulunid state and accelerated its downfall. More recently—well, from June to September 1904—the five children of Malaysian Sultan Abdul Hamid Halim Shah married in a 90-day-long ceremony.

- **Shortest wedding ceremony:** Westminster, Colorado, couple Corey and Autumn Pottratz married in 6 minutes and 36 seconds due to rain on July 7, 2007. But Reverend Robert E. Coté claims he performed a four-second ceremony in Los Angeles by skipping the "dearly beloved" mumbo-jumbo and asking both bride and groom, "Do you take _____ to be your lawfully wedded husband/wife?"

- **Longest wedding dress:** Though a 5,180-foot dress debuted in Bucharest, Romania, at the E-Marriage Fest on April 1, 2009, it was quickly overtaken on August 6, 2009, when Chinese bride Lin Rong sported a 7,093-foot gown handmade by her husband's relatives and pinned with 9,999 red silk roses. The dress took three months to make—and three hours to unroll on the morning of the wedding.

- **Tallest wedding cake:** The world's tallest (and heaviest) wedding cake debuted on February 8, 2004, at the New England Bridal Showcase. The seven-tiered, 17-foot-high spectacle weighed in at a whopping 15,032 pounds and could feed 59,000 people—roughly the entire town of Council Bluffs, Iowa.

# Bad Brides

*These ladies may have gone a little over the top on their wedding days. And we don't mean with the decorations…*

## Married Mugshot

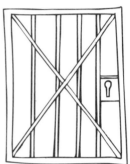

In March of 2009, newlyweds Jade and Billy Puckett left their wedding reception, only to be caught in a "March Madness" DUI sting that was being conducted by deputies in Harris County, Texas. When Billy was charged with driving under the influence, Jade became belligerent and was charged with public intoxication. But it didn't end there! Jade claimed she was not allowed to change clothing and was humiliated when an unidentified male in the courtroom took photos of her in her wedding dress—photos that wound up on the Internet. She filed a formal complaint with the Harris County Precinct 8 Constable's office just days after her arrest.

## Bridezilla Indeed!

Mark Allerton and Teresa Brown were friends for 16 years before they got hitched in a 2007 fairy-tale wedding at a castle in Aberdeen, Scotland. The castle is used in the popular British soap opera *Monarch of the Glen,* but the fight Mark and Teresa got into after the ceremony was even more dramatic than the show. According to police, Teresa attacked Mark with one of her stiletto heels, leaving him with a bleeding puncture wound on his head. Teresa spent two days in jail, but Mark stood by her, saying they had no plans to split. The bride claimed her freak-out was caused by a reaction to the antidepressant she was taking. Note: Might want to adjust those meds before the wedding.

# Breaking up the Band

Elmo Fernadez and his wife Fabiana had been married in a civil ceremony long before, but in 2008, they decided to renew their vows in a religious ceremony in Port Chester, New York. Everything was going swimmingly until the reception, when the band explained that they could only play music when the DJ was not playing. Fabiana didn't care for that excuse and went on a rampage, knocking over a set of $600 conga drums and destroying other equipment valued at $350. Girlfriend just wanted her money's worth! The cops hauled in Fabiana, her husband, and her daughter that night.

# Celebrity Wedding Ruckus

In 2007, groom Carlos Barron and bride Tara Hensley were arrested on their wedding night after partying at a Huntington, South Carolina, nightclub called Envy. Police said they had no choice but to arrest the couple and three other members of the wedding party after they received a report of shots fired, and the crowd refused to disperse. But when it was revealed that one of the arrestees was Cincinnati Bengals running back Quincy Wilson, the boys in blue had a little more 'splainin' to do.

# Two Birds with One Threat

Diane Carnes did something not-too-bright on the day before her March 2008 wedding. It seems Diane thought it would be convenient to schedule her wedding at the Scotts Bluff County, Nebraska, courthouse while she was already there taking care of a pesky suspended license violation problem. Her license had been revoked after a DUI, but she got caught driving again. At her trial, Diane threatened one of the jurors, but no matter—she scheduled her wedding for the next day and went on home. The thing is, threatening a juror is a little bit illegal, so when Diane showed up the next day for her wedding, she was arrested. What a way to start a new, married life!

# Wedding Chatter

"My wife and I were happy for 20 years. Then we met."

—Rodney Dangerfield

"Marriage is the triumph of imagination over intelligence."

—Oscar Wilde

"I think men who have a pierced ear are better prepared for marriage. They've experienced pain and bought jewelry."

—Rita Rudner

"One good husband is worth two good wives; for the scarcer things are, the more they are valued."

—Benjamin Franklin

"Never get married in the morning, because you never know who you'll meet that night."

—Paul Hornung

"Marriage is a great institution, but I'm not ready for an institution yet."

—Mae West

"'I am' is reportedly the shortest sentence in the English language. Could it be that 'I do' is the longest sentence?"

—George Carlin

"My husband and I didn't sign a prenuptial agreement. We signed a mutual suicide pact."

—Roseanne Barr

"Saw a wedding at the church. It was strange to see what delight we married people have to see these poor fools decoyed into our condition, every man and wife gazing and smiling at them."

—Samuel Pepys

## Weddings 'Round the World
# The Couple Who Saws Together

*Some of the German wedding traditions are reminiscent of summer camp prankster cruelty.*

### Short-Sheet the Bed, Too?

After a long day and night of being the center of attention, many newlyweds are exhausted and ready to retire to their room for their first night as husband and wife. Do candles and rose petals await? No way. In Germany, guests sneak into the honeymoon suite ahead of time to make the wedding night as unromantic as possible. This may include every unpleasantry from taking apart the bed to hiding multiple alarm clocks throughout the room.

### A Smashing Good Time

The night before the wedding, Germans may engage in *Polterabend.* This is an informal party where guests intentionally break fancy china dishes with the head-scratching logic that broken plate pieces will bring good luck. And the bride and groom get to clean up the mess! Or, in a more positive light, this allows them the opportunity to practice working together as a team.

### Getting off on the Right Foot

A hopeful mother may place salt and dill in her daughter's right shoe. For years, they will also stash pennies in the shoe until they have accumulated enough to pay for her wedding shoes.

### Sawing Logs

There is an old Bavarian tradition that the bride and groom would exit the church and encounter a log on a sawhorse. The act of the couple sawing the log in half symbolizes their tackling of tough tasks together.

# Weird Weddings

❦ ❦ ❦ ❦ ❦

*From a Ferris wheel to a public toilet, these couples said*
*"I do" in their own wacky ways.*

As weddings become more personalized than ever, some couples are putting their own wacky stamp on their big day. If creating a new "normal" is right up your alley, consider saying "I do" in one of these unusual ways.

## Cotton Candy Couple

When Tabitha Lund and Chris Brown look back on their wedding day, it's difficult to know what they'll treasure most: The Ferris wheel or the corn dog and cotton candy reception.

After dating for several years, Lund and Brown tied the knot amidst fairgoers and rodeo fans at the Benton Franklin Fair & Rodeo in Kennewick, Washington. Although they'd been up in the air about a theme, when Tabitha and Chris discovered a carnival-style wedding offered by a local radio station, they took the leap.

With just three days to find a dress and assemble her bridesmaids, Lund managed to pull off a massive to-do list and present herself as a bride before a roaring midway crowd. The couple, accompanied by a minister wearing the radio station's furry wolf costume, boarded a Ferris wheel. Within two rotations, they were pronounced man and wife.

True to form, the reception included stacks of freshly dipped and fried corn dogs, along with plenty of cotton candy. The best part, however, is that the couple will never wonder how to spend an anniversary. They received 60 years of fair tickets.

# Toilet Paper Couture

Jennifer Cannon of Lexington, Kentucky, wanted a custom wedding gown. But when she walked down the aisle in a New York City venue, her designer dress was far from traditional couture. Cannon and fiancé Doy Nichols won a contest sponsored by Charmin (yes, the toilet paper maker), and Cannon received a gown created by designer Hanah Kim using Charmin Ultra Soft and Ultra Strong.

To keep the theme, the couple wed in a public restroom in New York City's Times Square. Their wedding may take the cake for ingenuity, but we don't want to know where they spent their honeymoon!

# Walmart Wedding Vows

As Debra Bechtel and Mark Champagne planned their nuptials during the height of the spring wedding season, they ran into a snag: Every wedding hall in the area seemed booked to capacity. Then, the couple's boss had an idea.

Bechtel and Champagne, who both worked at a Palm Harbor, Florida, Walmart, were invited to wed at their workplace. Before long, in a cozy aisle between the men's and women's clothing sections, the couple exchanged vows.

As one might expect, the couple's wedding registry included plenty of Walmart items. This was a convenient option for attendees who arrived early to do a little shopping before the big event. But before you start wondering if the Champagnes took their work too seriously, consider this: They aren't the only couple to marry in a Walmart store.

According to a corporate spokeswoman, there have been several weddings at Walmart locations. The nuptials have included an 83-year-old greeter who met her husband while at work, and Crystal Newsome and Robert "Vick" Vickrey, two coworkers at a York, Nebraska, Walmart.

For Newsome and Vickrey, their union was a match made not in heaven, but in the deli department. The duo shared their first kiss in the Walmart Supercenter, so it seemed only fitting that they gathered friends and loved ones to exchange vows within its walls. They invited their fellow employees, thanks to a notice posted near the employee time clock.

# Maid of Honor = Man of Honor?

❦　❦　❦　❦　❦

*The times, they are a-changin', and weddings reflect
the tastes and cultural shifts of the times.*

Traditionally, a woman getting married selects her closest friend, a
sister, or the sister of her groom to be her maid of honor. It's a big
role and holds a special distinction in the wedding party. But more
than a few women in the past decade or so have chosen to put a man
in the maid of honor spot, eschewing traditional gender roles. So
how does it work? We're all still figuring it out, but here's something
to get you started…

## Maid of Honor, Project Manager

The role of the maid or matron of honor ("MOH" for short) is not
one that should be taken lightly. The MOH serves as head bridesmaid, taking charge of much of the production that is a wedding.
Jobs include: throwing the bridal shower; recording the gifts given to
the bride and groom at the shower, along with those brought to the
wedding (and then keeping track of that important list); dress shopping; addressing and stamping invitations; and of course standing up
in the ceremony next to the bride. This is an abbreviated list—the
jobs the MOH ends up doing are usually too many to count—but
one thing is for certain: The MOH is a special role for a responsible
person who really loves the bride. And sometimes that's a guy.

## A Trend Is Born

Over the past ten years or so, as alternative family arrangements
have garnered more attention and social acceptance than in the past,
the idea that a man could be a woman's "man of honor" has gained
popularity. If a woman's best friend is a man who is willing to serve
as the MOH, it may feel silly to go with someone else based solely
on what a set of people see as outdated gender roles. Over the past

few years, online bridal message boards and letters to the editor features of bridal magazines have lit up with questions about the etiquette of placing a man in what was traditionally a woman's role. By large, the answer was and continues to be: Why not?

Casting men in the MOH role is still rare, and your Aunt Bea might freak out a little at first, but the trend is here to stay. In fact, it's become widespread enough to have formed the story line of the romantic comedy *Made of Honor* in 2008, a movie in which heartthrob Patrick Dempsey is the MOH in his female friend's upcoming wedding. (Maybe invite Aunt Bea over to watch it with you—she'll warm up to the idea.)

## Does He Wear a Dress?

Should you give the MOH honor to your best guy friend, there are some changes that can and probably should be made to make the arrangement work. The MOH usually holds the bouquet for the bride during the exchanging of the rings, but if your guy isn't too keen on doing so, he could hand the bouquet to the bride's mother or grandmother after she's made her way to the front of the church—another way to win over any matriarchs who pooh-poohed the idea in the first place. Once the ceremony is over, the male MOH can exit solo, like the Best Man usually does.

It's up to your male friend as to whether or not he wants to attend fittings and/or dress selection meetings: Some will be thrilled to be there for the shoe-shopping type of errands, and some won't. No matter who is picked for the MOH role, as long as it's someone who can handle the job and do it with a glad heart, the bride should feel free to choose whomever she likes.

- *Oldest best man: At age 93, Gerald Pike performed the best-man honors for Nancy Joustra and Clifford Hill in Michigan on March 26, 2004.*

# Ooh La La: The World's Most Fabulous Honeymoon Suites

*Separating the ho-hum fun from the down right fabulous,
over-the-top hotel suites are sure to give "I do" swooners
forever memories or—in some cases—lifetime debt.
Below is a list of the most jaw-dropping, eye-popping,
wallet-squeezing honeymoon resorts found around the world.*

**The Westin Excelsior's Villa Cupola (Rome, Italy):** Valued as one of the most expensive hotel suites in the world, this $29,000 (and change) per night palace gives its guest the full-on royal treatment. With the ability to present a list of "pre-arrival" preferences, freshly married folks are made to feel like celeb-utantes. Even though the regal room is already adorned with authentic Italian frescoes, stained glass windows, and vaulted ceilings, every guest has the opportunity to fill the Villa Cupola with their favorite flowers, cigars, and amenities. The spoil-splurging stay also includes a private welcome massage, a fully stocked kitchen with more than 150 of the finest wines, a clandestine library, a Jacuzzi-bedecked fitness and spa center, and an exclusive cinema, complete with surround sound.

**Atlantis Paradise Hotel's Bridge Suite (Bahamas):** Newlyweds will be able to hobknob with the best of 'em after staying in this über-lavish suite. Soaring above the competition, the crown jewel of the Atlantis is suspended between its two Royal Towers and has housed some of the world's most recognizably wealthy clientele, such as Bill Gates and Oprah. For a staggering $25,000 per night, a couple can live it up in a luxurious ten-room suite featuring marble floors; a 22-karat gold chandelier;

an ivory-tickling grand piano in the 1,250-square-foot living room; an 800-foot terrace overlooking the island; and a ten-foot, four-poster bed.

**The InterContinental's Terrace Suite (Hong Kong, China):** This suite is all about its incredibly effervescent, state-of-the-art veranda, and for a meager $14,139 per night, the InterContinental will gladly open its doors to honeymooners everywhere. Fashioned with plush cushions for comfort, scented candles for ambiance, rose petals for whimsy, and mosquito netting for calming convenience, this hideaway's balcony is a force to be reckoned with. Putting even Romeo to shame, the Terrace Suite makes sleeping under the stars and Jacuzzi-ing by moonlight a simple credit card charge away. After couples are welcomed with a bottle of Dom Pérignon, they can toast to the amenities they'll receive, such as Rolls Royce transportation, 24-hour butler service, private spa treatments, yoga and tai chi classes, "romance" baths, and privately catered meals fit for a king.

**Eagle Island Camp's Private Suites (Okavango Delta, Botswana):** Couples looking for a little more bang for their buck will delight in the unmistakable atmosphere of Eagle Island's Private Suites. The most cost-conscious choice on the list ($2,010 per night), these adventure-driven abodes will provide all the excitement of a safari within the confines of luminescent luxury. Featuring outdoor plunge pools and copper tubs and showers, each sensationally secluded suite offers an enormous view of the heart of the Delta, giving honeymooners the chance to catch a glimpse of the island's inhabitants: hippos, crocodiles, and elephants (Oh my!). Not to mention, every honeymooning couple that reserves a suite also reserves the right to view game with an experienced guide.

**The Palm's Sky Villa 2 (Las Vegas, Nevada):** Playboy Bunny approved, this $25,000 per night hotel suite takes sexy to the extreme. With its virtually floating, cantilevered terrace, the Sky Villa 2's veranda features a full-size Jacuzzi with an unmistakable view of the Vegas strip. The lap of luxury continues indoors with three bedrooms—the largest of which sports a rotating bed—a media room, a private fitness center, and a personal butler. And what Vegas spectacle would be complete without its very own poker table? That's right, this ostentatious honeymoon bungalow even has its own private gambling area. Come on, big winner!

# How to Marry a Prison Inmate

*There has been an insurgence of people taking the plunge after their honey-to-be is already behind bars—some with no chance of parole and even some on death row. (Sounds appealing, right?)*

All rules and regulations will vary from prison to prison and state to state. However, generally speaking, there are a few provisos that should be followed... not to mention some serious consideration, mental reflection, and soul searching. After all, the divorce rate for a spouse incarcerated for more than a year is 85 percent.

- **Request a Marriage Packet:** The inmate needs specific marriage request forms. In order to *Jailhouse Rock* accordingly, both parties will have to fill out the forms completely and have the appropriate amount of money available through a money order.

- **Have All Required Documentation:** Proper identification, proof of age and citizenship, and all the necessary forms from the prison need to be polished and completed. (Lamination not required.)

- **Find and Keep the Correct Prison Contact:** Mainly done through the prison's family visitation coordinator, each couple should remain well connected to the person who will make sure all t's have been crossed and i's have been dotted.

- **Make Arrangements with Officiant:** Most prisons will have a list of approved pastors, as well as their own provided chaplain, who can offer succinct advice. (This ain't his/her first rodeo.)

- **Witness Needed:** Like all marriages, someone is required to be present to provide proof that this match is, in fact, legally binding.

- **Other Costs and Fees:** And like most things in life, love—legally speaking, of course—isn't free. Couples considering inmate matrimony will also need to make sure they have all their mandatory state debts paid in full. Well, minus the time served.

# Quiz

*Test your nuptial knowledge: Show what you know about these love songs, often used in weddings and ceremonies.*

**1.** The love song, "Longer" has been in many weddings over the years. Who wrote and recorded it in 1979?
a. Eric Clapton
b. Barry Manilow
c. Dan Fogelberg
d. James Taylor

**2.** What group sang the songs, "Truly Madly Deeply," "I Want You," and "I Knew I Loved You?"
a. 98 Degrees
b. Savage Garden
c. Boys II Men
d. 'N Sync

**3.** In "Always and Forever," Luther Vandross sang that what is "just like a dream to me?"
a. Your face
b. Loving you
c. The time we share
d. Each moment with you

**4.** The Temptations sang that they had "sunshine on a cloudy day." What made them feel this way?
a. The month of May
b. Love
c. My girl
d. Your smile

**5.** Faith Hill sang a song with which of these lyrics?
a. I can feel you breathe
b. I could stay awake just to hear you breathing
c. Every breath you take
d. You take my breath away

**6.** The song, "Unforgettable" was rerecorded as a duet with what father-daughter duo?
a. Frank Sinatra and Nancy Sinatra
b. Billy Ray Cyrus and Miley Cyrus
c. Brian Wilson and Carnie Wilson
d. Nat King Cole and Natalie Cole

*Answers: 1. c; 2. b; 3. d; 4. c; 5. a; 6. d*

# Stop the Wedding!

*The invitation to "speak now or forever hold your peace" was
too tempting for these ceremony interlopers,
who simply couldn't resist saying what was on their minds.*

**Caught on Camera:** When a 23-year-old MBA student decided
she couldn't "hold the peace," she took a camera crew with her. The
woman barged into a wedding ceremony in India, where she claimed
the groom had promised to marry her, impregnated her, and then
left her for another woman with a more attractive dowry. Expecting
trouble, the groom had changed the ceremony's time and, moments
earlier, had already married.

**Parental Prevention:** When Lemuel and Julia Redd decided they
opposed their daughter's marriage, they took action long before
the minister had a chance to ask if there were any objections. The
couple kidnapped their daughter and kept her out of the state—until
after her wedding day passed.

**An Official Interruption:** German police stopped a wedding by
leading the groom away from the altar. And just when shocked
guests began to believe something quite serious was afoot, they
learned the officers were simply quizzing the man about the theft
of wedding presents from his bachelor party the night before.
After guests began to boo, the officers quickly ended the ill-timed
interrogation.

**Between a Groom and a Hard Place:** In Hokuto City, Japan, a
man—who was already married—found a unique way to stop his
impending nuptials with another woman. He set fire to the hotel in
which his second wedding was to take place. Investigators reported
that the man, who lived with his wife, child, and his parents, ignited
a hotel hallway simply to avoid his wedding ceremony the next day.

# Fast Facts: Superstitions

- *Tying tin cans to the bride and groom's car will frighten away evil spirits.*

- *Victorian bridal couples were said to have very good luck if they married on the groom's birthday.*

- *Rain is the bride's old boyfriends crying over her.*

- *After toasting, it is good luck for the bride and groom to smash their glasses. That ensures the glasses will never be used for a better reason.*

- *It is bad luck for the bride to make her own dress.*

- *Bridesmaids dress similar to the bride to confuse the evil spirits.*

- *In Mexico, it is bad luck for the bride to wear pearls. It signifies the tears she will cry in her marriage.*

- *Don't let the groom see the bride in her wedding dress before the ceremony!*

- *If it rains and everything still goes smoothly, that means the couple was able to work under pressure to overcome obstacles and will continue to do so throughout their marriage.*

- *A penny in the bride's shoes will bring wealth in her marriage.*

- *It is good luck to encounter a frog on the way to the church. Just don't kiss it!*

- *Rain on the wedding day means the couple will be blessed with good fortune and fertility.*

- *If the new mother-in-law throws a shoe over the bride's head as she leaves the church, the two of them will be friends forever.*

# A Long-Ago Wedding Remembered

❧ ❧ ❧ ❧ ❧

*Though there are many medieval pageants, parades, and "faires" all around the world, one of the biggest and best reenactments of the Middle Ages is in Landshut, Bavaria (Germany), and celebrates a wedding that happened long, long ago.*

## To Marry Means to Ally

The Landshut Wedding is held every four years in remembrance of the wedding of George (Georg) of Bavaria to Princess Hedwig (Jadwiga) of Poland, which took place in 1475.

In 1474, the Ottoman Turks threatened the borders of Bavaria and Poland. And the leaders of these two countries knew they must appear to be strong allies against any possible invasion. What better way to show their combined strength than to marry the offspring of the two royal families? The marriage was negotiated in Cracow before the bride and groom ever met, but that was no big deal back in those days; royal children knew it was their duty to marry for political and religious reasons, not for love. Most "regular" people didn't even marry for love at that time, so the elaborate prenuptial arrangements wouldn't have struck anyone as strange or cold. That was just the way it was.

## Hedwig and George Get Hitched

Hedwig Jagiellonica was the eldest daughter of King Casimir IV Jagellion and his wife, the Archduchess Elisabeth of Austria. In a portrait painted in her youth, she appears quite pretty, with dark eyes; a long, straight nose; and a rather small, prim mouth. Her groom, who was also known as George the Rich, was the son of Louis IX the Rich and his wife, Amalia of Saxony. It took Hedwig two months to travel from her home in Poland to Landshut, but once she got there, she certainly couldn't complain that they didn't "put on the dog" for her. Numerous members of the royal family, the aristocracy, and the Catholic hierarchy feted her, plus, Salzburg's Archbishop Bernhard von Rohr agreed to perform the wedding.

Hedwig and George were married in St. Martin's Church in Landshut. Construction of the church had begun in 1380, and it would not be finished until 1500, but enough of it was standing so that the wedding could be held. After the ceremony, the couple led a parade through the Old Town to the Town Hall as 10,000 spectators cheered them on. And it's a good thing Louis IX was "the Rich," because all those people had to be fed and supplied with alcoholic beverages. It's estimated that they gobbled up 40,000 chickens, 320 bullocks, 1,500 sheep, 1,300 lambs, and 500 calves. The amount of beer and wine consumed is not known, but one can assume that it was enormous.

## Landshuter Hochzeit

In 1902, a group of Landshut citizens formed a society called *Die Förderer* (The Sponsors) and proposed to reenact the famous wedding of Hedwig and George every four years. The first bridal procession took place one year later, and the pageant has grown larger and more extravagant with every production. Over a century later, more than 2,000 participants (out of a population of 60,000) don medieval costumes to re-create the spectacle, and thousands more attend just to enjoy the show. The pageant goes on for three weeks, usually in late June and early July. Reenactors portray "life in the quarters"; joust as knights on horseback; play the music of 1475 on historically correct instruments; and dance as their ancestors once did, masquerading in colorful masks and regaling the crowds with juggling and jokes as jesters and fools.

It is considered a great honor to be one of the official actors in the Landshut Wedding, as the costumes are very expensive and maintained with the greatest care. One must have been born in Landshut to participate; however, all the citizens of Landshut and all the tourists who come to Landshut to see the pageant are encouraged to get into the spirit. The men of the town even grow their facial hair out for months before the pageant begins!

# Wedding Police Blotter

*In these real-life examples of weddings-gone-wild, there's plenty of fodder for front page headlines. When police arrived at these nuptials, they encountered all sorts of disturbances, from fistfights to shouting matches.*

**Crowbar Crasher:** When Lisa Coker showed up at her ex-boyfriend's wedding reception, she didn't come empty-handed. Coker, in her late-teens/early-20s, brought a crowbar and a razor blade to the Tampa, Florida, affair. After fighting with the mother of the groom, who then required 16 stitches, Coker was arrested.

**Groom vs. Fashion Police:** John Lucas, age 53, was arrested during his own wedding reception when a police officer working the event attempted to enforce the venue's dress code. Apparently, Lucas's nephew appeared at the Kenner, Louisiana, reception dressed in sagging pants. A police officer asked the teenager to pull up his pants, and he refused. Before long, the groom entered the fray and was arrested for disturbing the peace.

**Outspoken Ex-Girlfriend:** When Marie Salomon attended the Bridgeport, Connecticut, wedding ceremony of her ex-boyfriend, the minister uttered the weighted phrase: "Speak now or forever hold your peace." Salomon stood and yelled her objections in the middle of the ceremony. Eventually, police were called to the scene, and Salomon was charged with breaching the peace and trespassing.

**Attack of the Bride's Sister:** Annmarie Bricker wasn't invited to her sister's Hebron, Indiana, wedding reception, but she went anyway. Bricker wanted to talk out a few family problems, and by the time police arrived, the 23-year-old had wrestled the bride to the ground and pulled out clumps of the woman's hair. Bricker was arrested on a misdemeanor battery charge and later resigned from her job as a 9-1-1 dispatcher.

**Newlyweds Cash In:** Brian Dykes and Mindy McGhee wed at a quaint chapel in Sevierville, Tennessee, then promptly robbed the place. After the wedding, the couple waited until the cover of darkness and then stole a cash-filled lockbox from the chapel. They were later found at a local restaurant where they confessed to the $500 theft and were jailed on $10,000 bonds.

**Right in the Kisser:** How can a prenuptial party go wrong? When the groom kisses the bride's friend, for starters. Apparently, the bride's 12-year-old son reported that her fiancé smooched one of the female attendees. The bride-to-be tackled the groom, punched him in the face, threw his watch in the bushes, and broke his glasses. The Poulsbo, Washington, woman was jailed on assault charges.

**Bride and Groom Brawl:** Pittsburgh, Pennsylvania, newlyweds David and Christa Wielechowski spent the night in jail after duking it out in a hotel hallway. The couple insisted they were joking when the groom kicked his vociferous bride squarely in the rear. When hotel guests came to the bride's rescue and restrained the groom, the bride attacked them. The brawl then moved into an elevator and to the hotel lobby, drawing more guests to the fracas. The groom—a local dentist—was booked into the county jail with a black eye and only one shoe. His bride, still wearing her wedding gown, was in a separate holding cell.

**Makin' It Rain:** In Tampa, Florida, in 2009, groom Markeith Brown finished off his wedding reception by tossing dollar bills onto the dance floor while the younger guests snatched them up. Apparently, this didn't go over so well with one of the other guests, who made that fact known. And an all-out brawl followed: More guests got involved; non-guest reinforcements were called in; a policeman got punched; and the groom's grandma ended up with hands around her throat. Fortunately, the groom managed to avoid arrest, and he and his bride (who was none to happy about the whole thing) were able to go on their honeymoon cruise.

# Diamonds Are Forever

*While there's little doubt that the billion-dollar diamond industry has captured the romantic machinations of modern couples, some are beginning to challenge the notion.*

### So What Is a Diamond, Anyway?

The birth of a diamond is not as exciting as you might think. Diamonds are made of carbon, one of the most commonly occurring substances on the planet. Carbon is found in unimpressive forms, such as graphite (also known as pencil lead). But, when crystallized and pressed for millennia, something rather interesting happens. Eventually, all this pressure and a good dose of heat work to create diamonds—the hardest naturally occurring substance in the world. When harvested, cut, and polished, a diamond becomes the kind of shiny object that's desired the world over.

### What's Behind the Demand?

Committed couples have been wearing simple metal bands since ancient Rome, and by the 13th century, *sans* diamond betrothal rings were a mainstay of Christian tradition. In 1477, the first recorded instance of a diamond engagement ring appeared: The Archduke Maximilian of Austria commissioned a diamond ring (modest by today's standards) for Mary of Burgundy. By the 1800s, Americans were offering diamond rings to their betrothed as a matter of course.

The 1930s, however, changed everything. Smartly mastered diamond advertising campaigns upped the ante. These advertisements played on emotion and captured the attention of an entire nation. Behind it all: De Beers diamond company, who lobbied fashion designers to put the weight of their favorable opinions behind diamonds; talked Hollywood celebrities into flaunting large diamond rings during public outings; and convinced men everywhere that they should spend three months' salary on an engagement ring. And the campaigns worked. By 1941, diamond sales were up more than 50 percent in the United States.

To prompt continued sales, jewelers marketed diamonds as a rarity and as a symbol of eternal devotion. Indeed, what is arguably the most successful marketing campaign slogan of the 20th century still rests on the lips of many: "A diamond is forever." Frances Gerety, an on-deadline copywriter at Philadelphia-based advertising agency N. W. Ayer & Sons, authored the phrase for De Beers in 1947.

The diamond's popularity was cemented in 1953, when Marilyn Monroe sang the now famous line: "Diamonds are a girl's best friend" in the movie *Gentlemen Prefer Blondes.* Anita Loos's 1925 book of the same name seemed to capture Americans' future love affair with this sparkly gem: "So I really think that American gentlemen are the best after all, because kissing your hand may make you feel very, very good, but a diamond and sapphire bracelet lasts forever."

Still the world's largest diamond mining company, De Beers continues to fund advertising campaigns that seem to marry myth with emotion, and today, nearly all women who are engaged wear a ring—with at least one diamond.

## Why All the Fighting?

For many betrothed couples, knowing that some diamonds cost not only money, but also human lives, is troubling. Dubbed "blood diamonds" or "conflict diamonds," these stones are used to fund wars, particularly in central and western Africa, before they ever become part of a romantic setting in the West.

The problem became so widespread within the diamond industry that, in 2003, the United Nations adopted a system to track the origins of all rough diamonds. The idea was to stem the flow of conflict diamonds by ending sales of diamonds from areas that were hot spots for conflict. The process was also meant to encourage the humane treatment of those who mined the diamonds. Today, the Kimberley Process Certification Scheme (KPCS) is an international effort that's had debatable success. And while the average American may not follow the inner workings of the United Nations, some of the controversy surrounding diamonds became a part of the cultural landscape in 2006 with the movie *Blood Diamond,* which was set against a backdrop of enslaved diamond miners and fueled a growing debate.

Despite the intentions of many brides and grooms to buy "conflict-free" diamonds, it's still difficult to determine if this is the case. The jewelry store where a diamond engagement ring is purchased isn't likely to guarantee the stone has conflict-free origins. Fortunately, there are other options. Some companies, like Brilliant Earth, offer buyers a certification of diamond origin that tracks each diamond back to its conflict-free source. The iconic Tiffany & Co. reportedly deals only with suppliers using conflict-free, environmentally conscious mining. Some jewelers provide a KPCS or System of Warranties statement that illustrates the diamond's journey from mine to store. Other jewelers are taking a different, "greener" approach.

### What if You Just Want a Shiny Ring?

Enter the cultured diamond. A far cry from the cubic zirconia monstrosities of decades past, the modern version of a faux diamond is a brilliant imposter. Cultured diamonds, also known as synthetic diamonds, are gemstones created in laboratories. These gems are large and pure enough to mimic the real diamonds typically atop engagement bands—without the hefty price tag. Plus, the process doesn't create toxic byproducts or pollutants, according to Diamond Nexus Labs, one of the largest players in the cultured diamond manufacturing market.

Diamonds were even usurped during the 2009 Miss USA pageant, when Miss Venezuela, Stefania Fernandez, received a crown comprised entirely of cultured diamonds. Later that year, the Miss Universe and Miss Teen USA pageants followed suit.

Before long, it may be impossible to tell whether a "diamond" engagement ring is sporting the real deal—unless you're the one who paid for it, of course.

# Registries Gone Wild

*You've just gotten engaged, and you're excited to start planning
your wedding. It will be your big day. But don't forget
the gift registry! After the wedding day is long over, these gifts will
be yours to use and appreciate for years to come.*

## Gift Registry Evolution

The earliest wedding gift was food, which was brought to, and often
consumed at, the reception. That gradually branched out into things
that were needed for the home. Linens, candles, and baking dishes
were popular. Colonial Americans delighted in the gift of a handmade quilt for warmth on those cold winter nights.

But as handmade gave way to mass-produced, suddenly brides
were receiving duplicate gifts. Returns were probably not encouraged in those days—and how many cake plates or lemon juicers can
one household use?

Young H. C. Winkle changed that in 1901 at China Hall in
Rochester, Minnesota. The prestigious shop was known throughout
the area as an esteemed purveyor of fine china and crystal. Unable
to remember exactly what each bride wanted—and what had already
been purchased—Winkle came up with the idea of keeping a list. He
recorded each bride's china pattern and other preferences and then
recorded each item that was purchased. And the gift registry was
born. (Winkle went on to buy the store in 1924, and it remained in
the family for decades to come.)

In 1924, Marshall Field's in Chicago began using a gift registry
system of their own, and other stores soon began to follow suit. The
idea worked well and became
a staple of American weddings.
Then in the 1960s, Chuck
Williams of Williams-Sonoma
shook up the gift registry with a
new wrinkle: The gifts shouldn't

have to be china and crystal. Why not let brides register for everyday items? And so they did.

Then in 1993, Target launched an electronic self-service gift registry in their stores. And with the advent of the Internet, brides and grooms were soon able to register for gifts online, and their guests could view, order, and have a gift wrapped and shipped directly to the happy couple—all from the comfort of their own homes.

## Help for a Happy Honeymoon

Today's bridal couples are taking the gift registry concept even further. In addition to the traditional—albeit automated—registry, couples are now choosing to register for non-traditional items such as honeymoons, home improvements, and charities.

The honeymoon registry idea began in the 1990s. It was originally just an added service offered by travel agents when couples booked their honeymoon, but it has since evolved into a trendy, full-blown gift registry for every aspect of the honeymoon itself.

To get started, the couple contracts with a honeymoon registry company. This service generally takes about seven percent of the profits for their cut. A wedding website is set up, and guests have the opportunity to view the honeymoon site along with the add-ons the couple might enjoy. They can actually see what it looks like to parasail or get a massage at the couple's honeymoon location. Guests can choose an activity or service in their preferred price range and pay for it online. Some common offerings on a honeymoon registry include: dinner at an elegant restaurant, massages or other spa services, sightseeing trips, entertainment such as plays or concerts, scuba diving lessons, an upgraded hotel room, or even a portion of the airfare or hotel cost.

The perception of a honeymoon registry differs from person to person with some calling the idea tacky, and others calling it sheer genius. Peter Post, president of the Emily Post Institute, however, gives it the social graces seal of approval. He says it's a perfectly appropriate gift from an etiquette point of view.

One reason that the honeymoon registry idea has taken off is that today's couples are often older and more established in life than their counterparts of a few decades ago. Many already have a lot of the household things they need. Some are even already living together. And when that's the case, the couple just doesn't need one more toaster. But when the average American wedding costs more than $20,000, newlyweds might appreciate help in getting the honeymoon of their dreams.

## Give unto Others—Not Just the Bride and Groom

Another option for the couple that has everything is a charity registry. Wedding guests usually feel compelled to give something to the happy couple, even when they know they already have everything they need. So why not set up a charity registry? Guests can make donations to the couple's favorite charity in the newlyweds' names.

Or consider a home improvement registry. Unless the couple registers for it, no one is likely to give them a gallon of paint or pieces of flooring. Sometimes the bride and groom are buying or remodeling a house together, and they can save money by taking on a fixer-upper if they know that help will be coming through their dream home registry. The couple can register by the room, and friends and family can pay for items needed to complete each one. Through a special website, the gift-givers can even follow the improvement progress as it gets done.

## Easy as 1-2-Register

But whether you're looking for a traditional registry or something a little more out-of-the-ordinary, gift registries are easier than ever these days. Many couples create a bridal website that lists the places where the couple has registered. Bed Bath & Beyond, Macy's, and Target lead the pack as the stores most often used. And of course, guests can access the store's website and do the shopping right on their computer.

Most brides register about six months before the wedding, and nowadays two out of three grooms are involved in the process as well. While the registry is all about the couple, 40 percent of couples say their guest list influences where they decided to register.

Couples choose an average of 142 items for the registry, typically in a variety of prices. Whether you're just starting out, combining two households, or paying for a dream honeymoon, there are a lot of options—enough to please the gift-giver and gift-getter alike!

# White Blindness

*Your wedding is a once-in-a-lifetime event, right?*
*So why not splurge just this once?*

Weddings are all about love, and planning one can certainly tug at your emotions. Why, even the normally strong and levelheaded Carrie Bradshaw of *Sex and the City* let her fantasies take over when she was presented with the dress of her dreams. She couldn't wear that gorgeous designer gown to a city hall wedding—and suddenly the whole event began to spin out of control. That's what the wedding industry hopes will happen to you.

## Where the Money's At

There are more than two million weddings in the United States each year, costing an average of $22,000 apiece—that's a lot of revenue for the wedding industry, even if only half of the brides decide to splurge. Think of all the decisions for the bride, and thus, all the possibilities for the bridal shop. It's enough to make your eyes cross. Maybe that's why the industry calls it "white blindness."

The demand stays pretty much stagnant—it's not an industry driven by fire sales. So if they can't increase business, the wedding services need to set the bar higher. Brides are reminded that this is their one special day. How can you scrimp on your special day?

Even brides who are normally very practical women tend to get a little misty-eyed when they start thinking about their own wedding. It's an event that many little girls start planning with Disney-enthusiasm at a very young age. So when the day rolls around, it's easy to say yes to the dress—and everything else.

## Everyone Else's Expectations

Of course there are wedding professionals who have the bride's best interest at heart. Some of them have a soft spot for romance. But sometimes it seems as though this whole wedding planning thing is at cross-purposes with the bride. In your head, you may know that you should stick to your dress budget. But when the bridal consultant shows you a $1,000 to-die-for dress, it might be very hard to get excited about the $500 one. One wedding industry executive put it this way: "You are selling dreams, and you can charge anything."

But it's not just the industry that promotes wedding extravagance. Sometimes the bride's family is just as much at fault. Maybe your mother wants you to have the wedding she never had. Maybe she wants you to keep up with the Jones's daughter. Some parents save for their daughter's wedding for many years. Then when the bridal couple wants to have a small outdoor wedding, they succumb to the pressure of someone else's dreams—and finances.

And then there's the peer pressure. If your cousin had chair covers at her wedding last June, surely you need chair covers as well. And if your maid of honor got a $3,000 designer gown when she got married, you might suddenly feel awkward about shopping at David's Bridal.

## Head Versus Heart

The wedding business is a bit like the funeral business. There are decisions to be made when emotions are running high. Somehow, a second-tier wedding dress or cake or band may make the wedding less magical—and the love less perfect. Of course, we all know deep down that that's not true, but it's hard not to get swept up in the moment. That magical moment. And you find yourself choosing the dress or cake or band that makes you feel special, even if it is a little over budget.

You're not alone. Most brides exceed their initial budget by about 15 percent. There are ways, however, to cut back in areas that aren't as important to you. Receptions are often less expensive in the off-season or on a Friday night instead of a Saturday. Maybe you could skip the limo. And the engagement ring doesn't really have to be worth two to three months' salary.

So remember that it's *your* special day. Figure out what really matters most to you—whether it's the dress or the venue or something else. That's your dream, and yes, maybe they *can* charge you anything. Just skip those chair covers.

# The Man-gagement Ring

❧ ❧ ❧ ❧ ❧

*This male accessory has even-steven intent in Scandinavia but takes on other connotations in western parts of the globe.*

## Diamonds Aren't Just a Girl's Best Friend

In the United States, it's not unusual to see a woman sporting an engagement ring. It is, however, a bit more rare to see her male counterpart doing the same. Not so in Scandinavia, which includes the countries of Finland, Iceland, Denmark, Norway, and Sweden. In this part of the world, when a couple gets engaged, they both wear rings that publicly symbolize their intent to wed. It's also a way for both people in the relationship to signal that they're "taken" during a pre-marriage period that may last up to four years. In Scandinavia, couples have plenty of time to explore their relationship and get to know prospective families-in-law.

These male/female engagement rings also are a symbol of equality in a region with a historic reputation for gender fairness. Norway, for example, is one of the most gender-equal countries on the globe. There's even a law requiring women to occupy at least 40 percent of the seats on corporate boards.

## Equally Betrothed

In Scandinavia, male engagement rings come with a few etiquette rules to follow. A man should wear his engagement ring on the ring finger of his left hand—the same spot reserved for a wedding band—until the wedding ceremony. At that time, the engagement ring should be transferred to the ring finger of his right hand.

And the idea of a man-gagement ring is spreading. In early 2009, a jeweler in Great Britain began marketing engagement rings for men. Although the rings are significantly less expensive (by about $1,900) than women's engagement rings, they're still being met with mixed reviews.

# Wedding Chatter

"Keep your eyes wide open before marriage, half shut afterwards."

—Benjamin Franklin

"Lovers don't finally meet somewhere. They're in each other all along."

—Rumi

"I love being married. It's so great to find one special person you want to annoy for the rest of your life."

—Rita Rudner

"Love is an irresistible desire to be irresistibly desired."

—Robert Frost

"Love is life. And if you miss love, you miss life."

—Leo Buscaglia

"Never go to bed mad—stay up and fight."

—Phyllis Diller

"You come to love not by finding the perfect person, but by seeing an imperfect person perfectly."

—Sam Keen

"Love has nothing to do with what you are expecting to get—only with what you are expecting to give—which is everything."

—Katharine Hepburn

"Never feel remorse for what you have thought about your wife; she has thought much worse things about you."

—Jean Rostand, *Le Mariage,* 1927

"There is no more lovely, friendly, charming relationship, communion or company than a good marriage."

—Martin Luther

# Jumping the Broom

*For hundreds of years, African American slaves had no power or control over their own lives—yet they continued to marry, bringing their own tradition to a well-known ceremony.*

## A Bittersweet Tradition

As slaves, they could be sold away from their spouses, parents, children, and friends at a moment's notice, and once sold, they almost never saw those loved ones again. Yet despite knowing this awful reality, slaves continued to fall in love and marry, hoping against hope that one day they would have the legal right to possess their own bodies and call themselves families.

Of course, the marriages of slaves had no standing in the white world and were either ignored or debased by slave owners. To most slave owners, all that mattered was that their slaves were having children and creating more human property—whether they called it "marriage" or not was irrelevant. But many slaves had adopted the Christian religion of their masters, and the marriage ceremony meant a great deal to them, even if it meant nothing legally. Other slaves usually performed slave weddings, though once in a while a white minister would agree to preside.

Though the customs that grew out of slave weddings varied from place to place in the southern United States, one was almost universal: jumping the broom. After the vows were taken, a broom would be placed on the ground before the couple, and the two would jump over it—into the land of matrimony. This act may not have meant anything to people in the "outside world," but it meant something to the couple's immediate circle, as well as to the entire slave community: These two people were now married. Everyone else, hands off.

The roots of the tradition of jumping the broom go all the way back to Africa, where brooms were a potent symbol of domestic life. In Ghana, brooms were waved over the heads of the newlyweds at the feast following the wedding ceremony. In other parts of Africa, on the day after her wedding, the young bride would be expected to participate in a ritual in which she and her female in-laws swept out her new home. This signified her willingness to adapt to her new family and cooperate with them in communal work. Like many other African customs and symbols, the broom ritual followed slaves to America and evolved over hundreds of years.

## Bringing Back the Broom

In the mid-20th century, many whites had never heard of jumping the broom, and even some African Americans were unaware of it. But Alex Haley's 1976 book, *Roots: The Saga of an American Family*, changed all that. In one of the most famous scenes in the reality-based novel, Haley's ancestor, the slave Kunta Kinte (or "Toby"), is married to Bell, the cook on his master's estate. After taking their vows, Kunta and Bell jump the broom. When a blockbuster miniseries based on the book was aired in 1977, 130 million viewers watched actors John Amos and Madge Sinclair recreate this moment.

*Roots* was not the only thing in the 1970s to stir memories of slave traditions, however. Black leaders, civil rights groups, and black churches were encouraging African Americans to learn their history and take pride in their customs, even those—*especially* those—that grew out of great pain and suffering. Black couples began to reincorporate jumping the broom into their weddings, and now it is an almost expected part of the African American matrimonial experience. When discouraged at a church ceremony—for example, a Catholic wedding mass—it can easily be moved to the reception, but it's a tradition many African American brides and grooms insist on honoring in remembrance of those who had nothing else.

"Love: a temporary insanity, curable by marriage."

—Ambrose Bierce

# A Rocker Weds, a Career Is (Almost) Dead

*In 1957, Jerry Lee Lewis had it all after clawing his way to the top of the rock 'n' roll world with his electrifying piano playing and howling, sexy vocals. That is, until he married his 13-year-old cousin.*

## The High Climb to Fame and Fortune

It hadn't been easy for Jerry Lee Lewis. He was born in 1935, into grinding poverty in Ferriday, Louisiana. Though his family was devoutly Christian (his cousin, Jimmy Swaggart, would one day gain fame and notoriety as a preacher), the young Lewis was drawn to the rhythm and blues he heard on the radio and at Haney's Big House, an African American juke joint "on the other side of the tracks." When Lewis's parents mortgaged their farm to buy him a piano, they hoped he would make music for the Lord. Instead, Jerry began to tour the southeast playing rockabilly, an early form of rock 'n' roll.

Lewis was signed by Sun Records in Memphis, Tennessee, in late 1956 and immediately began backing such important artists as Carl Perkins and Johnny Cash on piano. But Lewis wanted to be a star in his own right, even though some told him it would be impossible unless he abandoned the piano for the guitar. He soon proved the naysayers wrong with two huge piano-driven hits, "Whole Lotta Shakin' Goin' On" and "Great Balls of Fire." Although many early rock 'n' roll artists traded on sexual innuendo, very few matched Lewis in their brazenness. His sex-drenched lyrics and orgasmic yelps caused some radio stations to boycott him, but this forbidden fruit aspect only made "the kids" want his music more.

## Lewis's Lolita

Lewis knew he could get away with a lot in his personal life, and he took full advantage of that. He married his second wife, Jane Mitcham, 23 days before his divorce from his first wife, Dorothy

Barton, was final. Then he divorced Jane, too. No one seemed to care or expect any better of him, so Lewis continued with his wild ways, womanizing and carousing his way across the United States on booze-soaked tours. Fans liked their rock 'n' roll devil to be as bad as could be, so perhaps by the age of 22, Lewis figured there was nothing he could do to push them too far. Oh, but there was: He married a 13-year-old girl who still believed in Santa Claus. And she was his cousin!

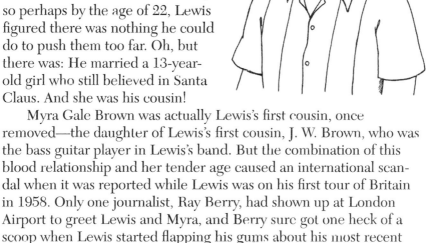

Myra Gale Brown was actually Lewis's first cousin, once removed—the daughter of Lewis's first cousin, J. W. Brown, who was the bass guitar player in Lewis's band. But the combination of this blood relationship and her tender age caused an international scandal when it was reported while Lewis was on his first tour of Britain in 1958. Only one journalist, Ray Berry, had shown up at London Airport to greet Lewis and Myra, and Berry sure got one heck of a scoop when Lewis started flapping his gums about his most recent plunge into matrimony. The British tabloids had a field day with the story, and the tour was canceled after only three performances.

## Rock 'n' Roll Repercussions

Back home in the United States, Lewis was blacklisted from both radio and television, and his career was nearly destroyed. His reputation as one of the hottest, most exciting stage acts in history saved him from complete ruin, however. Though his nightly concert fee dropped drastically from the $10,000 it once was, $250 a night wasn't exactly peanuts in the 1950s. Lewis was at least able to afford a comfortable, if not luxurious, lifestyle for him, his child bride, and the two children they eventually had.

Jerry Lee Lewis and Myra Gale Brown were married for 13 years, divorcing in 1970. Lewis, who was inducted into the Rock 'n' Roll Hall of Fame in 1986, toured the United Kingdom, the scene of the scandal, as recently as 2008. Brown is now a real estate agent in Atlanta, Georgia.

## Variations on a Theme: Weddings

# Lord of the Wedding Rings

*What does a medieval-themed wedding look like?*

### Going Medieval

For the vast majority of the couples uniting in medieval-themed wedding ceremonies (mostly members of Generations X and Y), medieval times have been romanticized since their early childhoods. The fantasy role-playing game *Dungeons & Dragons* was often the "gateway drug" that got them hooked on the age of valiant knights, fair ladies, and fierce monsters. Another strong influence was fantasy fiction. While the Middle Ages have been a subject in literature since . . . well, the Middle Ages, in the mid-20th century, a distinct publishing genre began to emerge to cater to those who wanted adventure stories full of medieval magic, heroes, and monsters. And in 2001, J.R.R. Tolkien's *The Lord of the Rings: The Fellowship of the Ring* was made into a film that was wildly successful around the world. That first film was then followed by two more *Lord of the Rings* films in 2002 and 2003, helping the medieval wedding trend get an even firmer foothold. And this trend is at the peak of its popularity; it shows no signs of slowing down anytime soon.

### Get Thee to the Church (or Forest) on Time

The setting of the medieval wedding is important. For Christians planning a medieval-themed wedding, a gothic-style church—the older the better—is the perfect place to celebrate their union. Obviously, the Brits and the Europeans are much luckier than Yankees when it comes to finding this type of church, but such old-world, ornate places of worship can be found in the United

States with a little effort (Episcopalians and Catholics would probably have the best luck). Christians whose denominations don't require them to be married in a church, those of other faiths, or those with a more pagan bent often choose an outdoor setting for their medieval wedding. There is definitely no better match for medieval dress than a woodsy area, and watching the appropriately clad bridesmaids and groomsmen walk (or sometimes run) out of a grove of tall trees on a bright, sunny day is truly a sight to behold. Some grooms even gallop to the ceremony on horseback.

## With My Hand, I Thee Wed

As for vows, again, the couple's religion (or lack thereof) would determine how much liberty they have to infuse them with medieval language and symbols. It is not uncommon to hear words like "m'lord" and "m'lady" or for a phrase like "in sickness and in health" to be replaced with "for fairer or for fouler." The pagan medieval marriage ceremony is called the "handfasting ceremony," where each guest ties a ribbon around the couple's bound hands to symbolize their approval of and support for the union. The rings exchanged at a medieval ceremony are often more colorful and elaborate than those in traditional weddings, many set with gemstones rather than the now-traditional diamonds.

## Men in Tights

So what does one wear to get married medievally? Deep blue is a popular color for brides, due to the fact that in the Middle Ages, blue, not white, was the color that represented purity. The style of the medieval wedding dress is usually longer, often with a train. The bodice can be tight or loose and belted, but there is almost always a drop waist. For the guys? Tights. Now, one would think it would be hard to get men into tights, even for their weddings, but in fact, it is often the grooms who initiate the idea of medieval weddings, and the brides who must be convinced!

# "Inked" for Life

*Wedding band tattoos may not work for every couple!*

## True Love Tats

One symbol may signify eternal unity more than a wedding ring: the tattooed version. A tattoo encircling one's ring finger has a lot going for it: It will always fit, will never need to be resized, and won't get lost. Plus, it's certainly less expensive than the precious metals at jewelry stores—a simple wedding band tattoo costs about $100.

Some couples that opt for tattooed rings choose an uncomplicated design. Others take a more elaborate route by selecting custom designs that show intertwined names or include a wedding date. Celtic patterns or Irish wedding knots are a popular choice for couples ready to get "inked" for life.

## Think Before You Ink

There are downsides to declaring "forever" with tattoos. Ring tattoos fade, so tattoo retouching will be part of at least one wedding anniversary. Some couples report that because of fingers' thickened skin, the design becomes distorted.

There's also the issue of buyer's remorse. D-listed comedienne Kathy Griffin had laser treatment to remove a ring tattoo after her five-year marriage ended. And when actor Colin Farrell vowed eternal love to wife Amelia Warner by getting a ring tattoo, he probably didn't expect the marriage to end just four months later.

Before former Motley-Crüe drummer Tommy Lee and *"Baywatch* babe" Pamela Anderson married, she had his name tattooed on her ring finger. When

they divorced, she simply changed the tat to "Mommy" rather than "Tommy," which would have been a bit awkward had they not had two sons.

# Always a Bridesmaid...

&#x269C; &#x269C; &#x269C; &#x269C; &#x269C;

*From multiple walks down the aisle to record-breaking bridal parties, these weddings are history in the making.*

## "...never a bride."

One thing's for certain: If you've donned more than one bridesmaid gown in your lifetime, it leaves an impression. Few women are competing to win the "most times as a bridesmaid" award, but there are a number of women who've come close. There's no official record of a bridesmaid walking down the aisle in multiple instances—at least not according to *Guinness World Records,* anyway.

In 2008, when the movie *27 Dresses* depicted a frazzled single woman fulfilling bridesmaid duties for more than two-dozen friends, her plight captured the imagination of women who'd experienced similar situations. Soon, cocktail parties and Internet blogs were filled with tales of frilly dresses and unfortunate color pairings.

## The More (and Older) the Merrier

When it comes to weddings with the largest number of bridesmaids, however, the record is clear. Suresh Joachim and his fiancée, Christa, married in the company of 79 bridesmaids. According to *Guinness World Records,* not only did this couple break the record for most bridesmaids, the 47 groomsmen set a new record, as well. (The average wedding party often includes five attendants on each side.)

Joachim didn't stand a chance when it came to the oldest bridesmaid category, though. That honor goes to Edith Gulliford. In 2007, when Gulliford was 105 years old, she was a bridesmaid for a wedding ceremony in Chatham, England. The stint earned her a place in *Guinness World Records.*

According to The Wedding Report, which tracks statistics and conducts market research for the wedding industry, more than 2 million couples married in 2008 (the most recent year with data available). Certainly more record-setting nuptials were among them!

##  Weddings 'Round the World
# Japanese Wedding Traditions

*While a modern Japanese bride won't likely find a fan at her doorstop to begin the marital journey, plenty of century-old habits remain.*

In olden-days Japan, the process of matching a young man to a well-suited lady was a formal interview called the *Mi-Ai*. The gentleman caller would visit his prospective bride's home and submit to some mutual judging. If he was satisfied with what he saw and learned, the suitor would leave behind a token of his intentions: a Japanese fan.

### Lady in White

Along with a white kimono, a traditional Japanese bride paints her skin pale white from head to toe. She may also wear a white hood that serves as a veil to hide her face. Or she may sport an elaborate ornamental hat. In either case, the headgear is said to cover her "horns," or imperfections, such as jealousy or selfishness.

### Bottoms Up

While alcohol is often a key component of Western wedding receptions, it's actually incorporated into the traditional Shinto Japanese wedding ceremony. The bride's and groom's families face each other, and nine sips of sweet sake are taken. After drinking, the couple is considered unified and may be officially introduced to each other's respective families.

### Wife Garb Swap

After the ceremony, the bride will change into a different kimono and may later change at least one more time, often into more modern or Western-influenced attire. Symbolically, this demonstrates that she is prepared to return to her daily life.

# Fast Facts: The Numbers

- *In 1945, the average cost of a U.S. wedding was $2,240.*

- *In 2006, the average cost of a wedding in the United States was $26,400, which was a 3 percent increase from 2005. The numbers went up until 2008, when they fell below $25,000 due to the economic recession.*

- *Anywhere from 28 to 50 percent of a wedding budget is spent on the reception.*

- *A wedding cake will cost you, on average, about $700.*

- *A wedding photographer will run you approximately $1,570, according to statistics from the past few years.*

- *Each year, Americans spend around $60 billion on items and services directly associated with weddings (i.e., gowns, formalwear, cakes, etc.). If you include items indirectly related (i.e., transportation, hotel accommodations, etc.), the industry rakes in about $140 billion every year.*

- *The average age of a first-time bride today is 26, the first-time groom, 28.*

- *There are more than two million weddings every year in the United States.*

- *Seventy-seven percent of couples use the Internet to help plan their wedding; 43 percent use it to research products and services; and about 13 percent use it to buy items for the wedding, though that number is going up.*

- *Eighty percent of all brides book services or buy goods from 16 wedding-related industries, including wedding planning agencies, bakeries, and dressmakers.*

# God-Awful Wedding Gifts

*Bad wedding gifts have been around as long as weddings themselves, but these examples are particularly egregious.*

- **Statue of Limitations:** When Arnold Schwarzenegger married Maria Shriver in 1986, he made the politically incorrect decision to invite his old pal Kurt Waldheim, a former Nazi who was then the President of Austria. Waldheim didn't show up, but he committed a crime against taste when he sent the couple a life-size statue of Arnold in lederhosen, carrying a dirndl-wearing Maria.

- **Fo' Swizzle:** In her infamous 1991 biography of Nancy Reagan, Kitty Kelley exposed the former first lady's rather tacky habit of re-gifting to friends and relatives. The Reagans received tons of free stuff from everyone—from clothing designers to wealthy donors. Whatever they didn't want for themselves went into a huge closet in the White House, waiting to be re-gifted by Nancy. So Nancy's stepdaughter Maureen was probably not too shocked when she learned that the 36 ugly, pewter swizzle sticks (topped by little GOP elephants) that she received as a wedding gift came from "the closet."

- **Bee Mine Forever:** When actress Scarlett Johansson married Ryan Reynolds in 2008, guest Samuel L. Jackson made a stinging impression with his very wild wedding gift. Jackson gave the couple a beehive, matching beekeeper outfits, and a lifetime subscription to *Beekeepers Journal.* While most couples would run screaming from the buzzing benefaction, Ryan jokes that there's

 an upside as far as security: "Some people are afraid of guard dogs, but I don't know anyone who's not afraid of swarms of bees." He and his lovely new wife are now making their own honey—literally.

# Proposals: The Perfect vs. the Poorly Planned

*What woman doesn't want her proposal to be perfect? But not every one goes that way. It seems that when the romance genes were passed around, some people got a few more than others.*

## Going to Extremes

Justin Firestone has an abundance of romance genes. When he was planning his proposal to his girlfriend, Natalie Abreu, he took her to Hawaii. As if that atmosphere wasn't enough, he also took her on a helicopter ride around the islands. But the big surprise came when she looked out the window to see "Will you marry me Natalie?" spelled out on the beach in giant letters made from hundreds of coconuts painted white. Her answer? A resounding yes.

At the opposite end of the spectrum is the guy who proposed to his girlfriend while they were vacuuming. She probably accepted as well, but the story isn't apt to be passed down to the grandchildren, unless it's used as an example of what *not* to do. You have to wonder, was a proposal that lame really planned in advance, or was he just overcome by the great job she was doing?

These are the extremes—most proposals probably fall somewhere in the middle. But to make it more complicated, there are some possible settings that get mixed reviews. So what's a guy to do?

## Public Proposals

One controversial method is flashing a message on a sporting event scoreboard (or finding someone to hold up a hand-lettered sign from the opposite side of the stands). Some people think this is both romantic and fun. It certainly fulfills the goal of being a surprise. But others are horrified by the thought: What if the woman says no? The key here is probably to make sure you know the answer to the big question before you pop it in public.

The same idea holds true for the plan of proposing in front of family or friends. Some guys think being surrounded by loved ones makes it even more special. This may be true—but only when the intended answers the way you intend.

## Have Your Ring and Eat It, Too

One surprisingly bad idea: putting the ring in the drink or dessert. Yep, it sounds romantic, and it would definitely be a surprise. But all too often the surprise is on the groom-to-be. Just ask Reed Harris. Knowing his girlfriend was partial to Wendy's Frostys, he took her to the fast-food joint with a couple of friends. He dropped the ring into her ice cream and—here comes the second bad idea—he suggested a race to see who finished their dessert first. His intent, of course, was to make her find it sooner, rather than eating at a snail's pace. But when his girlfriend started gulping spoonfuls, all that was left at the end was an empty cup. She had swallowed the ring (but hey— she won the race). In an anticlimactic and embarrassing moment, Reed had to tell her what he'd done. She got an x-ray that, yes indeed, showed a ring in there. She spent the next few days "looking for it." Fortunately, the ring eventually got put in the right place on her finger, and she definitely has a story to tell.

Actually swallowing the ring is the extreme case, but other things could go awry. If you have the dessert delivered to your table, an employee might steal the ring in advance. Or what if it's delivered to the wrong table, causing distress for the real groom and confusion—at best—for the other couple.

## The Pros and Cons of Places

One romantic boyfriend planned a weekend getaway with his girl-friend, who was really looking forward to the trip. On the morning they were supposed to leave, he presented her with a day at a salon instead. He sent her off for pampering while he laid out a new dress and jewelry on her bed, along with instructions that he would pick her up at 5:00 P.M. He arrived in a tux and a limo, presented her with roses, and took her to a fabulous restaurant. On the way home, they stopped at a park where two dozen roses and a bottle of champagne were waiting. He then got down on one knee and gave her the ring. She said yes. Note: If you try this yourself, just make sure she won't be mad that you never did go on that trip!

It's also important to make sure that the place you propose isn't dangerous. When one man proposed to his girlfriend on a rocky trail of a national park, she got so excited she fell off a ledge and had to be rescued by helicopter. Slightly less dangerous, but just as much of a fiasco, one couple climbed 14,092 feet to the top of Snowmass Mountain, where the guy thought he was setting the scene for a beautiful view and a romantic proposal. Instead, tired from the climb and sick from the altitude, when he reached for her hand, the girl pulled it away saying she thought she might puke. All romance was lost as he quickly said, "Don't throw up, marry me!"

Sunsets and scenic views are usually a good idea, however. So is writing the question in the sand—just don't forget to add her name. You don't want another girl shouting "Yes!" to some poor sap who had no intention of proposing.

And what about the guy who shared dog duties with his live-in girlfriend? They took turns cleaning up around the doghouse, and one day he asked if she'd take care of it. In a moment of sheer romance, what did she find perched on the dog poop but an engagement ring! You've got to give him points for originality.

## Happily Ever After

So perhaps a bookstore proposal would be more romantic. It is, if it's done right. When Jarrod wanted to propose, he took his girlfriend Emily to Barnes and Noble. They headed to the children's section where he pulled out a book called *Fun with Emily and Jarrod.* He read her the illustrated book, which told the story of their relationship. At the end, the fictional Jarrod proposes to Emily. Pulling out a ring, the real Jarrod did the same. Now that's a proposal right out of a fairy tale.

## Weddings Through the Years
# The Waxing and Waning of Honeymoons

*The honeymoon is time alone with the one that you love. Or a much-needed rest after the stress of planning and attending your own wedding. However you look at it, the honeymoon is a wedding tradition that couples treasure. But it wasn't always that way.*

- **2500 B.C. and earlier:** In ancient Babylonia, it was tradition for the bride's father to give the groom honeyed mead (a type of wine). He drank this every night for 30 days after the wedding to promote fertility. Some consider this the origin of the word honeymoon.

- **A.D. 400:** The earliest honeymoons were a period of function rather than fun. In the Scandinavian regions of Europe, during Viking times, the groom stole his new bride away for about a month or "moon." During this time, her family and friends searched for her. The hope was that the new bride would be pregnant with the couple's first child by the time she was "found."

- **16th century:** For the first time, the honeymoon became a romantic vacation for the newlyweds. Fun at last. Another possible origin of the word honeymoon cropped up during this century when Thomas Blount, a political representative from North Carolina, referred to the period just after the wedding by saying, "It is honey now, but will change as the moon."

- **1820s:** Europeans—probably noticing that newly married Americans were taking vacations abroad—adopted the honeymoon for themselves. The French called them *les voyages à la façon anglaise* or English-style voyages.

- **1830s:** American couples discovered Niagara Falls as a honeymoon destination. It was closer

and less expensive than a European vacation—and every bit as beautiful.

- **Victorian era:** In Victorian times, the honeymoon finally became a wedding tradition. Typically, the groom's family would pay for this romantic vacation after the wedding. The honeymoon—or bridal tour—was initially taken only by the wealthy, since it frequently lasted for weeks or even months. Wedding couples took these earliest honeymoons by train, with the best man accompanying the couple to the station. He was the only one who would know their destination, so they wouldn't be disturbed. The bad news: The bride and groom were kept apart during the engagement and used the honeymoon to get to know each other better. Italy was the most popular destination for English couples during Victorian times. Family members who couldn't attend the wedding often went with newlyweds on their honeymoon. There goes the romance!

- **20th century:** At the turn of the century, the idea of taking a honeymoon spread through all classes of people in the United States and into Canada, as well.

- **1940s:** Wartime took its toll on the honeymoon tradition. Many grooms were already in the service or heading off to war. Weddings were often small affairs, and honeymoons frequently took place in a hometown hotel or within a few hours' drive. Sometimes the bride-to-be traveled to the military base, and the groom was able to get a few days furlough to get married and enjoy a night or two with his bride before the realties of war separated them again.

- **2000s:** Now, many American couples are choosing exotic destinations for their getaways. Aruba, the Cayman Islands, Cancun, Greece, Spain, and England are among the most popular spots, perhaps gaining popularity because they are far away from the couple's hometown. Some locations are quiet, offering a chance to relax and regroup, while others have plenty of activities to keep the couple active. For couples choosing to stay in the United States, the most popular destinations are now Hawaii, Florida, and Las Vegas. For the newly married but young at heart: Disney World.

# When Pets Marry

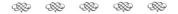

*Does your pet have a best friend in the neighborhood or at doggy day care? Does he always sniff around the same pooch at the dog park? Well, maybe it's time to think about having a pet wedding.*

## Do You, Rover...

Don't laugh. Well, okay laugh. But pet weddings are more common than you might think. And for those companies who have already jumped on the gravy train, pet weddings are a big business.

If the idea of a pet wedding makes you think of two little girls dressing up their rabbits and singing, "Here Comes the Bride," you don't know the half of it. Sixty-three percent of Americans own pets—and a surprising number are buying into the pet wedding industry.

## The Maltese Millennium Marriage

Shelley Johnson and Bunny Heller—and their husbands—actually became friends because of their dogs. The foursome met when each showed up at a Florida Safari Club rally driving the same motor home—and carrying nearly identical Maltese dogs in their arms. Shayna and Dusty hit it off right away. And so did the humans. Two years later, the moms decided it was time to make it official.

It all began with a diamond collar for Shayna at Labor Day. And then the moms had to hurry to get a wedding ready by New Year's Eve. They sent out 60 invitations, and 25 people showed up for the festivities—one guest even came all the way from Texas.

There were bridal clothes, flowers, vows, a maid of honor, and even a blessing by an ordained minister. The canine couple exchanged gold dog tags shaped like hearts. The Maltese Millennium Marriage, as the moms call it, was a big hit. Although the dogs have a long-distance relationship, they were reunited the following summer for a honeymoon when their parents took the motor homes to Maine.

## For As Long As You Both Shall Bark (or Purr)

Not too many doggy weddings can top that, but they're still taking place on a smaller scale. Two young girls in California talked their parents into having a wedding for the family's two Jack Russell Terriers. The girls felt sure that if the dogs were married, then puppies would soon be on the way. The girls dressed the dogs up and had a brief ceremony attended by the family. The girls thought it was fun; their mom thought it was a good teaching moment. And the dogs? Well, they tolerated it.

One not-so-tolerant animal was Comfrey the cat. When the Baltimore Humane Society planned a feline wedding to celebrate Valentine's Day, they shouldn't have had the bridal shower on the same day. After a whirlwind shower in the morning, Comfrey had had enough. She hid under a cabinet and refused to come out. So the staff pulled a switcheroo, substituting another black cat as the bride. Winslow, the groom, had never met Luna, but he didn't seem to mind. The pair was united in front of a crowd of well-wishers. They were given new collars and a slice of special wedding cake.

The Humane Society in Naples, Florida, celebrated Valentine's Day with pet nuptials as well, but this one was open to the public. A Pet Minister was on hand from 4:00 P.M. until 7:00 P.M. to unite pet couples in marriage. Dogs and cats, dressed in their bridal finery, arrived with their owners in tow. Two shelter animals got the ball rolling with the first ceremony, and then the other eager brides and grooms were married a pair at a time for a $35 donation. In addition to the minister, there was music, photographs, and wedding cake.

## Pet Wedding Planning

So if you're thinking of a wedding for your pet, there are numerous Web sites that offer bridal attire for prospective brides and grooms, big and small. You can even register the little critters at Pet Smart. My Best Friend Pet Bakery in San Diego will ship a pet-friendly cake anywhere in the country, with prices starting at $99. And if you're having an open bar, don't forget to order enough Bowser Beer and Pinot Leasheo for all the thirsty guests!

# The Other Cake in the Room

*There's not a lot you can count on in this world,*
*but one thing's for sure: People like cake!*

In some regions, among some families, the groom's cake is an important part of the wedding festivities. Here's a little background on the other cake in the room.

## Let Them Eat (More) Cake!

The groom's cake comes to us by way of Victorian England. Somewhere during the Victorian "Let's show off our money!" heyday, it was popular to create not just the wedding cake, but two *additional* cakes: one for the bride, and one for the groom. These cakes, usually cheese- or fruitcake, were sliced up and given just to the bridal party. Rumors started that bridesmaids who put the box of cake under their pillow later that night would dream of their future husband (and probably wake up with cake in their hair, but go for it, ladies).

The tradition made its way across the pond and took root particularly in the South, where it's more common today to find the groom's cake ritual played out, though the trend is coming back into vogue across all of North America.

## Today's Groom's Cake

These days, if a groom's cake has a place at the table, it's not just for the bridal party, and no one's expected to take it into bed with them later.

The groom's cake has become about the bride doing something thoughtful for her groom, since she knows most of the attention is being paid to her throughout the whole wedding process. This (literally) sweet gesture therefore often reflects the interests, hobbies, or personality of the groom: Cakes are often in the shape of a football, a roulette wheel, a motorcycle, etc.

## Make It Manly

It's hard to know how to make a cake "masculine," but there are a few elements that are usually incorporated into the groom's cake to make it appeal to male sensibilities. Chocolate is the favored flavor, and many opt for rum or other liqueur-soaked cakes. Skipping a million frosting flowers is probably a good idea, too. No matter what you serve up, it'll get eaten, so don't get caught up in too many details—the cake should never outshine the actual wedding cake, so keep that in mind. Also keep in mind that the groom's cake, while delicious and fun, is not a wedding necessity, and many couples choose to skip it altogether.

## What to Do with the Groom's Cake

Groom's cakes can be served at the reception, as an alternative to the regular wedding cake; however, many brides choose to serve the groom's cake as dessert at the rehearsal dinner or have the cake delivered to the bachelor party.

Typically, if used at the reception, the groom's cake is presented next to the wedding cake. Later, it's cut and placed in boxes for wedding guests to take home. Some couples even use these boxed slices as wedding favors. If this is the route you decide to take, have fun with it! Take creative packaging to a new level and make it reflect your bridal style.

- *In the 1700s, a groom's cake was usually dark brown in color from the fruits baked inside. Similarly, modern groom's cakes are still often dark in color because they're usually chocolate.*

# Brazen Bigamists

*Some people really like the institution of marriage.
In fact, some like it so much they get married again and again.
Most of them get divorced between weddings—
but a few are just brazen bigamists.*

Bigamy is a felony in 37 states, carrying a sentence of up to ten years in prison. The problem? Prosecutions are not that common, and many times, offenders come away with a slap on the wrist.

## Making (Serial) Marriages Work

Anthony Glenn Owens was a man of God, pious and devoted to his church. At least that's what one Texas woman thought when he proposed to her in 2002. He even traveled all the way to Mississippi to ask her father for permission for her hand. Maybe her dad would have said no if he'd known what the new bride discovered. Owens was already married—to seven other women. Apparently he didn't believe in divorce.

After the couple established a new life and a church in Georgia, a female pastor told the woman that she'd seen Owens with seven other women over the years. She said he had cheated on them and stolen from them. The new Mrs. Owens began to investigate her husband's past, and she found several marriages and no divorces. So she took her findings to the police. Four of the wives came forward, claiming that Owens had used them and left them broke.

Owens was sentenced to two years in prison and four more years of probation. His defense? He never meant to hurt anyone, and as a man of God, he was misled by teachings of the Mormon faith (although he was not Mormon himself). He was released in 2005 but was back in jail by 2007 for parole violations. What did he do with his free time in those 18 months of freedom? He proposed to four more women.

## When You Love Love Too Much

Ed Hicks is another man who just can't get enough of a good thing. In fact, his profile on an Internet dating site claims he is "in love with love." When the law caught up to him in 2005, he was married to two women and had been married to at least five others. In three cases, he didn't bother with divorce between the ceremonies. Unlike the devious Owens, who stole from his many wives before moving on, Hicks appears to be a sweet-talking romantic who is handy around the house. In short, the wives liked the guy.

"He could be a real nice husband," explained Sharon Hicks Pratt, wife number two. "But he had to have more than just one woman." Hmmm. That could be a problem.

What was once a problem for the women turned into a problem for Hicks when the ladies began to find out, and the dominoes began to fall. The last three wives have even formed an unofficial support group—and are committed to warning future wives about his secret past. Even after his arrest, Hicks began an online relationship with at least four other women. The wives must know his type by now, because three of those "pen pals" were fictional women created by wife number six to see if he'd take the bait. He did.

## Equality of the Sexes

Lest you get the idea that women are constant victims, and only men can cheat in the name of love, consider the case of Kyle McConnell (a woman) from Roseville, Michigan. She was charged with felony bigamy and sentenced to 22 months to ten years in prison.

The popular McConnell had a talent for finding lonely men, marrying them, and stealing their money, according to sheriff's Detective Tim Donnellon. Apparently, her pattern was to drain their bank accounts and move on to the next guy by the time the current husband found out.

It worked pretty well, too. All in all, she managed to marry about 15 men. Isn't love grand?

# What Price, Love?

❦ ❦ ❦ ❦ ❦

*Can't afford the wedding you've always wanted?*
*Make someone else pay for it! And we're not talking about*
*Mom and Dad or your in-laws...*

## The Ceremony Goes Corporate

By the time lawyer-turned-talk show hostess Star Jones married investment banker Al Reynolds on November 13, 2004, most of America was sick of hearing about it. Like a lot of brides, Jones loved to talk about her wedding plans—but unlike most brides, being head-over-heels in love may not have been one of her reasons. She had set up an elaborate Web site to celebrate her upcoming nuptials and began to solicit donations from corporate sponsors: freebies for the ceremony and the reception. Hungry for the publicity that Jones could provide on *The View,* the talk show she cohosted, these sponsors scrambled to offer her complimentary invitations, tuxedos, bridesmaid dresses, and airline tickets for the honeymoon. And the bride didn't let them down: Soon, Jones was mentioning the names of these businesses on air as often as she could. Federal regulations actually prohibit trading products for on-air plugs, but Jones denied any accusations regarding that. According to her, she was just a happy bride chatting about the things all happy brides chat about.

## Bridezilla Rears Her Head

Legalities aside, it struck viewers as tacky and boastful. The press took to calling Jones "Bridezilla." Even Jones's cohosts on *The View,* Barbara Walters, Joy Behar, and Elisabeth Hasselbeck, seemed visibly annoyed with her near-constant shilling. Relations with

Walters, who was not only her coworker but her boss, went rapidly downhill, and in June 2006, Jones left the show under a cloud of controversy. It could have been an omen: Almost two years later, her marriage to Reynolds disintegrated, and some of the same corporate sponsors who had been so generous while she was planning her wedding began demanding financial compensation. "Those wedding vows said 'til death do us part' and so does our contract," said a spokesperson for the company that donated the bridesmaid dresses.

## Will You Sponsor My . . . Wedding?

Perhaps Jones's experience should have served as a warning, but it sure didn't. If anything, it only sparked the imaginations of those who longed for dream weddings but couldn't afford them. One groom convinced the manager of KeySpan Park in Brooklyn, New York, to allow him to get married in the ball park in front of thousands of baseball fans, and then started lining up sponsors. An online florist donated flowers in return for prominent logo placement. "It was attractive due to the fact that there were 7,000 people there," said a representative. The groom claims that he cut his costs from $100,000 to $20,000.

A Midwestern bride turned her search for wedding sponsors into an almost full-time job, spending six to eight hours a day, five days a week, on the phone. But she claims the time and effort were worth it. The cost of her wedding plummeted from $30,000 to $5,000; she received free invitations and other materials; and she was able to wear the kind of dress she had fantasized about since she was a child. The Dr Pepper Snapple Group approached another bride after she auctioned off a bridesmaid spot on eBay. The company gave her $10,000 in exchange for the publicity.

Unsurprisingly, etiquette experts are aghast. The editor in chief of a popular online wedding site argues for other budget-friendly options such as cutting the guest list or throwing a low-key party, "Have hamburgers and hot dogs before you have a sponsored wedding." But as long as sponsors are willing to hand out money and gifts, there will be frugal brides and grooms who won't mind being viewed as "tacky."

# Happily Ever After

*"Fairy tales do come true, it can happen to you . . . "*
*If you're willing to play the part.*

Almost every little girl has fantasized about having a fairy tale wedding. You know, the one where the handsome prince weds the most beautiful girl in the land in an extravagant affair with stunning gowns and horse-drawn carriages—the whole enchanted enchilada.

Apparently, enough prospective brides and grooms want to transform their fantasy nuptials into fanciful realities that Disney has marched into the wedding biz. Wanna-be Princess Brides can choose from a dazzling array of gowns inspired by animated royalty, including classics like Cinderella, Snow White, and Sleeping Beauty, along with more modern Disney princesses such as Jasmine, Belle, and Ariel (in her "above" the sea stage).

But that's not all! For upwards of $1,200 (center stone not included) brides can add some serious princess bling to their ring fingers. Disney's designers have created a line of wedding and engagement rings for Prince Charming to present to his fairest-of-them-all. And for a minimum of $25,000, the happy couple can even secure the ultimate fairy tale wedding venue: Sleeping Beauty's Castle at Disneyland.

## Peter Pan and Tinkerbelle

Some people never grow out of their fairy tale dreams—and some just never grow up. Enter Peter Pan, aka Randy Constan, a 50-something computer software engineer who embraces the "I'll never grow up" lifestyle. Sporting a brilliant smile and thick, dark hair coiffed in a perfect Prince Valiant pageboy, the androgynous Constan describes himself as "openly unique."

Constan generally dresses à la Pan, although he also enjoys wearing an assortment of other fancy-dress costumes, including faerie-wear, tutus, and Little Lord Fauntleroy get-ups. In fact, he was dressed in one of his personally designed, too-too cute outfits on August 13, 2006, when he first met the love of his life, Dorothy (which Constan pronounces with three syllables). It was love at first sight.

On his Pixyland.org Web site page dedicated to Dorothy, Constan describes their meeting as "a wonderful collision of Fairy Tales." Although he reports Dorothy "didn't have many childlike or fairylike outfits to wear back then," the self-described "Eternal Child" took her under his wing and transformed the girl from Oz into his magical Tinkerbelle. Today, they share a love for pixy couture and often share the same wardrobe.

Upon her engagement to Constan, Dorothy left the corporate world behind and entered the Pixyland of her fiancé's dreams. Although some may doubt her choice of life partners, Dorothy declares, "Randy is my soul mate." Regarding her companion's ambiguous gender, straight-girl Dorothy reveals that Constan represents the best of both worlds, "but when it matters—he's a boy!"

The deeply spiritual "Sire Randy," who established the Through the Cracks Christian ministry, was united in holy matrimony with his "Princess Dorothy" on March 29, 2009, in the shire of Tampa, Florida. The two faerie spirits pinky-swore their allegiance to each other at the city's annual Bay Area Renaissance Festival before King Henry VIII.

Both the bride and groom were visions in green. She wore a green fairy frock complete with wings and green ballet slippers; he was adorned in a green belted tunic, matching spandex tights, pointy Pan shoes, and a green plumed hat.

Friends came from both coasts to toast the happy couple. Some dressed in their Ren-fair best, others wore attire ranging from Batman and Catwoman to faerie "bois" and "grrls." The newly "faeried" groom expressed these hopes for the enchanted couple's future: "With faith, trust, and a little Pixie Dust, I'm sure we'll be flying together a long time!"

# Fiona & Shrek

Although more and more couples want to go green for their wedding, newlyweds Christine and Keith Green (yes, that's his given surname) took their green wedding over the top. The happy couple spent three hours prepping for their walk down the aisle as Fiona and Shrek lookalikes, adorned from the top of their ogre-ish ears to the tips of their fingers in green theatrical paint.

Mrs. Green, the former Christine England, is a children's hospice nurse, so it's easy to see how she would need a bit of whimsy in her real life. Mr. Green is a builder. The couple married in April 2009 in Broomhill near Barnstaple in Devun, England, after a nine-year engagement.

Wanting to throw a fancy dress party for her 40th birthday, Christine thought about springing a wedding on her friends in the midst of the merriment. But when she realized how hard it would be to keep the secret, she opted to let the ceremony out of the bag.

The decision to costume themselves as Shrek and Fiona came naturally to Christine. While she felt she resembled the rosy-cheeked Fiona, she deemed her husband a dead-ringer for the lovable lout, Shrek.

Walking down the aisle to REM's "Shiny Happy People," the bride and groom wore replicas of Shrek and Fiona's wedding attire. Clever poems replaced stuffy readings, and the couple left the ceremony to a tune from *Toy Story*. The wedding confection featured a tower of colorful cupcakes topped by a small cake with mini ogres.

The Greens asked their 100-plus guests to dress like TV or film characters, and the crowds complied. Among the fanciful attendees were Mary Poppins and her chimney sweep companion, Snow White and a rather tall dwarf, and Cruella de Vil. Christine's 18-year-old son declined the invitation to dress as Donkey.

# Wedding Disasters

*Wedding disasters come in all shapes and sizes. Some are little bumps in the road; others send the marriage down a path of no return. There are very few weddings that go off without any hitch at all. Sometimes, it's how you handle it that makes or breaks the day.*

## Too Much of a Good Thing

Lynda chose a cake design that was unique. A round bottom layer was topped with a couple layers in the shape of hexagons and trimmed with plaid ribbons for a spectacular effect. Her baker assured her it was no problem. Did we mention the cake was rum cake? It turns out the baker was more interested in the rum than the cake. Instead of the smash hit Lynda expected, she got a smashed baker and a smashed cake.

## Double Trouble

Just how important is the groom? Not important at all for two sisters in Saudi Arabia. At their double wedding, their faces were covered with the traditional veil, causing their father to accidentally give each sister away to the wrong groom. The marriage was official before anyone noticed the problem. When their father asked them a few days later if they would be getting divorces, they both said they were happy with the husband they had married by accident.

## Awkward Acceptance

In 1906, a Missouri bride found herself facing divorce after she married the wrong man. Mrs. Amy Sturgeon had two serious suitors after she moved to St. Louis, and she was forced to choose between them. She wrote a proper note to each, stating her acceptance to one's marriage proposal and her polite rejection of the other. Unfortunately, she put the notes in the wrong envelopes before sending them to the young men. Upon receiving her acceptance, a delighted Mr. Sturgeon raced to her house where she was unable to tell him he was not the man she loved. They married but divorced soon after when the new husband discovered the mistake.

## You're Out!

What do you do when someone changes the date of your wedding? That's what one bridesmaid tried to do when the date the couple selected conflicted with her son's Little League game! She started calling guests and telling them there was a new date. Fortunately, those guests checked with the bridal couple, who assured them that the real date was still valid. The bridesmaid (a sister-in-law) then proceeded to complain loudly about everything from the food to the bathroom conditions. She was so belligerent and unpleasant that when she finally made her exit to attend her son's ball game, the other guests all broke out in spontaneous applause. A happy ending after all.

## Say Yes . . . to Her Dress

The kindness of strangers can be a godsend on your wedding day. Amy Orr of Seattle left the hair salon four hours before her wedding only to discover that her car had been stolen—with her wedding dress, shoes, bridesmaid's dresses, rings, and marriage license all inside. She hurried to a nearby restaurant to call her fiancé and found herself walking in on another wedding reception. The bride had already changed into a suit for travel, so when she heard Amy's story, she offered her own dress for the occasion—and it fit perfectly. Friends raced to replace the other missing items, and the marriage went off without another hitch. The bonus? The two married couples are now good friends.

## Hair Today, Gone Tomorrow

When a New Jersey bride started feeling sick the day before her wedding, she wrote it off as stress, but by evening, her temperature reached 102 degrees. Her hairdresser and make-up artist, who were booked into the same hotel, invited her down to the bar for a drink, but she passed in favor of sleep. A few hours later, there was a commotion in the hall complete with banging, slamming doors, and screaming. The bride heard her maid of honor telling the people to be quiet and went back to sleep. When the bridal party arrived at 6:30 A.M. the next day for the beauty treatments, the maid of honor launched into the story of the noise, explaining that she had asked the hotel manager to call the police on the two offenders. An hour later, the hairdresser and make-up artists had failed to arrive, and after multiple calls to their cell phones, the bride was getting worried. When she went searching for them, she ran into the manager who had called the police the night before. And—you guessed it—her make-up artist and hair stylist were now sitting in the slammer. The bride's sister, brother-in-law, and hotel staff quickly scrambled to find someone else to do the women's hair. They missed the scheduled time for photos but arrived just in time for the bride to walk down the aisle.

## Braving the Blackout

When weather reports predicted a 90 percent chance of rain, Brandi and Anthony Robinson decided to move their wedding indoors. Good idea. It stormed throughout the evening, causing the electricity to go out during the reception. Worried that guests might leave, Brandi discovered the answer to the question, "What are friends for?" Her bridesmaids found and lit dozens of candles, and the band brought out their acoustic guitars. Guests pulled their chairs closer together, and what might have been a disaster turned into a cozy campfire—a memorable end to a wonderful day.

## A Colorful Consolation

Julia Sturges also had a little trouble with rain during her outdoor wedding to Jordan Eisenberg. The clouds rolled in, but the couple managed to get through their outdoor ceremony before the rain began in earnest. Guests were hurried under the waiting tents, and women were offered colorful flip-flops to replace their heels as they walked on the sodden ground. The weather couldn't dim the couple's happiness in their special day, however, and they were rewarded with an unexpected surprise—a beautiful rainbow. The photographer was able to get some fabulous pictures of the newlyweds and their wedding party against the rainbow backdrop. How many couples can say that they started married life with an omen like that?

# Weddings 'Round the World
# Getting Lassoed

*What do lassos, coins, and donkeys have in common? You might encounter one or more at a Mexican or South American wedding.*

## And Now a Word from our Sponsors

Conventionally, engaged Hispanic couples rely on the guidance of two carefully selected mentors. These "sponsors" are friends or family members, typically a male and female, who stand in as godfather and godmother. The sponsors are tasked with everything from spiritual guidance to financial assistance along the road to the altar.

## Lucky 13

A traditional Mexican wedding ceremony may include the 13 coins ritual. The priest blesses the coins, and the groom bestows them upon his bride. This symbolizes the groom entrusting his new wife with his possessions, as well as his promise to support her. The bride's acceptance of the coins infers that she will honor his unconditional trust with dedication and prudence.

## Bondage: El Lazo

Yee-haw! There are a couple variations to the Mexican lasso tradition, which symbolizes eternal unity. After vows are exchanged, a long, circular string of rosary beads or lasso chord is wrapped around the couple's necks, shoulders, or wrists in a figure eight. The "lasso" may first be blessed three times with holy water in tribute to the Holy Trinity. Often times, the couple will wear their lasso for the remainder of the ceremony.

## Heart-Shape Box

During the reception, guests may hold hands and surround the bride and groom in the shape of a heart during the first dance.

# Ouch!

You've heard of tossing rice or confetti at newly married couples. One Mexican custom has guests pelt the bride and groom with red beads, a wish of good luck. It's not as bad as some European countries that go hardcore by throwing eggs at the happy couple!

# Now You See Them...

...Soon you won't! In Venezuela, the bride and groom may play a disappearing act on their guests and vanish at some point during the celebration. It is believed to be good luck for a newly betrothed couple to sneak out of their own party. It also eliminates the time-consuming practice of saying good-byes to everyone!

# Breaking the Rules

A traditional Argentinean wedding excludes some common wedding customs. They nix the groomsmen and bridesmaids from the wedding party. Only the groom's mother and bride's father are permitted to escort the couple down the aisle. Also, the bride and groom are forbidden from exchanging rings during the vows and, instead, trade rings at the time of the engagement. Why wait?

# Donkey Kong

Brazilian weddings are among the most festive and grand in the world. Vivacious receptions are marked by the *Caipirinha* (a cocktail of rum, sugar, and lime), *Casadinhos* (Brazilian "marry well" cookies), and *Pagoda* (a Samba-like dance). The bride is expected to arrive at least ten minutes late, and the groom had better be there first! For weeks prior to the ceremony, the bride may refrain from "eating directly from the pot," which is believed to ensure good weather on the big day. And how about this for a patriotic fashion statement: Instead of wearing floral boutonnieres, groomsmen may hold Brazilian flags. Perhaps the most intriguing aspect of Brazilian tradition, practiced only in certain parts of the country, is the *Bumba-Meu-Boi*. In this test of brawniness, the groom must tame an unbridled donkey to prove his worthiness.

## HOW IT ALL BEGAN

# Toppers, Tossed Shoes, and Truisms

*We all know that brides need something old, new, borrowed, and blue; that no cake is complete without a topper; and that every newlywed has to drive away in a car with old shoes dangling from the bumper. But why?*

### Shoe Stopper

In ancient Egypt, shoes represented authority and possession—transactions of all kinds ended with the exchange of the goods as well as a shoe, just to seal the deal. So it only makes sense that when a father handed over his daughter to a groom, he included one of her shoes. (It also meant she couldn't run away!) In Anglo-Saxon England, grooms would strike the heel of their wife's shoe during the ceremony to demonstrate their new position over her.

Fortunately, the authoritative connotation of shoes disappeared during the Middle Ages, when shoes came to represent the union between the bride and groom. In some cultures, shoes were thrown at the couple (ouch!) to invite good luck. Today, shoes are tied to car bumpers for the same reason.

### Top Notch

Little is more mysterious than the origin of the wedding cake topper, but chances are some kind of good luck symbol—like a horseshoe—topped wedding cakes as early as the 17th century. As for the traditional bride-and-groom cake topper, legend has it that it dates back a few centuries to when a baker's daughter asked her father for a special topper to represent her and her groom's love for each other. Inspired, the baker whipped up bride-and-groom figurines, and the rest is history.

Nice as this story is, it's probably pure fiction. Most likely, the bride-and-groom cake topper comes from Queen Victoria (who, by the way, also inspired the tiered wedding cake, wedding veil, and white wedding dress). Her 1840 wedding cake featured miniature replicas of herself and Prince Albert in bridal attire. American brides clamored for similar cake toppers, which enjoyed a major resurgence in the 1950s, when postwar prosperity sparked a return to lavish princess weddings.

## Old, New, Borrowed, Blue

*Something old, something new, something borrowed, something blue, and a silver sixpence in her shoe.* This tried-and-truism dates back to Victorian times as a good luck wish to the bride and groom.

"Something old" suggests a hope that the couple will welcome friends and family from their past lives into their new life as husband and wife. Usually, a bride will carry or wear a family heirloom to fulfill this obligation.

"Something new" speaks to the new life the bride and groom are embarking on, and though typically most of the bride's outfit qualifies as "something new," the wedding ring traditionally fulfilled this role.

"Something borrowed" serves as a reminder that the couple's friends and family will always be there to help. It also stems from a belief that carrying or wearing something borrowed from a happily married woman on the wedding day will bring similar luck to the bride. Any of the new, old, or borrowed items can also double as the "something blue"—blue being the color of purity and fidelity.

The final phrase—to carry a "silver sixpence in her shoe"— dates back to the 1600s, when a lucky sixpence was placed in the bride's left shoe to ensure financial prosperity. Why the left shoe? Possibly because the ring was worn on the left hand, or maybe because the left side has traditionally been associated with the bride—for instance, the bride typically stands on the left side of the altar.

And why's that? In ancient times, men carried a sword on their left side, so they could easily draw it with their right hand. Should anyone try to attack or steal the bride, the groom needed to be ready to fight. So the bride stood on his left.

# The Long Tradition of Wedding Drunkenness

*Still steaming mad at Uncle Ralph for getting totally wasted and ruining your reception? Just comfort yourself with the knowledge that folks have been getting blotto at weddings for thousands of years.*

Even Jesus Christ seemed annoyed at the prospect of drunken revelers when his mother informed him that the wine had run out at the wedding at Cana. "Dear woman, why do you involve me?" he asked before giving in and working a miracle to keep everyone happy. Since then, weddings and liquor have gone together like Courtney Love and cosmetic surgery: It *should* make everything better, but does it, really?

## Cog Stand

Though heavy drinking at weddings happened all over the world throughout history, the United Kingdom is really hard to top when it comes to nuptial boozing—plus they wrote everything down for our enjoyment. Communal cups added to the feeling of alliance and kinship, but they also made excessive drinking harder to avoid due to peer pressure. On the Orkney Islands, for example, it was traditional for two types of round, wooden drinking vessels—or *cogs* as they were known—to be passed around at every wedding celebration. The *cog-gilt-cogs* were kept at each table of 24 guests, while the *menye-cogs* were circulated throughout the entire dining hall. The menye-cogs themselves were broken down into three categories—the best man's cog, the priest's cog, and the bride's cog. See? These people took their wedding drinking seriously!

## Driven to Drink

Even worse than a guest getting drunk at the reception is a groom being drunk at the ceremony. Perhaps the most famous historical example of this is George, the Prince of Wales, who arrived at his 1795 hitching loaded to the gills. The 32-year-old George didn't want to get married at all—he was perfectly happy with his mistress, the 42-year-old Lady Jersey—but his father, King George III, was often ill. The heir to the throne needed to step up and reassure the people that all would be well in case of his dad's death. He was thus forced to marry his cousin, 26-year-old Caroline of Brunswick, a woman who utterly repulsed him. George rebelled by showing up at the Chapel Royal at St. James Palace in a hopelessly inebriated state. He proceeded to pout, cry, screw up the vows, and repeatedly glance over at Lady Jersey, who must have been thrilled to be in attendance.

## Death by Drunkenness

Two hundred years later, it's easy to laugh at the Prince's drunken antics, but we would do well to remember that excessive drinking can turn what should be a beautiful day into a horrible nightmare. Take the case of 35-year-old Wu Cheng-feng. The Taiwanese insurance executive was so excited and happy about his wedding in the spring of 2009 that he invited every classmate he had known at Tamkang University to the reception at a ritzy Taipei restaurant. Following a Chinese custom that dates back to the 12th century, Wu drank more than he should have—one and half bottles of red wine and four beers. Technically, this should not have been enough to kill him, but combined with recent overwork and a preexisting asthma condition, the binge proved fatal.

Despite such cautionary tales, wedding drunkenness will no doubt go on for a very, very long time. A search of "drunk wedding" on YouTube turns up all kinds of embarrassing videos from all over the world—even places where drinking alcohol is prohibited by law or religion. While excessive drinking at weddings may never be abolished, brides can only hope that it can be somewhat controlled.

# I Now Pronounce You Man and Dog

❧ ❧ ❧ ❧ ❧

*This Indian farmer took an odd path to break a curse.*
*At least the reception must have been interesting!*

## The Happy Couple

In November 2007, a 33-year-old Indian farm laborer named
P. Selvakumar married a four-year-old female dog named Selvi.
There's no word as to where the couple registered for gifts.

The family of the groom had selected Selvi from an array of
strays, then bathed the bride-to-be and dressed her in an orange sari
and garland of flowers. In the style of a traditional Hindu marriage
ceremony, the betrothed strolled at the head of a celebratory procession toward the Hindu temple in Manamadurai, a town in the
Sivaganga District. There, Selvakumar formalized the marriage by
tying the *mangal sutra,* or sacred string, around Selvi's furry neck.

Nearly 200 guests attended the reception—enough of a crowd to
spook the bride into making a run for it. Selvi was later captured and
placated with a bun and some milk. After all, making arranged marriages work can be difficult, and the ways of the heart are often
a mystery.

## Star-Crossed

Selvakumar actually wed Selvi on the advice of his astrologer in an
attempt to rid Selvakumar of a curse that had followed him for more
than a decade and a half, ever since he had stoned two mating dogs
to death and hung their bodies from a tree. The contrite farmer
claimed that ever since the incident he suffered from hearing loss
in one ear, paralysis of his legs and hands, and speech impairment.
Medical doctors were unable to help him.

Such unions are not uncommon in the more rural areas of India,
particularly to banish bad luck or evil spirits. After the curse is lifted,
Selvakumar will be free to marry a human bride without the incon-
venience of a divorce lawyer or Animal Control.

# Fast Facts

- All across Europe, eggs are used to tell fortunes. The most popular method is to carefully pierce the shell and catch drops of the egg white in a glass of water. The shapes that form in the water are examined and interpreted by an unmarried woman who is looking for clues to her future husband's profession. A ship means marriage to a sailor, a shoe means she'll wed a cobbler, and so on.

- The tradition that inspired the phrase "You may kiss the bride" likely originated in ancient Rome. To seal the marriage contract, couples kissed before a large group of people. The Romans had three different categories of kisses: osculum, a kiss on the cheek; basium, a kiss on the lips; and savolium, a deep kiss.

- The Greeks were among the first to use flowers in weddings, representing a gift from nature to the bride, groom, and their families. Bridesmaids were in charge of the flower bouquets and garlands and often made posies (small nosegays) for each guest as a symbol of thanks.

- The phrase "Often a bridesmaid but never a bride" comes from an advertisement for Listerine that first appeared in 1925 and ran for more than ten years.

- Paulette Goddard was Charlie Chaplin's companion from 1936 to 1942. Their relationship was scandalous for the time because it was never clear if they were actually married. Goddard lost the role of Scarlett O'Hara in Gone with the Wind because she could not validate the relationship by showing producer David O. Selznick a marriage certificate.

- Before marrying Marc Antony, Cleopatra was married to two of her brothers. But not at the same time! She married one brother, Ptolemy XIII, when he was 11 years old. When he died, she married her other brother, Ptolemy XIV. He died not long after they were married.

103

# Destination . . . Unique

*In the market for a destination wedding but don't want
the usual beachside fare? Here are a few offbeat locations that may
have you saying "I do" sooner than you think.*

## Dive-in Wedding

Deep-sea diving enthusiasts may think the idea of an underwater
wedding is romantic. The rest of us, however, are left wondering
about the logistics of an underwater kiss. After all, there are dive
masks involved in this creative ceremony.

An increasing number of locations around the globe are proof that a
"dive-in" wedding can be done—and
done well. From a state park in
Florida to exotic locales in Malaysia
and Thailand, there are more spots
than ever catering to couples opting
for an underwater "I do."

Pennekamp Coral Reef State Park
in Florida is home to Key Largo Dry
Rocks Reef, along with an impres-
sive number of wedding ceremonies. In addition to the obvious
scenic attractions—clear, shallow water and an intricate dome-shape
reef—there is a larger allure: a nearly nine-foot bronze sculpture of
Jesus Christ anchored under water.

The 4,000-pound figure known as Christ of the Abyss was a mid-
century creation of Guido Galletti, an Italian artist. It has become
one of the most sought-after underwater destinations in the world.
Why? Legend purports that good luck will come to anyone who
touches the statue—which is especially good on a wedding day.

# "I Do" at the Zoo

An African safari is an undeniably offbeat destination, but not everyone wants to plan their dream wedding through a travel agency. The truth is that an exotic setting may be closer than you realize.

Chances are a local zoo will let you and your betrothed wed within its bounds. The San Diego Zoo's Wild Animal Park, for example, offers several themed destinations in its 1,800 acres, from an intimate spot along the Mombasa Lagoon to a scenic vista overlooking free-roaming herds of giraffes or rhinos.

The Blank Park Zoo in Des Moines, Iowa, also offers wedding parties the use of its property, including an indoor wedding ceremony and reception area. After saying "I do," the happy couple—and guests—can roam around the zoo's grounds to get a closer look at exotic animals.

The good news is that zoo weddings can be surprisingly economical. There's no need to hire a wedding singer because the entertainment is built right in.

## In-Flight, Almost

Until recently, it seemed couples would be able to wed in-flight, thanks to British budget airline easyJet. The company announced plans to host wedding ceremonies while flying over terra firma—with the pilot officiating.

The idea, unfortunately, didn't fly with local officials. According to British law, marriages require one thing a moving aircraft doesn't provide: a licensed building permanently affixed to the ground.

## Whirlwind Wedding

*Wizard of Oz* fans, look no further for the wedding destination of your dreams. The Land of Oz theme park on Beech Mountain is North Carolina's answer to a Hollywood set.

Here, couples can forgo a traditional walk down the aisle to traverse an actual yellow brick road. The Judy Garland Memorial Gazebo provides a pitch-perfect ceremony spot, and a honeymoon stay can be booked in "Dorothy's House"—an exact replica built to scale. Really in the mood for a theme? The Land of Oz theme park also rents costumes to wedding parties.

# Internet Brides

❧ ❧ ❧ ❧ ❧

*While many people use a regular dating site to find an American mate, there are a steady number looking for foreign brides—and women wanting to move to the United States.*

## Easy Way to Find a Mate

Mail-order brides were popular in early America as pioneers traveled west to make their fortune. Sometimes these pioneers went alone; sometimes their wives didn't survive the long and difficult journey. There was a shortage of women in the west, and the men were lonely. Many of these men sought a bride for companionship, to run their household, and to mother their children. Maybe the men answered an ad, and a correspondence began with a young woman. Soon, this woman arrived in the new land, bag in hand.

It might be a different world today, but the idea of mail-order brides is not so far-fetched. The technology and transportation might be different, but the concept is much the same. Today, the lovelorn search the Internet, correspond by e-mail, travel by plane, and send money by electronic transfer. Ah love.

## Traditional True Love

Many men seek foreign mates because they feel those women might be more traditional than American women. Brides from Asia and Russia are often depicted as family-oriented, hard working, and maternal—women who love to keep house and please their husbands. There are certainly women who fit that mold. Some are anxious to move to the United States, where they imagine that life will be better than their lives in their home countries.

Sometimes this change of lifestyle is the primary incentive—and love is secondary. Each person gets something out of the relationship, and maybe love will come later. Unfortunately, there are many more cases involving fraud, deceit, and lies than true love. In short, they're scams.

# Be Careful What You Wish For

There are definitely things to watch out for if someone is thinking of using the Internet to find a foreign bride. For example, while it may be flattering if the "bride" says she is in love after only a few letters or conversations, she may be trying to hurry things along. Does she want money sent to her for a plane ticket? Most legitimate brides would be pleased to have their future husbands make the trip. Most times a request for money means that money will never be seen again.

The same is true if she suddenly needs money for a personal emergency, family illness, hotel reservation, or some English lessons. These are common scams. The money is sent, and she splits.

Letters or e-mails that read like form letters are warning signs. They might have some personal information added, but it's usually at the very beginning or the end. One test is to contact the bride under a different name, and see if the response is the same.

Sometimes there is no "bride" at all. Scammers post bogus photos and try to get the prospective groom to send money. If a photo of the same woman can be found on numerous sites, it can be a red flag. Paying steep fees to any agency in advance is definitely not wise. And explicit instructions on how to wire money is another suspicious marker. Why is the "bride" so familiar with how to do this?

## Unsuspecting Brides

It's not always the man who is innocent and the prospective bride who is a con artist, however. Mail-order bride Web sites can be dangerous for prospective brides as well. There are equally disturbing stories of women who move to the United States and are abused by their new husbands. Here, the motive is not money, but rather the need for power. The idea that a woman from a third-world country will lack the English skills, personal finances, and worldliness to fight back is very appealing to these men.

Maybe bars and churches aren't such a bad way to meet people after all.

# A Truly Haunting Wedding

*What holiday speaks of love more than ... Halloween?*
*Wait. That's not right ...*

## Tie the Knot on Halloween

Maybe Valentine's Day still has a slight edge with lovers, but
Halloween has the Bride of Frankenstein. For a fun fall wedding,
October 31 seems to fit the bill. Halloween weddings offer a lot of
options. The more conservative or traditional bride might choose
to stick with a fall harvest theme. But the more daring bride—the
woman who chooses Halloween because it's *Halloween,* rather
than because it's the only free Saturday in October—can take this
holiday and run with it. If you love Halloween, you can create a
wedding that's, well, to die for.

## Set Up a Howling Good Time

Let invitations set the mood for Halloween nuptials. Brides can
make their own by using black cardstock with white, silver, or even
orange calligraphy. One bride printed her invitations on mottled
gray cardstock in a font appropriately called Ghost Town. And

don't forget the wedding cake. A pumpkin, spice, or red velvet cake can suit the
theme. For a traditional cake, black frosting
and flowers can help the Halloween theme
along, or the cake itself can be shaped like a
haunted house or a jolly jack-o'-lantern.

## What to Wear?

Black lace might not be for everyone, so an antique white or cream
wedding gown is a nice way to fit the mood and still have wedding
photos that are loved well into the future. Bridesmaid dresses in
purple, black, or navy with cameo necklaces add a nice touch.

## Location, Location, Location

An evening wedding is often popular with Halloween brides as darkness creates a spookier ambiance. The only problem is that it's often quite cool by sunset on October 31 in many parts of the country. It's always possible to rent outdoor space heaters or use a building such as an old stone church, a museum, or a historic mansion for the ceremony.

Destination weddings are all the rage these days—how about a "haunted" setting? These five hotels are perfect spots for Halloween weddings: Belcourt Castle in Newport, Rhode Island; the Stanley Hotel in Estes Park, Colorado; the Lemp Mansion in St. Louis, Missouri; Hawthorne Hotel in Salem, Massachusetts; and Hotel Provincial in New Orleans, Louisiana. Not only are they hauntingly beautiful, they're also rich in history. But beware . . . because they are all well known and popular, they need to be booked well in advance.

## Two Boo-tiful Brides

One Halloween bride went all out, wearing a gown of black lace (like a sexier Morticia Addams). Her husband was dressed in a turn-of-the-century frockcoat that conjured up images of the Abe Lincoln era. The venue was lit with flickering candlelight. Skeletons danced. And many of the guests came dressed in costumes. At the reception, a Jell-O Brain mold served as both salad and centerpiece. The happy bride reported that many of the guests said it was the most fun wedding they had ever attended.

Another Halloween bride, dressed in black velvet, wore jewelry complete with spiders and skulls and completed the look with very long, blood-red nails. Her bouquet was made of dried roses, wheat, and curly willow, all tied up with black lace and ribbons.

# Marriage en Masse

*Imagine sharing your wedding day with hundreds of other couples.
As crazy as it sounds, many people have.*

Living in a culture that has created a lucrative industry out of *"your
special day,"* mass marriage is almost unthinkable to us. It seems to
fly in the face of the individualism on which our society was built.
But marriage means different things in different places—even in
different subcultures right here in the United States. To some, a
wedding isn't an opportunity to express one's romantic love or creativity, but a covenant made to further the cause of something much
larger than one's self, whether that be religion, politics, or cultural
traditions. Not all the reasons for mass weddings are quite so lofty,
however. In the Arab world, it is often simply a matter of economics,
with governments, corporations, or wealthy individuals sponsoring
mass weddings for those who cannot afford their own.

## Moon Marriages

When most Americans think of mass marriage, they think of the
Reverend Sun Myung Moon. The leader of the Unification Church
started small with a wedding for 24 couples in 1954. By 1997, he
was hitching as many as 30,000 couples in an elaborate ceremony at
Robert F. Kennedy Memorial Stadium in Washington, D.C., and in
2009, he hit a whopping 45,000 in his home country of South Korea.
In many cases, Moon's church pairs the couples—many of them
barely know one another before taking their vows. Moon does not
see this as negative, however, but as a way of building a more multicultural, tolerant world.

## Celebrate Wedding Style

In October 2002, more than 500 couples took part in mass weddings all over Iraq to celebrate Saddam Hussein's new term in office.

Never mind that the election was no doubt stolen—at least it was a chance for impoverished couples to celebrate their marriages in a way they could otherwise never afford. Everything, from the Western-style white wedding dresses to the musical entertainment, was picked up by the state. In Baghdad alone, 155 couples took advantage of this rare generosity, relaxing for two nights in luxury hotels before returning to a world of sanctions and rationing.

## Nondiscriminatory Nuptials

On March 21, 2007, 692 couples were married or renewed their vows in Sint-Niklaas, Belgium, as a protest against racial discrimination. It all started when Wouter Van Bellingen became the first black registrar of the city (and of all of Belgium). Three couples declined to be married by Van Bellingen because of the color of his skin. At first Van Bellingen shrugged it off as "their problem," but after thinking it over, he formed a multicultural action group and planned a mass wedding. Couples came from the Netherlands, Germany, the United Kingdom, and Norway to participate in the event.

## Olympic-size Ceremonies

China set one heck of a record when, to celebrate the opening day of the 29th Olympic Games, at least 314,224 couples were married across the country. In Beijing, the host city of the Olympics, 15,646 lovebirds took the plunge, and all major cities saw spikes in their wedding registrations. It didn't hurt that the opening date of the games was 8/8/08—the number eight is a symbol of wealth and good luck for the Chinese.

## Marriages Made for Everyone

While mass weddings are quite common in the Arab world, the one held on October 13, 2009, in Riyadh, Saudi Arabia, was pretty unique: 102 disabled couples were married that day in the first ceremony of its kind for the handicapped. The wedding was well-publicized by the Saudi Arabian government, which is taking steps to eradicate the stigma attached to disabilities, allowing those with special needs to have fuller, more active lives.

# Sustainable Ceremonies

*It ain't easy bein' green. But for brides and grooms who care as much about the environment as they do about their betrothed, planning and hosting a green wedding is a labor of love.*

For serious-minded conservationist couples who are ready to go green all the way, the GreenBrideGuide.com offers a carbon calculator. Simply input the number of guests, the number of miles they will fly/drive to arrive at the nuptials, and the number of hotel nights they will stay, and the calculator will output the ceremony's carbon footprint. A medium-size wedding might rack up 63 tons of carbon emissions, for which the couple could purchase $882 of carbon credits to offset the costs of environmental remediation (at 2009 prices). Alternatively, they could employ the following real-life solutions to reduce the size of their carbon footprint.

## Invitations

Why kill a tree when there are so many green options available for getting the word out about a wedding? Some tree-hugging brides embrace electronic invitations, which divulge details of the big day without adding to landfill waste. One bride used the Internet to encourage her guests to interact and arrange car pools to her wedding festivities.

For those who want to stick with tradition by mailing formal invitations, recycled paper is the green way to go. Several companies now sell paper embedded with seeds, which serve to inform guests of wedding details now and remind them of the event later with wildflower displays.

## Attire

When it comes to wedding apparel, green brides tend to rely on something old—as in recycled gowns. Whether they favor vintage or retro, second-hand stores, as well as the Internet, are brimming with choices. Another popular option is to borrow or rent a dress.

Brides who favor something new for their special day can still go green—although not literally the color green as in Scarlett O'Hara's green velvet drapery gown. Rather, they can opt for a custom-made creation assembled from earth-friendly fabrics, like hemp, organic cotton, or "peace silk." Peace silk, aka "vegetarian silk," is processed in a humane manner, which lets the silk worms naturally emerge from their cocoons, rather than being boiled alive.

## Rings

Eternal symbols of love, rings comprised of precious metals and gems can become a source of contention for socially conscious couples. Astute fiancés who want to please their activist mates will select rings made from conflict-free diamonds and investigate to find out the source of origin for the gold in their wedding bands.

## Gifts

Eco-friendly couples can share their passion for conserving resources by gifting their guests with sustainable favors. Canvas tote bags are a popular option. One couple designed a removable pin to tie the totes in with their wedding theme. Potted herbs and flowers often pull double duty as wedding decorations and take-home favors.

Some socially responsible couples embrace the "it's better to give than to receive" philosophy by asking guests to donate to the couple's favorite environmental charities in lieu of purchasing wedding gifts.

## Menu

When it comes to food and beverages for the wedding feast, the green trend is to incorporate local ingredients into the menu whenever possible. Many environmentally conscious couples also follow a vegetarian or vegan lifestyle. However, when planning the menu, it is wise to consider your guests' palates along with your own passions. After pushing a tofu concoction around her plate like a finicky toddler, one meat-loving grandmother-of-the-bride was overheard to say, "If we could open a hamburger stand outside this reception, we could pay for the entire wedding.

# "Mazel tov!"

❧  ❧  ❧  ❧  ❧

*A glass is wrapped in a cloth (usually white), set on the ground before the couple, and then crushed by the foot of the groom. Loud cheers and shouts of good luck are sure to follow.*

## "Tradition, tradition!"

If you've been to a Jewish wedding, you've probably witnessed the breaking of the glass at the end of the ceremony. Where does this tradition come from? What does it mean? Those of the Jewish faith who are a bit superstitious believe that the sound of the glass breaking will drive away evil spirits. Some scholars believe it once represented the breaking of the hymen. Still others theorize that it is a symbol of God's command to "be fruitful and multiply"—the couple's offspring will eventually number as many as the broken shards of glass. Wherever the truth may lie, it is a custom rich in history.

## A Symbol of Permanence

For Orthodox and more traditional Jews, the breaking of the glass symbolizes the destruction of the Temple at Jerusalem in A.D. 70 during the First Jewish-Roman War. The future Roman emperor, Titus, and his army captured the city, which had been under Jewish control since A.D. 66, and the Temple was razed. A devastating event in Jewish history, it is still mourned once a year as the Tisha B'Av, a day of fasting and prayer. By remembering the destruction of the Temple at their wedding, a Jewish couple affirms that they "set Jerusalem above their highest joy" (Psalm 137). For reformed or secular Jewish couples, the breaking of the glass may represent the permanence of marriage: Just as a broken glass can never really be put together again, so is the couple ever changed by the vows they have just taken.

# May the Best Man Win

*The garter, once a symbol of virginal proportions,*
*still signals the next to wed.*

### Proof of Purity

While the garter toss may be one of the oldest wedding rituals on record, few grooms probably realize its symbolic nature. As early as medieval times, brides wore garters under their wedding gowns as sign of their virginal status. After the vows, the groom slipped the garter off his new wife's leg, the risqué move illustrating the relinquishment of her virginity.

### So Much for "Get a Room"

After the bride and groom made their eternal commitment, wedding attendees drew near the bridal bed to make sure the happy couple sealed the deal. As they waited for confirmation, the interlopers also vied for their chance to snag the no-longer-needed garter. Thankfully, a more civilized tradition eventually evolved, which allowed the groom to toss the garter from the bridal chambers before shutting the door for the night.

### All the Single Guys

Today, the garter toss ritual seen at many wedding receptions is largely for entertainment. Still, it can sometimes exhibit questionable taste as grooms crawl head-first under bridal gowns to remove garters—all the while wiggling their feet as if trapped.

One common practice is simply removing the garter from a seated bride's leg, then sling-shotting it to waiting single men who may (or may not) be eager to catch it. Why? As the tradition has it, the man who catches the garter will be the next to wed.

# Just Eloped!

*It happens every day: The bride and groom, overwhelmed by
the gathering storm of a big wedding (or interested in discretion
from the start), choose to slip away and say their vows in secret.
Here's a little history and etiquette surrounding
this alternative wedding custom.*

## 'Twas the First Elopement

As you probably know by now, until the mid-19th century, marriage
was less about love and more about economics. Parents arranged
unions that would benefit the families, and their kids didn't have
much to say in the matter. For those youngsters who happened to be
passionately in love with someone other than their betrothed, these
arrangements could be a real pain in the neck. So what did some of
the more daring kids do? They ran away! Together! Defying convention, culture, and their parents, the first elopers snuck away to get
married, often literally leaving in the dead of night, never to return.

Over the next century or so, elopements changed a bit. In the
West, marriage became more about the couple's relationship and less
about politics, so couples that were in love could marry each other
out in the open, no running away necessary. But around this time,
the wedding-as-big-business began to take hold, too, and the bigger
the weddings got, the warier some couples got of the whole process.
In the '60s and '70s, it was trendy to scale back a bit (think barefoot
beach weddings with friends and family), but some couples were still
less than excited about making their wedding about anyone but the
two of them. Whether for financial reasons or personal ones, eloping
has become a viable option for couples that want to wed.

## Elopement or Not?

Purists believe that to truly elope, a couple has to get married
completely in secret—not even mom or dad should be present. But
for many, the modern definition of "elopement" is more generous.

Today, eloping can mean having anything other than a large, traditional, structured wedding. Going down to the courthouse or arranging a dinner with the family, where the ceremony happens over dessert, are both now considered versions of eloping.

By and large, couples that choose to elope do so by jetting off to an exotic or otherwise exciting locale, such as Italy, Mexico, or Vegas, and having their marriage made official by a city clerk. Plenty of travel agencies and online companies offer "elopement packages" for those who want to get out of town.

## Elope-iquette

Not so long ago, elopements were seen by many as a kind of thumbing of the nose by the couple to their friends and family. This is less so these days, as more and more people realize that the cost and stress of a big wedding (even a small big wedding) is simply not necessary. But in order to keep from hurting the feelings of the people you love the most, there are some important things to keep in mind if you're planning on eloping.

When you get engaged, consider sending out engagement announcements. Not everyone does, but for a couple that has their eye on an elopement, engagement announcements assure friends and family that you didn't just run off with the milkman.

Engagement announcements are considerate, but it's largely recognized that a couple that elopes does need to send out an announcement of marriage after the fact. Not only does it let people know that you're married now, it implies parental approval, which may save you from having to answer lots of questions over the next few years. The announcements can include pictures if you like, which is another way to include loved ones in the celebration of your marriage, even if they weren't there in person.

Weddings Through the Years

# Let Them Eat Cake

*Wedding cakes are not a new tradition. The idea dates back thousands of years, but the type of cake and its appearance has changed considerably over the years.*

- **40 B.C.:** During the Roman Empire, wedding cake was not really cake as we know it. This cake was more of an unsweetened bread made with flour, salt, and water. The wedding couple tasted the cake, which was then broken over the bride's head by her groom to encourage prosperity, happiness, and fertility in the coming years.

- **Medieval Times:** Brides of the Middle Ages didn't need to worry about choosing their wedding cake. The guests brought small cakes—more like sweet buns—which they stacked as high as possible before the newlyweds. The couple kissed over the pile for good luck. This was the forerunner to the stacked cake that we know today.

- **17th Century:** Many wedding receptions in the 1600s featured a bride's pie—a crust filled with sweet breads, mincemeat, or mutton. Probably the best ingredient was a small glass ring baked inside. Custom said that the lady who discovered the ring in her slice would be the next to marry.

- **18th Century:** Victorian cakes were frosted in white to represent the purity of the bride. But pre-Victorian brides valued white cakes as well. White icing called for the best refined sugar, an ingredient not readily available. So white wedding cakes were considered a symbol of affluence.

- **1850–1900:** Credit the Brits with the wedding cake as we know it today. When Queen Victoria's daughter married in 1859, her cake was a frosted three-tier masterpiece—but only the bottom was cake. The top was just sugar. Prince Leopold's wedding in 1882 featured an all-cake structure, but it took 20 more years for columns to appear. The top layer of these three-tiered wedding cakes was saved for the christening of the couple's first child.

- **1930s:** Cake toppers such as a bride and groom, cupid, or horseshoe were molded from food products, bisque, papier-mâché, and celluloid.

- **1940s:** Wartime sugar rationing made it hard for brides to have the traditional wedding cake, thus, the cakes were much smaller. Some were even made to look like the typical cake by pairing it with a box made of plaster of Paris. Yum.

- **1950s:** After the war was over, couples went all out on cake decorations, often using silver trinkets, such as horseshoes, leaves, hearts, and flowers. Fruitcakes iced with marzipan were a popular choice for the base.

- **1960s:** The '60s were a cross between the elegance of Jackie Kennedy and the hip look of Twiggy. Daisies and bright colors made their debut and cake toppers were all plastic for the first time.

- **1970s:** Even in the era of free love, cakes were not forgotten. The traditional three tiers were still common but the style was "anything goes."

- **2000s:** Creativity reigns in modern wedding cake designs. Elaborate tiered cakes are common but so are cupcake arrangements, flavored cakes, and cakes sculpted into practically every size and shape imaginable. They're almost too pretty to eat!

# How to (Not) Marry a Multimillionaire

꧑   ꧑   ꧑   ꧑   ꧑

*When Darva Conger and Rick Rockwell said "I do," it wasn't a match made in heaven. It was a proposal—and a wedding ceremony—made in front of viewers who watched the reality show* Who Wants to Marry a Multi-Millionaire?

The creators of *Who Wants to Marry a Multi-Millionaire?* invited 50 single women from across the country to fly to Las Vegas and compete for the heart of an unknown multimillionaire. The women never saw Rick Rockwell—a self-described real estate investor and motivational speaker reportedly worth more than $2 million—except in silhouette. When the two-hour FOX network show aired on February 15, 2000, it ended with a real wedding ceremony.

## 'Til the End of the Series Do Us Part

During the show—a competition much like a beauty pageant—the women paraded the stage and were eliminated in rounds based on Rockwell's criteria. Darva Conger, a blonde, curvaceous emergency room nurse, edged out the other contestants to take the top spot. Rockwell proposed to Conger, who donned an ill-fitting wedding gown and married him in front of the millions who tuned to the broadcast.

In addition to winning the man of her dreams, or at least the man of the moment, Conger also won an Isuzu Trooper, a $35,000 diamond ring, and other prizes. Then the newlyweds did what any couple would do: They cruised to the Caribbean. However, their fairy tale ended before the ship even docked. The couple slept in separate beds, and the marriage remained unconsummated. Conger later said she spent more time with their chaperone than her new husband. An annulment was filed just weeks afterward.

## The Downhill Slide

Unfortunately for viewers, as the show aired in February, the proposal and marriage seemed to be happening in real time. However, by then, Conger had already filed for an annulment and returned to her life. She said she just wanted a free trip to Las Vegas.

After word leaked that the marriage wasn't legit, Conger was fired from her job. She faced mortgage payments but had no income. Enter *Playboy*. In August 2000, the magazine published nude photographs of Conger, for which she reportedly earned six digits.

By the time the *Playboy* issue hit newsstands, Conger's marriage to Rockwell had been annulled for months, but rumors were gaining steam. Information surfaced that shed doubt on the validity of Rockwell's fortune, and it didn't help when the public learned he'd once told jokes for 30 straight hours to get into *Guinness World Records*. There was also troubling news that nine years before Rockwell married Conger, he'd been the subject of a restraining order after threatening to physically harm his girlfriend.

## Reality Is Better Than Fiction

The FOX network said they'd checked into Rockwell's history, and that the controversial marriage, though not long-lasting, had been legal. But Rockwell's sketchy past only added fuel to the fire. Within weeks of airing *Who Wants to Marry a Multi-Millionaire?* FOX threw a blanket on the show's franchise. It was never repeated.

Two years later, Conger again planned to wed—this time for real. And to pay for the wedding, she cashed in on her pseudo-celeb status. For $35,000, Conger took a beat-down from a former Olympic gymnast in *Celebrity Boxing II*.

Although Conger's first marriage and her newly earned money lacked staying power, *Who Wants to Marry a Multi-Millionaire?* was a glimpse into a new genre of American television: The reality show. *Who Wants to Marry a Multi-Millionaire?* spawned modern celebrity: ordinary people courting the media, trying to gain public image.

# Spoken For: Commitment Customs

*First comes love, then comes marriage . . . or so the saying goes.*
*However, some couples prefer to stretch the period of time*
*between love's first blush and the culminating bonds of marriage*
*by "engaging" in practices that publicly express their commitment*
*without taking it all the way to the altar.*

## Rings . . .

Precious metals that are forged into circular shapes without beginning or end, rings are a time-honored symbol of love and commitment. However, different rings signify different things. Back in the day, high-schooler Biff would announce his intention to enter into an exclusive relationship with Susie by giving her his senior class ring. Susie would proudly display this token of affection by wearing it on a chain around her neck or lovingly wrapping it with yarn to secure it on her slender finger. Without the benefit of this "upper classman" advantage, younger Romeos resorted to cigar bands and even adhesive bandages to express their ardor.

A promise ring was the next stop on the love train. More feminine and mature than a class ring—not to mention custom-fit—a promise ring held the pledge of a future engagement and signified the first tentative step toward the aisle.

## And Things . . .

Rings are not the only items used to express commitment. Letter sweaters, jackets, and ID bracelets also symbolize a "going steady" status. Some college men present their sweethearts with lavalieres—necklaces with their fraternity letters—to signify the seriousness of their relationship. But the ultimate Greek act of commitment occurs when a frat boy "pins" his intended life partner.

The Catholic Church took a dim view of the monogamous trend that began among youth in the 1950s. In 1957, *TIME* magazine reported on a Catholic high school in Connecticut that had expelled four students for going steady. An article in a Paulist Fathers publication warned it was "impossible" for a young boy and girl in an exclusive relationship to be alone together "without serious sin." (Amen.)

## Gestures of Love

Exchanging trinkets isn't the only way to express commitment. Some couples feel the need to memorialize their undying affection for each other by publicly linking their names for all to see. Whether scrawling their names on trees, water towers, bathroom stalls, or their own skins via tattooing, the whole world is a canvas.

In Rome, the Eternal City, couples often express their commitment in a "novel" way. Recently young lovers have been mimicking a scene from *I Want You,* a best-selling-book-turned-movie in which the protagonist padlocks a chain around a lamppost on a bridge; he then tosses the key into the Tiber River to signify his everlasting love. Since then, so many love locks have been wrapped around lampposts over Rome's Ponte Milvio bridge that the authorities have had to install special steel posts to preserve the light posts.

## Commitment Ceremonies

Ceremonies are sometimes used to signal commitment without entering into a ball-and-chain contract. Handfasting, an ancient Celtic ritual where the couple's wrists were symbolically tied together, was practiced by the upper class as an engagement of sorts, to signify a promise of marriage before the dowry details were worked out. For the peasant class, for whom dowries often weren't an issue, handfasting was kind of a trial marriage signifying that the couple would stay together for a predetermined length of time, generally a year, and then reevaluate their relationship. The phrase "tying the knot" reportedly originated from handfasting.

# Dearest Regard

*Two historically popular rings spell out one's feelings.*

## For Your Dearest

The diamond engagement ring is the mainstay of modern marriages. However, this hasn't always been the case. While the diamond has long been a part of the jeweled rings used to signify a couple's intent to marry, it hasn't always been the centerpiece. The "dearest" ring, which was popular in the Victorian era, included seven gems placed in order from left to right: Diamond, Emerald, Amethyst, Ruby, Emerald, Sapphire, and Topaz.

Although a beautiful addition to any ring finger, the dearest ring was a piece of jewelry that did more than symbolize an upcoming marriage. It contained a special message for the woman meant to wear it. Not sure what that means? Look closely at the first letter of each gem, which spell: D-E-A-R-E-S-T. This style of jewelry, in which the first letter of each gem's name together spells a word, is known as "acrostic" jewelry.

## Nothing Says I Love You Like Lazurite

In addition to the dearest ring, the "regard" ring was another example of acrostic jewelry that peaked in popularity in the 1800s. The gems in this ring, from left to right, spelled "regard" and included: Ruby, Emerald, Garnet, Amethyst, Ruby, and Diamond.

Today, the dearest and regard rings aren't just for engagements. These rings also are given as pre-engagement promise rings or as anniversary rings. Modern acrostic rings may, for example, include gems that spell a name like Ashlee: Aquamarine, Sapphire, Hessonite Garnet, Lapis Lazuli, Emerald, and Emerald.

Some couples opt for an acrostic ring as a way to go against the norm, using the occasion to spell out their feelings for each other in creative ways. Possibly the most fitting expression uses Lazurite, Opal, Vesuvianite, and Emerald to spell L-O-V-E. Awww.

# Quiz

*True or False?*

Most of the traditions folks practice at weddings today come from ancient times, even if they've been tweaked or adapted over the years. Take this true or false quiz to test your knowledge of various ancient cultures and their wedding customs.

**1.** It's considered bad luck for a bride to put on her own veil.

**2.** The practice of wearing engagement and wedding rings on the fourth finger on the left hand comes from an ancient Asian tradition.

**3.** In China, it was customary for the groom to "obtain" the bride on the day of the wedding by traveling to her house while setting off firecrackers and beating loud gongs and drums.

**4.** Some African American couples incorporate the "jumping the broom" ceremony in their wedding rites.

**5.** In Greek weddings, it's customary for the bride and groom to be connected by ribbons tied around their waists.

**6.** The traditional Irish wedding cake is a rich, dark chocolate.

**7.** Particularly in the smaller villages of Germany, sometimes friends and family would "kidnap" the bride and hide her.

**8.** Historically, Korean families would employ the expertise of a fortune-teller to ensure that the betrothed couple was a suitable pair.

**9.** The largest religious faith in Japan has long been Buddhism. Therefore, orthodox Japanese weddings were performed in Buddhist temples.

*Answers on the next page.*

### Answers:

**1.** True. This notion comes from Ireland, where it's considered much better to have a well-married woman affix the bride's veil for her.

**2.** False. The practice comes to us from ancient Rome, where it was believed a nerve ran directly from this finger to the heart.

**3.** True. The loud noises were meant to scare off evil spirits.

**4.** True. This tradition allegedly began during times of slavery and is still practiced by some couples today.

**5.** False. In fact, in an ancient custom still practiced today, the bride and groom both wear crowns during the ceremony connected by a ribbon. This signifies the union of the couple and indicates the pair's rule over their household.

**6.** False. Traditional Irish wedding cake is a fruitcake, iced in white. The top tier of the wedding cake is traditionally an Irish whiskey cake, which is saved for the christening of the couple's first baby.

**7.** True. This required the groom to search high and low, or more accurately from one pub to the next, for his beloved. Excessive drinking naturally ensued, and often times, the groom would get stuck with the check for all of the pub patrons.

**8.** True. Assuming the couple passed the test, called *kung-hap,* the couple moved forward with their engagement and could claim all kinds of lavish gifts.

**9.** False. Acutally, Shinto has been the largest religious faith in Japan. Orthodox Japanese weddings were performed in Shinto temples, and finances permitting, many still do today. Second runner-up would be a Buddhist ceremony.

# 'Til Port Do Us Part

*The captain of a ship holds wide-ranging legal powers when that vessel is at sea, but it's a nautical myth that any ship's captain can perform a legally binding marriage.*

- Unless the captain of a vessel happens to also be an ordained minister, judge, or recognized official such as a notary public, he or she generally doesn't have the authority to perform a legally binding marriage at sea. In fact, a suitably licensed captain is no more qualified to perform marriages than a similarly licensed head chef, deck hand, or galley worker. There are a few specific exceptions: Captains of Japanese vessels can perform marriages at sea, as long as both the bride and groom hold valid Japanese passports. And thanks to a quirk in Bermuda law, captains with Bermuda licenses are also legally authorized to officiate weddings aboard ship.

- The myth that any ship's captain has the power to marry at sea has been propagated by countless romantic movies and is so widely believed, even among sailors, that the U.S. Navy specifically forbids it. Section 700.716 of the U.S. Navy Regulations reads: "The commanding officer shall not perform a marriage ceremony on board his ship or aircraft. He shall not permit a marriage ceremony to be performed on board when the ship or aircraft is outside the territory of the United States, except: (a) In accordance with local laws . . . and (b) In the presence of a diplomatic official of the United States."

- As an alternative to a wedding at sea, couples may want to consider exchanging vows aboard a ship that is docked in a port. Ultimately, though, if you want to avoid a legal battle to validate your cruise-line marriage, you may want to heed the adage displayed on many vessels: "Any marriages performed by the captain of this ship are valid for the duration of the voyage only."

# Mother-in-Law Mix-up

*Destination weddings are all the rage: Exotic location, beautiful beach. Just make sure to check your documentation. Check it twice.*

## Have Passport, Will Marry

Getting married on the Italian isle of Capri was a natural choice for Allison Gates and her fiancé, D. J. McCutcheon. After all, they got engaged there. So they did their homework and found out that a marriage license from the American Embassy and a three-day residency in Italy were required. Easy, right?

On the morning before the wedding, the bridal couple grabbed their passports from the hotel safe and set off on a boat to Naples to get the marriage license. At 11 A.M., Judy Gates got a frantic call from her daughter—she had grabbed her brother's passport by mistake, and the Embassy was closing at noon. No passport, no license. No license, no wedding. You see the problem.

## I, D. J., Take You, Mother-in-Law . . .

Judy got her daughter's passport from the safe, but discovered she had no cash for the boat. A sympathetic hotel manager loaned her 50 Euros, and she set off.

Wanting to call her daughter to have someone meet the boat, Judy searched for English-speaking tourists who might have a phone. Success. A nice couple from Baltimore helped her out.

Allison stayed at the Embassy, begging them to remain open until the passport arrived. D. J. ran to the dock. When Judy reached into her purse, D. J. quickly grabbed the passport and tore off down the street. It was then that Judy realized she had handed him her own passport. That's not the name they wanted on the license!

She yelled. No one heard. A crewmember on the boat sounded the horn and the wedding consultant raced back for Allison's passport. They arrived back at the Embassy at 11:59, and the staff stayed long enough to process the license. Whew. The wedding was on.

# Operation Royal Charm: A Wedding Bust

*Undercover FBI agents spent several years watching their targets—
members of an international counterfeiting and smuggling ring—and
developing a relationship with them. It worked so well that the
ultimate wedding sting operation just fell into place.*

## Nice Day for a Fake Wedding

Two of the agents, who had gained the trust of the criminals, posed
as bride and groom, with a fake wedding that was months in the
making. A date was set, and invitations were sent out. The wedding
was planned for 2 p.m. on a Sunday afternoon in August 2005, just
off the coast of New Jersey. A luxury yacht named *Operation Royal
Charm* was docked outside of Atlantic City, and guests started arriv-
ing from far and wide. No detail was forgotten: Guests and the bridal
party were decked out in wedding finery befitting the high rollers
that they were. There were even wedding presents, including a pair
of Presidential Rolex watches.

But when the guests boarded a boat that they thought would
take them out to the yacht, they got a bit of a surprise. There was
no wedding! And instead of a cruise on a luxury boat, eight wedding guests got caught in an FBI sting that led to the arrest of about
60 other residents of Asia and the United States, all involved in a
variety of international trafficking crimes.

## Quite the Wedding Gifts

Authorities seized $4.4 million in counterfeit $100 bills, $42 million
worth of counterfeit cigarettes, $700,000 worth of fake U.S. postage
stamps and blue jeans, and very real quantities of Viagra, ecstasy, and
methamphetamine. The criminals were also charged with conspiracy
to ship $1 million of automatic rifles, silenced pistols, submachine
guns, and rocket launchers—none of which were delivered.

## Weddings 'Round the World
# Lucky in Love

*A traditional Irish wedding can be a beautiful and festive setting for the special day. And it doesn't have to cost a pot of gold.*

### Luck o' the Irish

The first order of business is choosing a wedding date. In Ireland, weddings are usually held during one of the main Irish festivals in May, August, November, or February. New Year's Eve is also thought to be lucky because the newlyweds will wake up on the first day of the New Year to start the first day of their new life. And of course, St. Patrick's Day is a popular date for Irish weddings. But any date can be considered lucky if Irish traditions are added.

### Good Gear

Some people say the wedding is all about the dress, and following Irish tradition, this is easy. Ireland is known for its beautiful lace, so a gown made of lace, accented with lace, or accompanied by a veil of Irish lace is always the perfect choice. The bride may sew or pin a shamrock to the inner hem of her dress for good luck.

Some brides choose a green dress for their Irish wedding, but according to Irish folklore this is *not* a good decision. The fairies are attracted to green, and since they love to steal and keep pretty things, a bride in a green dress would definitely be in danger of getting kidnapped! It's much safer to stick with white. But if a bride wants to honor the oldest of Irish traditions, she chooses blue. This was the color of purity before the 15th century—many an Irish bride walked down the aisle in blue.

Irish brides also traditionally carry a horseshoe for good luck—with the open part facing upward so the good luck doesn't run out. This may sound a bit old, heavy, and rusty, so these days brides can carry a porcelain horseshoe or even choose a fabric horseshoe worn around the wrist as a bracelet.

## The Celtic Trinity

A shamrock is the traditional symbol of Ireland. The druids in Ireland looked at the shamrock as a sacred plant because its leaves formed a triad, and three was a mystical number in the Celtic religion. Shamrocks can show up anywhere and everywhere in an Irish wedding: in the bouquets, on the tables, even in the frosting of the cake. Some bridal couples give tiny potted plants to their guests as wedding favors.

An exchange of Celtic love knot rings is a great way to honor Irish heritage. They have no beginning or end and symbolize everlasting love. A Claddagh ring is also a popular choice. The Claddagh design is two hands clasping a crown and a heart, symbolic of friendship, love, and loyalty.

When the couple is ready to leave the church, someone is supposed to throw an old shoe over the bride's head for good luck. Here's hoping it's someone with good aim!

## *Sláinte*

What would an Irish wedding—or any wedding—be without food? Traditionally, Irish weddings were potlucks with corned beef and cabbage, Irish stew, lamb, and soda bread. Some couples, however, prefer a more elegant reception and incorporate some of these foods with others that are more to their tastes.

After the feast, an Irish wedding cake is a must. Unfortunately, that typically means a dense fruitcake with white icing. Thus, many wedding couples save this traditional cake for the top tier, with the cake's lower levels made of something a bit tastier for the guests. Served with Guinness, Irish whisky, and Bailey's Irish Cream, not too many people will remember what the cake tasted like anyway.

And here's a tradition most mothers-in-law must love: If the groom's mother breaks a slice of wedding cake over the bride's head, she and her daughter-in-law will be friends for life. Wonder who came up with that one?

# Wedded at the White House

*There have been many
White House weddings—21 in all.*

## I Now Pronounce You President and First Lady

Grover Cleveland was the second of three presidents to marry while in office (with John Tyler and Woodrow Wilson as the other two). He wed Frances Folsom in the Blue Room of the White House on June 2, 1886, an event that turned Folsom into the youngest first lady in our nation's history—Cleveland was 49 years old, Folsom was 21. Fortunately, the age difference didn't stop them from having a very happy marriage (also fortunately, the public didn't take exception to Cleveland's marrying a much younger woman). And when Cleveland was voted out of office after only one term, his wife cheerfully assured the White House staff that they'd be back in four years—and they were.

## Alice in White House Land

Nine White House weddings were those of children of various presidents: Maria Hester Monroe, John Adams II, Elizabeth Tyler, Nellie Grant, Alice Roosevelt, Jessie Wilson, Eleanor Wilson, Lynda Bird Johnson, and Tricia Nixon. Of these, there are two that stand out—not only for their glamour, but also for the media sensations they caused: the weddings of Alice Roosevelt and Tricia Nixon. Alice Roosevelt, the daughter of President Theodore Roosevelt, swept into the White House with her father in 1901. Alice's mother had died only two days after her birth, and she didn't get along with her stepmother. She was spoiled in a material sense, but never felt a part of her father's new family. Starting in her teenage years, and continuing well into young adulthood, this caused her to do a lot of what we like to call "acting out"—smoking, gambling, and carousing with male friends.

Regardless of her modern-day socialite behavior, the American people couldn't get enough of Alice—mainly her wild antics and flamboyant fashion sense. And when her engagement to Nicholas Longworth was announced in 1906, the press whipped the public into a frenzy with their breathless coverage of the wedding planning. Alice and Longworth were married in the East Room of the White House on a cold but sunny February day. True to form, Alice had no bridesmaids in attendance—she was determined that all eyes would be on her at every moment. Sadly, her fabulous wedding was the start of a miserable marriage: Her husband turned out to be an alcoholic and a womanizer, and her only child was conceived in an adulterous affair.

## It's Coming Up Roses

Sixty-five years after Alice Roosevelt's special day, another White House wedding captured the imagination of the public, but the bride was the exact opposite of her hard-partying predecessor. Tricia Nixon was so private, shy, and retiring that her outgoing younger sister Julie had once jokingly called her "The Howard Hughes of the White House." However, Tricia decided to make her wedding a grand affair: Not only would it take place at the White House, it would be held in the Rose Garden, on June 12, 1971. This caused much hand-wringing over possible weather problems, for Washington's summers are notoriously rainy, but on the big day, the sun came out, and Tricia herself also shone in a sleeveless Priscilla Kidder gown cut on the bias.

Oddly enough, the guest of honor at Tricia Nixon's wedding was none other than Alice Roosevelt Longworth. And the spry 87-year-old hadn't changed much. The kind invitation didn't stop her from later saying of Tricia, "She seems rather pathetic, doesn't she? I wonder what's wrong with her?"

## *Behind the Bride's Music*

*Mention the phrase "Here Comes the Bride" and most people in America—indeed, most people in the Western world—could hum the tune. But few know which opera it comes from or who composed it, and even fewer know of its pagan inspiration.*

### There Goes the Bride

"Here Comes the Bride" is properly known as the "Bridal Chorus" and is from the opera *Lohengrin.* German composer Richard Wagner began work on *Lohengrin* in 1845. He suffered from skin problems and thus was sitting in a medicinal bath one day, when he suddenly became inspired to write an opera based on Lohengrin, a legendary medieval knight. In Wagner's retelling of the tale, the mysterious knight saves the beautiful Elsa from the malicious Count Telramund—but only on the condition that she never ask his identity. After Elsa's rescue, they fall in love and are married. However, on their wedding night, Elsa can't control her curiosity and asks her new husband the question that shall not be asked. Lohengrin reveals his identity, kicks Elsa to the curb, and skips town. Consequently, Elsa freaks out and dies. So . . . a chorus from this opera is now commonly used on what is supposed to be "the happiest day of your life." Hmm. . .

### There's New Tunes in Town

Of course, not every bride uses "Here Comes the Bride" for her processional. Catholic priests discourage it because they consider it secular, Lutheran pastors discourage it because they consider it pagan, and rabbis . . . well, Wagner's anti-Semitism was not exactly a secret (and most Jewish weddings do not feature a processional anyway). Then there are many brides who insist on "something different." Don't read too much into it, though—Wagner's "Bridal Chorus" is still famous, it's just not as pervasive as it once was.

# Shot Through the Heart

*The term probably originated in 19th-century rural America, but shotgun weddings have been happening around the world for ages, in all social classes, and including, yes, celebrities.*

## Get Married . . . or ELSE!

When most people hear the phrase "shotgun wedding," they probably think of a firearm-toting father forcing his pregnant daughter and her boyfriend into a church. The purpose of such hasty marriages was almost always to maintain or restore the "honor" of the woman and/ or her family. But true shotgun weddings, in which the groom is threatened into marriage by the bride's father, are practically nonexistent in the Western world today, since there is not as much of a stigma attached to out-of-wedlock motherhood. However, the phrase still manages to rear its head and provide some friendly ribbing among friends whenever the bride happens to be pregnant.

## Shotgun Weddings Heard 'Round the World

In the celebrity world, shotgun weddings have been tabloid fodder since at least 1952. That's the year that Sid Luft married Judy Garland after getting her pregnant a second time (the first pregnancy was aborted). Another 1952 shotgun wedding was far more low-key, however—that of Ronald Reagan and Nancy Davis. They were married on March 4, and their daughter, Patti, was born on October 21. More recent celebrity shotgun weddings include Ashlee Simpson and Pete Wentz (married on May 17, 2008, with Bronx Mowgli born November 20, 2008) and Jessica Alba and Cash Warren (married on May 19, 2008, with Honor Marie born June 7, 2008).

# Can't Top This...

*Traditional cake toppers are giving way to irreverent, sometimes wacky, depictions of today's brides and grooms.*

Wondering what kind of bride and groom figurine to place on top of your wedding cake? The decision is certainly more complicated than ever before. In fact, the shear number of unique cake toppers available at online and specialty retailers makes the traditional bride and groom figurine seem like a relic of weddings past.

## The New Take on Toppers

Today's cake toppers are as individualized as the couples they represent. Customized cake toppers can be handcrafted to reflect the bride and groom's body measurements, facial features, and hairstyles. These sculpted figurines depict surprisingly realistic 3-D details or can take on a whimsical caricature effect.

Other cake toppers depict a bride and groom with their favorite pets or enjoying a pastime. Whether the bride and groom are wearing water skis, riding snowmobiles, or casting fishing lines, there's a collectible that captures nearly every hobby.

Some cake toppers take a more humorous approach. For example, a bride dragging a groom caveman-style to the altar, or a bride and groom each talking on a cell phone. Another figurine depicts the bride "in charge" as she wears the groom's tuxedo pants and he idly stands by wearing boxers.

For couples seeking something a bit more scandalous, there are cake toppers that catch the bride and groom figurines mid-action—as she leaps into his arms for a passionate kiss or wraps her legs around his waist. Others reveal enough leg to show the bride's garter or portray the groom as he removes the garter. Some toppers may even illustrate the couple's honeymoon plans, with a groom pulling playing cards from his sleeve and the bride trading her dress for casino-ready attire.

# Topper Timeline

Wedding guests have come to "expect the unexpected"—at least when it involves cake toppers—but one thing is a mystery: The origins of the cake topper are largely unknown.

The first recorded cake toppers appeared in the late 1800s. They were homemade and composed of molded sugar and sugar paste, making any surviving figurines a sought-after commodity for collectors. It wasn't until the 1920s that bride and groom figurines got the stamp of approval from one of the nation's most influential mavens of wedding manners—and became a fashionable part of popular culture.

In a book published in 1922, *Etiquette in Society, in Business, in Politics and at Home,* Emily Post wrote, "the wedding cake . . . is usually in several tiers, beautifully decorated with white icing and topped by small figures of the bride and groom."

By the late 1920s, the Sears and Roebuck mail order catalogue was devoting an entire page to wedding cake decorations, including cake toppers. The mass-produced toppers were made out of more durable materials, such as porcelain, glass, and eventually, plastic.

## Toppers Following the Trends

As the figurines became an iconic part of American weddings, they also began to reflect the times. As World War II loomed in the 1940s, groom sculptures often appeared in military uniform. Through the ensuing decades, miniature brides' and grooms' attire mirrored current fashions, from the empire waistlines of the '60s to the mutton-chop sleeves of the late '70s. Additionally, symbols of love and commitment were sometimes seen atop wedding cakes, such as doves, silver bells, and cherubs.

Cake toppers still play an important role in today's weddings. After a couple cuts the wedding cake, the topper is removed, cleaned, and saved. Sometimes the top tier of the cake is frozen, to be thawed and eaten on the couple's first anniversary—with the bride and groom that once topped the cake in attendance, of course.

# Gotterdammerung Wedding

*It was April 29, 1945, in Hitler's underground
bunker in Berlin...*

The Soviet Army is pounding what is left of the city into the ground,
fighting the small groups of old men and boys who are the last true
believers in the Nazi cause. Adolf Hitler knows that he has run
out of time. There is nowhere left to go in the world that he once
believed he would conquer; suicide is his only way out. However, he
doesn't have to face his death alone. With him until the bitter end
is his longtime mistress and new bride, Eva Braun. They will die
together mere hours after their bizarre, morbid wedding ceremony.

## Evaluating Eva

Hitler's Minister of Armaments and War Production, Albert Speer,
once said that Eva Braun would "prove a disappointment to historians." It's easy to see why. Braun lived in fascinating, complex times,
but she wasn't a fascinating, complex person. Hitler made it clear
that the role of German women was not to be intellectual, ambitious,
or clever. Their highest purpose, according to the dictator, was to
bear healthy children for the Reich, so it didn't really matter what
was between their ears. There are many theories as to why Hitler did
not procreate with Braun. According to Hitler, it was because any
son of his would feel he had to live up to Hitler's greatness. Whether
Eva Braun actually wanted children of her own is not known.

Hitler met Braun in 1929, when she was just 17 years old and
was working as an assistant and model in a photographer's studio
in Munich. As Hitler's mistress, Braun lived in a gilded cage. She
enjoyed the perks their relationship provided, such as a suburban
villa, a Mercedes, and a maid. She loved the luxury of Hitler's Alpine
retreat, the Berghof. Her days appeared to be filled with nothing
but reading romance novels, watching films, playing with pets, and

dining with friends. Like many Germans, she enjoyed strenuous exercise and nude sunbathing. Photography remained an interest all her life, and she often took both still and moving pictures of Hitler and others in their inner circle. Though Hitler disapproved of women wearing makeup, drinking alcohol, and smoking, he tolerated these things in Eva. Hitler and Braun's sex life was active in the  early years of their affair, but by 1943, she reported to Speer that their intimate encounters had dwindled to almost nothing. Hitler had become too preoccupied by the war.

## Hitler Gets Hitched

Hitler entered his bunker (the *Führerbunker*) on January 16, 1945. His senior staff, an administrative staff, and a medical staff joined him. This concrete basement, located beneath the New Reich Chancellery, did a good job of protecting its occupants from Soviet shelling. Even so, everyone there was miserable, planning either their suicides or last-minute escapes. Most miserable of all was Hitler, but he did brighten just a bit when Braun traveled from Munich in early April to be by his side at the end.

Refusing to leave Hitler, and thus knowing her fate, the bride wore black on April 29 when she married the Führer in a decidedly depressing civil wedding witnessed by top Nazis Joseph Goebbels and Martin Bormann. With a shaking hand, she almost signed the marriage certificate as "Eva Braun," but then crossed out the "B" and wrote "Hitler." Her new husband ordered the few loyal staff members who were still with them in the bunker to address her as "Frau Hitler," but he continued to refer to her as "Fraulein Braun." Just one day after their wedding, Adolf Hitler and Eva Braun committed double suicide, he with a gun and she with a cyanide capsule. He was 56 years old. She was 33.

# When Someone Else Knows Best

*If you think arranged marriages are a thing of the past,
or that they don't happen in the United States, think again.*

## Modern Arrangements

While arranged marriage traditions are certainly controversial, and
while abuse can definitely occur, they all can't simply be lumped
together into one category. They are practiced by so many different kinds of people and for so many different kinds of reasons. For
some, an arranged marriage may be for religious reasons; for others,
the motive is purely cultural. Most arranged marriages are encouraged or even insisted upon by one or both sets of parents, but in others, the bride and groom themselves decide to take that route and
have the freedom to give the final "yes" or "no."

## Matchmaker, Matchmaker

In American Orthodox Jewish circles, many, if not most, young
couples meet through the *shidduch,* a matchmaking process facilitated by parents, close relatives, or friends. They may even be paired
through a professional matchmaker (known as a *shadchan*). These
facilitators "check out" the prospective bride or groom as a way of
shielding a loved one (or client) from emotional pain. If the prospective spouse passes muster, a meeting, called a *bashow,* is set
up for the couple and both sets of parents. The parents break the
ice with small talk, and then retreat to another room so that their
children can speak privately. Some Orthodox Jews may even have
many bashows before finding their *bashert* (soulmate), but the more
conservative members of the Jewish community frown upon such
"dating around." A Hassidic rabbi's daughter, for example, would
be expected to have very few bashows—and ideally, just one. If a
bashow is considered successful, a relatively short engagement of
anywhere from a few weeks to a few months is entered into.

## Marriages Made to Last

Many Muslims in the United States also rely on family and friends to help them when it comes to finding an appropriate mate. This is necessary since very devout Muslims do not socialize with the opposite sex the way most young Americans do. For them, it is a way of keeping chaste and maintaining a modest demeanor. Though there can be pressure from parents to marry and have children, most Muslims deny that they would ever force a marriage on their child, citing a story in the Koran in which Mohammed spares a young woman from marrying a man she does not admire. Still, there are rare instances of adult children going through with marriages they do not really want for the sake of their parents.

## Shared Expectations

Young Indian Americans also feel parental pressure to marry other Indian Americans and honor their cultural heritage. Of all the immigrant groups in America, their matchmaking process seems the most high tech, with Web sites, such as Indianmarriages.com, popping up on the Internet every day. Though their parents and immediate family play large supporting roles in their quest to find a mate, Indian American spouse-seekers may be a bit more independent and picky than those in other ethnic groups, and their techno-savvy backgrounds afford them some liberty and freedom of choice.

## Bringing Back Betrothal

While most arranged marriages in the United States take place within immigrant communities, there is also a growing movement amongst homegrown, ultra-conservative Christians to revive "the courtship and betrothal process," and it's  gaining converts rapidly. There are those who may be wary of this anti-dating crusade, in which young people are warned to "guard their hearts," but it will be decades before the fruit of its tenets can be judged.

# Wedding Chatter

"Who, being loved, is poor?"

—Oscar Wilde

"When you fish for love, bait with your heart, not your brain."

—Mark Twain

"If you want to be loved, love and be lovable."

—Benjamin Franklin

"Do not marry a man to reform him. That is what reform schools are for."

—Mae West

"Marriage is an alliance entered into by a man who can't sleep with the window shut, and a woman who can't sleep with the window open."

—George Bernard Shaw

"Passion makes the world go round. Love just makes it a safer place."

—Ice T

"My most brilliant achievement was my ability to be able to persuade my wife to marry me."

—Winston Churchill

"A happy home is one in which each spouse grants the possibility that the other may be right, though neither believes it."

—Don Fraser

"Life without love is like a tree without blossoms or fruit."

—Kahlil Gibran

"Love comforteth like sunshine after rain."

—William Shakespeare

"Sometimes I wonder if men and women really suit each other. Perhaps they should live next door and just visit now and then."

—Katharine Hepburn

# Red Is for... Body Odor?

*Today's wedding flowers are largely symbolic,
but history reveals a different story...*

Long before the modern wedding emerged, flowers served a practical purpose. More than mere decoration, they masked the stench of rural life and the smell of infrequently bathed wedding parties. Thankfully, contemporary blooms are now used for beauty. Traditional wedding flowers symbolize everything from purity to desire, while some offbeat choices signify independence and hope.

### Traditional Choices

- **Red rose:** Love and desire
- **Lily of the Valley:** Greater measures of happiness
- **White rose:** Purity
- **Freesia:** Innocence and trust
- **Orchid:** Beauty and refinement
- **Stargazer lily:** Wealth
- **Tulip:** Declaration of love

### Offbeat Choices

- **Dahlia:** Dignity
- **Orange rose:** Fascination
- **Tuberose:** Secretive pleasure
- **Sunflower:** Adoration
- **Thistle:** Noble independence
- **Cornflower:** Hope
- **Daffodil:** Singular desire
- **Poppy:** Fertility

# Will the Real Buccaneers Please Stand Up?

*Don't rely on Edith Wharton's novel* The Buccaneers *for a glimpse into a gilded age. Its heroines had real-life counterparts: Women who crossed an ocean to rule the social world.*

## A Sense of Entitlement

In the late 19th century, many English aristocrats found themselves in the uncomfortable position of being "land rich and cash poor." Their lofty titles and grand estates couldn't save them from impending financial doom, but marriages to wealthy young American women sure could. And there were many, many "nouveau riche" American parents who were more than happy to facilitate these marriages of convenience—as long as it meant securing their social status on both sides of the Atlantic.

The girls who willingly (or unwillingly) traded their families' money for titles and breeding are sometimes referred to as "buccaneers," after Edith Wharton's unfinished novel *The Buccaneers*. (Wharton died during the writing process in 1937, and the novel was published unfinished in 1938.) Wharton, born Edith Newbold Jones, intimately knew the privileged world she wrote about. Indeed, her blood was so blue that some historians believe the phrase "Keeping up with the Joneses" began as a reference to her family. *The Buccaneers* followed five rich American girls as they traveled to London and made their debuts during "The Season," that lovely time of year when aristocrats left their country homes to search for suitable brides while living it up in the city.

## For Love? No, Mostly Money

But while Wharton's book was filled with glamour and drama, its stories were just that: fictional stories. Want the real scoop? Turn to the true "buccaneers" of the 1870s, '80s, and '90s—the accounts of these women are just as exciting, not to mention true. Perhaps the most famous was Consuelo Vanderbilt. Born in 1877 to a socially ambitious mother and a father who had made millions in the railroad, Consuelo knew from an early age that her most important duty—her only duty, really—was to marry as well as she possibly could. She was even named after a friend of her mother's who had "overcome" a part-Hispanic background to marry an English viscount.

Consuelo was a raving beauty and succeeded beyond her mother's wildest dreams—she attracted the attention of many European and English aristocrats. Unfortunately, however, Consuelo was in love with a respectable but relatively undistinguished American, Winthrop Rutherfurd. Her mother would hear nothing of it and went to great lengths—even faking serious illness—to get her daughter to agree to marry Charles Spencer-Churchill, the ninth Duke of Marlborough. Eventually, Consuelo gave in—and spent three miserable decades in the marriage before it was annulled.

## A Brazen Buccaneer

Consuelo had followed another "buccaneer" who had also married into the Churchill family: Jennie Jerome. The daughter of wealthy New York banker Leonard Jerome and his wife, Clara, Jennie grew into such an unconventional beauty that rumors flew about her true parentage and ethnic heritage (one observer noted that there was "more of the panther than of the woman in her look"), however no evidence was ever presented to validate the speculations.

Jennie was a passionate woman with a wild side, and her first marriage to Lord Randolph Churchill, third son (second surviving) of the seventh Duke of Marlborough, didn't slow her down. Soon after giving birth to their son Winston (Britain's future prime minister), she was back on the scene in London. Jennie's second son, John, is believed to have been squired by Evelyn Boscawen, the seventh Viscount Falmouth. And her third and last marriage was to Montague Phippen Porch, a man three years younger than Winston!

# Man's Best Friend Becomes His Best Man... or His Ring Bearer

*Weddings are meant to be shared with family and friends—and more and more these days that includes man's best friend. So if Fido holds a special place in your life, you might want to consider including him in your special day.*

## Going to the Dogs

British musician Gavin Rossdale walked down the aisle with his rose-bedecked sheepdog, Winston, when he married singer Gwen Stefani. Tori Spelling went a step further, dressing her pug, Mimi Larue, in wedding clothes for her role as ring bearer and flower "girl" at Spelling's wedding. And Adam Sandler's dogs, Matzoball and Meatball, were at his wedding, with Meatball standing in as "best dog," dressed in a little tux and yarmulke.

## Teaching Your Dog New Tricks

Taking your dog to your wedding isn't just for the rich and famous. One wedding planner says as many as 30 percent of her weddings include pets. So if your dog has his invitation, and you know he'll attend, what's he going to do?

Some dogs serve as ring bearers with a little pouch tied around their necks. Others proudly walk their owners down the aisle. And some are appointed best man or maid of honor. Some dogs just sit quietly in the audience, and others are only included in the photos. Occasionally, a bride will carry a small dog down the aisle in a basket—in place of a traditional bouquet.

But whatever the role, a little finery should be added to the dog's everyday coat. Some brides want to see their canine friend in a wedding outfit of his or her own. But a jeweled collar or bow tied around his or her neck can be an easy—and a little more dignified—alternative. A corsage attached to the leash looks cute, just be sure the flowers aren't toxic to dogs.

And it's totally fine to carry the dog theme over to the reception with dog-bone decorations on the tables or miniature dogs in wedding attire atop the wedding cake. After all, your pooch wants to be a part of the party, too!

## Getting Permission for Your Pup

Beware—having a dog at a wedding isn't for everyone. There are a lot of things to consider before going ahead with the plan. First off, think of the animal. Does the dog have the right temperament for the job? Does he or she bark or jump? Follow commands? Does he or she get excited, aka, is he or she apt to have an accident?

If you ask yourself these questions and feel your dog passes the test, there are other aspects to consider. Most churches—and many other indoor facilities—won't allow pets other than service dogs. Occasionally they will make an exception, but if the answer to this one is no, it's time to give up the dream or look into an outdoor venue. Parks, beaches, gardens, and private homes lend themselves well to a wedding with dog involvement.

Next, just because your feelings for Fido are all warm and fuzzy doesn't mean that the priest, pastor, or rabbi will feel the same way. He or she needs to be prepared for the addition ahead of time. And that leads to the next seal of approval: Be sure to check with your wedding party before you finalize your plans. If the maid of honor turns out to be allergic—or afraid—of dogs, it could spoil the whole day.

And once you have the go-ahead, beg, borrow, or hire someone to be in charge of your dog. You'll be far too busy—and in demand—to tend to Fido all day and night.

But most important of all . . . don't let the dog upstage the bride.

# Groomzilla: The Very Married Signor Vigliotto

❧ ❧ ❧ ❧ ❧

*"Love 'em and leave 'em" could not have been a more appropriate motto for serial bigamist Giovanni Vigliotto, who wed 105 ladies without bothering to divorce any of them.*

Vigliotto said "I do" in ten different countries as he traveled the world hawking tchotchkes and furniture at flea markets. Although he was short, paunchy, and something less than Romeo-esque, the raven-haired Vigliotto had no trouble attracting ladies. Starting in 1949 at age 19, Vigliotto perfected a method that brought in a bride every time.

## Something Borrowed, Something Boo-hoo'd

Vigliotto began each con by choosing an alias that seemed appropriate to whichever country or neighborhood he found himself in. (He later claimed he used too many aliases to remember them all.) After he carefully selected a woman of financial means, who also appeared lonely and vulnerable, he preyed on her sympathy by confessing that he was lonely, too. A proposal soon followed, but before the ink was dry on the marriage license, he'd find some reason to convince his new bride to sell her home and move. That left him in a position to zoom off in a moving truck laden with all his bride's possessions while she trailed behind in her car. He would then ditch her and sell her purloined belongings at the next flea market.

## Walter Mitty of Love

It was a profitable setup, but his luck ran out in November 1981. Earlier that year, he'd abandoned wife Sharon Clark of Indiana, leaving her in Ontario, barefoot, alone, and $49,000 lighter. With all the stubborn rage of a woman not only scorned but also robbed, Clark reasoned that if she went to enough flea markets, she would eventually find her runaway groom. Sure enough, she tracked him down in Florida and caught him peddling her possessions. By that time, he was wanted in Arizona for taking Patricia Ann Gardiner, wife number 105, for $36,500 worth of goods plus another $11,474 in profits from the sale of her house. He was hauled back to Phoenix, where he stood trial in early 1983. The 53-year-old Casanova spent his time before the trial researching the history of bigamy.

Vigliotto played the wounded victim in court, asking plaintively why it was so wrong of him to open doors for women and bring them flowers, insisting that most of his wives actually proposed to him. He also painted himself as a sort of Walter Mitty of love, innocently acting out fantasies of marriage. He never did admit that it was wrong to rob the ladies after he married them.

## I Do... Find You Guilty!

In less than half an hour, a jury found Vigliotto guilty on 34 counts of bigamy and fraud; the judge subsequently fined him $336,000 and slapped him with 34 years in prison, which was the maximum.

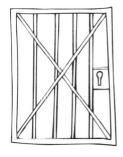

Vigliotto served eight years in a state prison in Arizona before dying of a brain hemorrhage in early 1991. Local papers reported various grandiose schemes hatched by Vigliotto during that time, such as a made-for-TV movie based on his life and a million-dollar deal to become the poster boy for a male virility drug, but his plans invariably fizzled, ensuring that Vigliotto's legacy will remain that of a record-setting bigamist.

- *In 1791, Andrew Jackson married Rachel Donelson, believing that her former husband had applied for a divorce. A few years later, they were informed that no divorce had ever been sought, and the couple was being charged with adultery. Once the situation was remedied, Donelson and Jackson quietly remarried.*

## Weddings 'Round the World
# African Wedding Customs

*There's an African proverb that says,*
*"A man without a wife is like a vase without flowers."*

Marriage in nearly every corner of Africa is considered an integral part of life, and many wedding rituals there have survived centuries. Because the African diaspora is so vast, traditions vary from region to region. The beauty of some of the rituals has enticed various Western couples with African roots to incorporate them into their own weddings.

### Ethiopia

Many African weddings begin with the paperwork, so to speak. Since a lot of marriages are still arranged (or at least seen as political moves), dowries are paid, and multiple meetings may take place between the bride's and the groom's family. This is the case for certain tribes in Ethiopia, where once the marriage has been approved and the dowry paid, the men in the groom's party go to the house of the bride for a mock standoff. The women "guard" the house, and the men must sing and entertain the women for passage.

### Kenya

Kenya's Swahili Muslims give weddings a lot of attention. For a full week surrounding the big day, participants live it up with singing, dancing, and feasting. But the men and the women party separately, which pleases both groups looking for a little time away from each other. After the public ceremony, the bride goes off with the women again, this time to learn more about how to be a proper wife before the marriage begins. The women wear their best jewelry to this party and sport fancy hairdos for the occasion, which includes live music and lots of good food.

## Namibia

If you're a member of the Himba people and happen to be a bride, sleep with one eye open. Members of the community kidnap a bride before the ceremony and dress her in a ceremonial leather headdress. Once the ceremony is complete, the bride is brought into the groom's house where the family tells her what her responsibilities will be as the wife. After that, they anoint her with butterfat from cows, which shows that she has been accepted into the family. Gee, thanks!

## Nigeria

In this West African country, brides stay sequestered in a special hut before the wedding. The groom must bring tobacco and chickens to all the guests that have gathered outside. Once they're satiated, the groom is allowed to come inside, and the marriage is official. The next day, a goat is slaughtered, and the blood is poured over the threshold. Then, refreshingly, the bride's mother asks her daughter if she's pleased with her husband. If she is, a party commences with lots of food and dancing. Guests at the party pay a penny to see the bride's face and give her sandalwood to rub on her body. (It should also be noted that ceremonies with Western influences are gaining in popularity in Nigeria, too.)

## Senegal

To propose in Senegal, you'll need some money and some kola nuts. A hopeful groom's family sends these items to the bride's family. If the family accepts the proposal, the kola nuts (which were once used in the making of Coca-Cola) are distributed to friends and family as a way of announcing the marriage. Before the wedding day, the groom's family throws a big party for the bride-to-be, welcoming her into their circle. When it's time for the ceremony, the groom's house is used, and guests bring gifts of spices, rice, and beverages, among other things. With the money she collects, the bride is expected to buy cooking utensils, which she takes with her to her new husband's home.

# Rules to Follow for the BEST Wedding Toast Ever!

*Here are some helpful hints to create a toast that will take the cake—figuratively speaking, of course.*

In order to create a speech that causes the crowd to "Wow!" not "Whoa!," it is central to keep a few things in mind when raising champagne glasses to honor the newlywed love. People who follow these guidelines and speak from the heart are guaranteed to deliver a speech that will surely make a fabulous impression long after the "I do's" are done.

- Above everything, a toastmaster needs to be mindful of the occasion and the audience. This is not Spring Break 2K7; this is Wedding Day 2K10. A person can still be witty without being over the top. If only one rule is remembered, it should be the one Aretha Franklin has been belting out since 1967—R.E.S.P.E.C.T!

- Avoid the use of overly offensive and profane language. Great-grandma Dottie and baby cousin Olivia do not need to be part of a sailor's rant. Sexual, racial, political, and religious jokes will probably always fall under this category. The basic rule of thumb: If there's a question as to whether or not something may or may not be appropriate, it probably isn't. So, one should probably nix it from the speech.

- For the most part, past marriages, relationships, and deaths in the family should be avoided at all costs in any wedding toasts. These are topics that generally make people uncomfortable, sad, or even angry, and this type of occasion should be kept light-hearted and celebratory.

NOTE: In order to adhere to all of the above, DO NOT drink too much! When people are under the influence of too much alcohol and equipped with a microphone, the results can be disasterous. No one wants to wake up the next day with a pounding headache, nervous stomach, and 15 disapproving voicemails.

- It's imperative to talk about the couple as a whole and not just as individuals. After all, the occasion is all about two becoming one, not how awesome they were apart. It's always good to bring up a fond memory of them as a team. For example, "I remember the first time I knew it was love..." or "It was obvious from day one these two crazy kids should be together because..."

- Always stand when giving a speech and refrain from fidgeting as much as possible. Even though the majority of the population has some level of stage fright, counteracting this fear with nervous ticks only makes matters worse. If you stand still, tall, and confident, no one will pay any attention to the fact that your insides are shaking.

- Never chew gum. Not only can it be seen as rude, but it might also hinder the clarity and pronunciation of your speech. Plus, it's just gross.

- Try not to overuse inside jokes. While they may be hilarious to those on the inside, the majority of the audience is on the outside, and their attention will be lost.

- Finally, keep the speech short, sweet, and to the point. The natives tend to get restless if the music is cut off for too long, and no one— especially the bride and groom—wants a long lull in the middle of a celebration. It tends to bring the party down when someone feels the need to list and provide examples of their "26 ingredients to a Healthy Marriage." Boooorrrrrrriiiiiing.

"A wedding is a funeral where you smell your own flowers."

—Eddie Cantor

"I was married by a judge. I should have asked for a jury."

—George Burns

# Fast Facts: Superstitions

- If a young child tastes a bit of the wedding cake frosting before it is cut, the couple's first child will be the same sex as that child.

- It is good luck if a chimney sweep kisses a bride on her wedding day.

- It is good luck to marry when the minute hand of the clock is on its way up, rather than down.

- Rain means the couple will be blessed with a lot of children.

- A full moon a couple of days before the wedding means a marriage filled with good luck.

- In England, an old tradition had the bride's father throw a plate of cake out the window. If the plate broke, the bride was destined to be happy.

- According to Chinese tradition, holding an open red umbrella over a Chinese bride will protect her from evil spirits.

- If the bride and groom wake up to rain on their wedding day, they should hang rosary beads outside their window or on a clothesline and it will clear up by the time of the ceremony.

- A bride shouldn't let anyone try on her engagement ring—if she does, it means that woman will steal her fiancé!

- When the bride throws her bouquet, and the groom throws her garter, it is good luck for the single woman and man who catch them. They are supposed to be the next to marry.

- If it rains, the bride will shed many tears during her marriage.

- Bells ringing at the church will keep evil spirits away.

# Proposals: The Preposterous

*Lovers who want to pop the question in a memorable way might be inspired by the following people.*

## Ready for Prime Time

In 2006, Rand Fishkin decided to propose to his girlfriend via a TV ad on Super Bowl Sunday. . . until he found out it was going to set him back $2.5 million. Fishkin spread the word online, which garnered attention from several media outlets, but he could only raise $85,000. However, CBS wouldn't lower their price, so for just $3,000, Rand purchased a local ad that ran during his girlfriend's favorite show. She saw the commercial, said yes, and the rest of the money was donated to charity.

## Baby, Light My Fire

In 2005, Todd Grannis of Grants Pass, Oregon, lit himself on fire, jumped into a swimming pool, and then swam over to his girlfriend, Malissa, to ask for her hand in marriage. This stunt, which nobody should ever try at home, was overseen by a stuntman and was executed while paramedics and a safety crew stood by. Grannis was shown how to wrap his body in protective garments before igniting for a few seconds. After recovering from the horror she must have felt when she saw her boyfriend go up in flames, Malissa said yes.

## From Crush to Crash

In 2006, Adam Sutton had it all planned out. He would take his girlfriend, Erika Brussee, up in a chartered plane and ask her to look out the window, high above Rome, Georgia, where family members would be holding a large sign with his proposal written on it. But instead, she saw flames just before the plane crashed onto the runway. No one was seriously injured, and Brussee did say yes, but the ring was lost in the rubble.

# Bride of Infamy

*Now that Elizabeth Taylor is a little old lady known for charity work and saying nutty things at awards shows, it's kind of hard to remember when she was considered a scarlet woman . . . but she was.*

The young Taylor always, always followed her heart, and that meant enduring a lot of slings and arrows from both the press and the public. She went from being one of the most beloved international stars in the history of show business to being a lightning rod for moral controversy, considered by many to be little more than a harlot who was destroying traditional marriage and family values.

## Marriages Made in . . .

Elizabeth Taylor shot to fame at the age of 12 in the wholesome 1944 family film *National Velvet.* Six years later, fans were excited to watch her grow into adult relationships both onscreen and off. In 1950, she starred in the huge hit *Father of the Bride,* and she married her first real-life husband, too. His name was one that is still very familiar to us now: Conrad "Nicky" Hilton. Her wedding to the hotel heir proved a publicity coup for Taylor's studio, MGM, but the marriage was a nightmare. Hilton was allegedly an abusive alcoholic, and they divorced less than a year later.

Taylor never had to go long without male companionship, however, and on February 21, 1952, she walked down the aisle a second time, marrying English actor Michael Wilding. Wilding was 20 years older than Taylor, and early on, during their just-shy-of-five-years marriage, he made her feel happy and secure. They had two sons, Michael and Christopher. But as soon as Taylor met another older man, Mike Todd, her marriage to Wilding was over. A high-school dropout who clawed his way to the top of Hollywood film production, the charismatic Todd married Taylor on February 2, 1957, just days after her divorce from Wilding became final.

## Losing Face

Taylor's reputation in Hollywood began to suffer and the public began to turn against her. On March 22, 1958, however, Mike Todd's private plane, *Lucky Liz*, suffered engine failure and crashed in New Mexico. Fans showered his grieving young widow and their baby, Liza, with sympathy, but it wouldn't last long. Soon, the press was reporting that Todd's best friend, singer Eddie Fisher, was too busy "comforting" Taylor to stay at home with his own wife, actress Debbie Reynolds, and their two children. Debbie Reynolds was beloved as "America's Sweetheart," so when Fisher divorced Reynolds, and Taylor converted to Judaism to marry him, not many people had much goodwill for the couple.

## The More Marriages the Better

For all the drama Taylor went through to win and marry Fisher, she still thought nothing of tossing yet another marriage away when she met the love of her life, the Welsh actor Richard Burton, on the set of the film *Cleopatra* in 1963. She would marry and divorce Burton twice and adopt one daughter with him. At this point, Taylor was the most famous human being on the planet, and the public clamored for information on every move she made. Even the Vatican weighed in when she took up with Burton, accusing her of "erotic vagrancy."

When Taylor and Burton finally split for good in 1976, she waited just months to marry again, this time to Senator John Warner. She was now in her "Studio 54" phase, a time of heavy substance abuse. Her marriage suffered, and she and Warner divorced in 1982. Cleaning up her act, she got married for the last time to blue-collar, every-guy Larry Fortensky in 1991. The marriage lasted five years, and she has been single ever since.

# With This Ring, I Thee Wed

*A wedding ring, traditionally a simple gold band, is a powerful symbol. The circle of the ring represents eternity and is an emblem of lasting love in many of the world's cultures. But the history of the wedding ring also includes less spiritual associations.*

Historians suggest that wedding rings are a modern version of the ropes with which primitive men bound women they had captured. This suggests that the phrase "old ball and chain" may have referred more to the passage of a bride from person to prisoner than to the husband's matrimonial outlook.

### Symbolic Circles

Our current perceptions of the wedding ring evolved over time and are rooted in a variety of ancient practices. In Egypt, a man placed a piece of ring-money—metal rings used to purchase things—on his bride's hand to show that he had endowed her with his wealth. In ancient Rome, rings made of various metals communicated a variety of political and social messages. In marriage, the ring holding the household keys was presented

to the wife after the ceremony when she crossed the threshold of her new home. Later, this key ring dwindled in size to a symbolic ring placed on the woman's finger during the wedding. Among Celtic tribes, a ring may have indicated sexual availability. A woman might have given a man a ring to show her desire; putting her finger through the ring may have symbolized the act of sex.

## Forget 14 Karat...

Wedding rings were not always made of gold. They could be made of any metal as well as leather or rushes. In fact, in the 13th century, a bishop of Salisbury in England warned young men against seducing gullible virgins by braiding rings out of rushes and placing them on their fingers. In the 17th century, Puritans decried the use of a wedding ring due to its pagan associations and ostentatious value, calling it "a relique of popery and a diabolical circle for the devil to dance in."

## The Ring Finger of Choice

Why is the ring placed on the fourth finger of the left hand? According to A.D. fourth-century Roman grammarian and philosopher Ambrosius Theodosius Macrobius, the fourth finger is the one most appropriate to that function. Macrobius described the thumb as "too busy to be set apart" and said "the forefinger and little finger are only half-protected." The middle finger, or *medicusm,* is commonly used for offensive communications and so could not be used for this purpose. This leaves only the fourth finger for the wedding ring.

It was once believed that a vein ran directly from that finger to the heart, the so-called *vena amoris,* or vein of love. Since the right hand is commonly the dominant hand, some scholars suggest that wearing a ring on the left, or "submissive," hand symbolizes a wife's obedience to her husband. The importance of the Trinity in Christian theology provides another explanation for the identification of the fourth finger on the left hand as the "wedding ring finger." In the early Catholic Church, the groom touched the thumb and first two fingers of his bride as he said, "In the name of the Father, Son, and Holy Ghost." He then slipped the ring all the way onto the next, or fourth, finger as he said, "Amen." This four-step placement of the ring was a common custom in England until the end of the 16th century, and it remained a tradition among Roman Catholics for many more years.

## Weddings 'Round the World
# Take This Goose...

*Gifts are a major part of the Korean wedding. Today some families spend upward of $30,000 on gifts alone!*

The emphasis on gifts dates back to ancient Korea: The night before the wedding, the groom's family would don costumes and smear dried squid ink on their faces. They traveled to the bride's home with a box, or *hahm,* of gifts, chanting *"Hahm* for sale!" The bride's family would greet their visitors with food and money.

## If It's Good for the Goose, It's Good for the Gander

Back in the day, a Korean groom would present his bride's mother with a live goose. Since geese mate for life, the goose represented the groom's pledge of fidelity to their daughter. In modern times, a groom may still honor that sentiment by presenting his future mother-in-law with a wooden goose.

## Rice, Rice Baby

As with most cultures, food and drink play an integral role in Korean weddings. Rice is prevalent, both as a sweet sticky rice dessert and a beverage. Two cups of rice liquor may be offered to the couple. In turn, they pour the liquid into a single cup to share, signifying their souls uniting. Central to the *kook soo sang,* or noodle banquet, is a noodle soup in beef broth. The noodles signify a long and happy life.

## Go Nuts

A bride may present her new in-laws with dates and chestnuts. The groom's parents will toss the nuts back to the bride. She will convert the skirt of her bridal gown into a sack and try to catch as many nuts as she can. This supposedly reflects how many children the happy couple will produce.

# Quiz

*Make a Match!*
*See if you can match the duty to the proper attendant—*
*and don't forget to say "thank you."*

**1.** Mail or e-mail tux measurement cards to male attendants with payment instructions

**2.** Seat guests, assist those with special needs

**3.** Toss flower petals or other decorations before the bride walks in

**4.** Read scripture, poetry, or prose selections during the wedding ceremony

**5.** Sign the marriage license as a witness

**6.** Pack and decorate the "getaway car," if needed

**7.** Accept and securely store any gifts brought to the ceremony

**a.** Ushers

**b.** Flower Girl/Flower Boy

**c.** Best Man

**d.** Groomsmen

**e.** Reader

**f.** Maid/Matron of Honor

**g.** Guest Book Attendant

*Answers: 1. c; 2. a; 3. b; 4. e; 5. f; 6. d; 7. g*

# The Return of the Backyard Bash

*You loved playing in the backyard as a kid.*
*Why not get married there, too?*

One of the few bright spots in tough economic times is that people sometimes look to the past to find the inspiration to live with less. This can be seen in the current trend of couples holding wedding receptions in their own backyards.

## Everything Old Is New Again

Backyard receptions were once quite common for American spring and summer weddings, and they seemed to reach their zenith during the Great Depression and World War II. They were popular in the 1930s for obvious economic reasons but continued throughout the war because so many weddings happened in haste, as soldiers hurried off to battle. With the coming of peace and prosperity in the 1950s, lavish weddings became all the rage—every girl wanted a country club reception. But now that many Americans are once again struggling to make ends meet, brides and grooms are returning to the simpler ways—and that includes backyard receptions.

## All the Comforts of Home

A backyard wedding reception need not be a shabby, thrown-together affair. It can be a charming alternative that allows the wedding couple and their parents to actually relax and have fun rather than worry about whether they're getting their money's worth. Friends and relatives are usually more than happy to help out, as the cost to them will be minimal. Male guests might even fight over who gets to tend the grill. A tent is a good idea in case of bad weather, but if the home is big enough, guests can simply be moved indoors if it rains. Draping retro decorations like gingham fabric, blasting big band music on the sound system, and using grandma's china to serve the guests creates a fun, nostalgic atmosphere.

# Wedding Chatter

"Being in a long marriage is a little bit like that nice cup of coffee every morning—I might have it every day, but I still enjoy it."

—Stephen Gaines

"We have the greatest prenuptial agreement in the world. It's called love."

—Gene Perret

"Behind every great man there is a surprised woman."

—Maryon Pearson

"Anyone can be passionate, but it takes real lovers to be silly."

—Rose Franken

"My heart is ever at your service."

—William Shakespeare

"True love comes quietly, without banners or flashing lights. If you hear bells, get your ears checked."

—Erich Segal

"I like her because she smiles at me and means it."

—Anonymous

"How much better is thy love than wine!"

—Song of Solomon 4:10

"The difficulty with marriage is that we fall in love with a personality, but must live with a character."

—Peter De Vries

"All weddings, except those with shotguns in evidence, are wonderful."

—Liz Smith

"If you live to be a hundred, I want to live to be a hundred minus one day so I never have to live without you."

—A. A. Milne

# The Domestic Goddess Goes Wedding

*In 1987, it seemed there was no one more suited to write a lavish, colorful coffee-table book about weddings than Martha Stewart. Who better to advise brides on their first step into domestic tranquility than the domestic goddess herself?*

## Martha's Publishing Prowess

After successful stints in both modeling and stockbrokerage, Martha Stewart decided to make a career out of what she really loved: home and family. And indeed, she appeared to be the perfect wife and mother. Her husband, Andy Stewart, was the president of the Harry N. Abrams, Inc. publishing house, her daughter Alexis was smart and attractive, and the family's restored 1805 farmhouse in Westport, Connecticut, was something out of a *House & Garden* spread.

Through her husband's connections in publishing, Martha had gotten her first book deal, and the result, a cookbook called *Entertaining*, was a *New York Times* Best Seller in 1982. This was quickly followed by three other cookbooks from 1983 to 1985, which all sold well but weren't the sensations that *Entertaining* had been. Martha wanted to achieve that kind of success again—or even go beyond it. Some publishing professionals thought the subject of weddings was too old-fashioned and conservative, but Martha guessed correctly: In the post-Vietnam, post-feminist era, many people were yearning for tradition, hospitality, and elegance.

# Plan Your Wedding with Martha

*Weddings* made its debut in bookstores on July 11, 1987, and was an immediate smash. Martha, at 40 years old, appeared on the cover looking fresh and lovely next to a five-tiered wedding cake and several enormous flower arrangements. Her shoulder-length, honey-blonde hair and antique-lace, off-white dress perfectly captured the preppy New England style that was all the rage at the time. The bride who stood behind her, back to the camera, almost seemed to be an afterthought. It was all about Martha, and readers loved it, shelling out $50 to see what she had to say. The book's success propelled Martha to even greater heights, and in that same year, she signed a $5 million deal with Kmart to be its "lifestyle consultant."

## Something Old . . .

*Weddings* may seem dated and quaint to us now—certainly some of the featured bridesmaid dresses are appalling to our 21st-century eyes—but it is also classic. Martha herself called it "a social document," a microcosm of the way the wealthy planned their weddings in the high-flying '80s. And it's a guilty pleasure to relive those times through the book's beautiful photography. Besides, a roast loin of pork is a roast loin of pork no matter what age you're living in, and when it comes to weddings, tradition will never get old. While a minority may continue to want something "different," Martha Stewart's *Weddings* will always be in demand. The book was so popular, it led to a magazine in 1994. *Martha Stewart Weddings* is the best-selling wedding magazine in America, beating both longtime favorites, such as *Brides*, and newcomers, such as *InStyle Weddings*.

Ironically enough, however, the woman teaching us how to live in wedded bliss may not have been following her own advice. In 1987, her marriage to Andy Stewart collapsed when he moved out of their home and obtained a restraining order against her. After their divorce in 1990, Andy married Martha's former assistant, Robin Fairclough. Neither Martha nor their daughter, Alexis, has spoken to Andy Stewart in over two decades.

# Honeymoon at the Falls

*A mecca for newlyweds, Niagara Falls is still one of
the nation's top spots for honeymooners.*

Niagara Falls and honeymooners: It seems like such an obvious
match, but have you ever wondered how this phenomenon began?
Starting in the mid-19th century, marketing campaigns paired with
well-timed publicity—all aimed at newlyweds—began putting
Niagara Falls on the map. Making sure this destination had the staying power to hold the number one spot, however, has proven a bit
more problematic.

## Birth of the Falls

Located in upstate New York, Niagara Falls is a landmark that's been
forming—and slowly migrating—for millennia. The Falls at Niagara
are about 12,000 years old. However, the story of their formation can
be traced back hundreds of millions of years to that era's last remain-
ing glaciers. As these giant ice cubes began to melt, they carved out
some of America's greatest landmarks, including the upper Great
Lakes and the Niagara River. When the Niagara River's continuous
torrent of water ran out of solid ground, it simply poured off a cliff
near Lewiston, New York. And thus, Niagara Falls was born.

Throughout its adolescence, the Falls continued to change.
Water forced a slow migration that carved a seven-mile canyon known as Niagara Gorge. Today, the Falls continue to move
upstream inch by inch. Still, it takes more than a few thousand gal-
lons of rushing water to create a honeymoon destination.

## A Mecca in the Making

The Falls first flirted with its romantic side in 1803 when Jerome
Bonaparte, the younger brother of Napoleon, became the site's
first recorded honeymooner. By the mid-1800s, newlyweds were a

common sight at Niagara Falls. Throughout the rest of the century, magazines such as *Harper's Weekly* helped cement Niagara Falls' image by printing pictures of couples honeymooning there.

In 1928, a campaign by the New York Scenic Trails Association and the Niagara Falls Chamber of Commerce debuted one of Niagara's most enduring logos: two hearts, both pierced by Cupid's arrow. The Falls were packaged as the ideal American honeymoon spot. And, just to make sure people noticed, nearly a dozen 50-foot billboards were erected to bear the Falls' signature logo. The billboards were stationed along a highway running from Rochester to Niagara, which was aptly renamed "The Honeymoon Trail."

The area's rise as a newlywed destination with deep American roots continued after World War II, when it was marketed by the Falls' chamber of commerce. The chamber launched the Niagara Falls Honeymoon Club for alumni honeymooners. It also offered an all-expenses-paid trip to a couple that had spent their honeymoon at the Falls and then celebrated the greatest number of wedding anniversaries. Newspapers across the nation publicized the giveaway.

## Lasting Impressions

Today, an estimated 12 million tourists trek to Niagara each year, including honeymooners. Many of them board the *Maid of the Mist*, which is billed as "North America's oldest tourist attraction," to voyage across the Niagara River, past the American and Bridal Veil Falls, and into the spray of the Horseshoe Falls. Since the *Maid of the Mist*'s first voyage in 1846, its many incarnations have carried visitors from the theme-park atmosphere of the Canadian Falls to Niagara's American side. Modern-day Niagara, however, seems to be resting on its laurels.

The Falls, which were a symbol of America's progress, are by some accounts now a bit shabby; perhaps Niagara Falls is a destination that's a bit dog-eared, dotted with vendors and lackluster tourist fare, and too "everyman" for the kind of luxury exclusivity breeds.

Still, that hasn't stopped Niagara Falls' continued association with romance and, of course, honeymoons. After all, where better to celebrate the next phase in your married life than in the shadow of one of the nation's most awe-inspiring natural wonders?

**Weddings Through the Years**

# A Bride's Crowning Glory

*Theories abound as to the origin of the wedding veil, but many historians believe it came from the tradition of arranged marriages.*

- **"You've Got to Hide Your Love Away…":** Since the bride's father didn't want the groom to change his mind before the marriage was finalized, he covered the bride's face with a veil, lifting it only after the wedding ceremony was finished. By the 20th century, arranged marriages were almost over in the Western world, but the wedding veil endured and evolved over the decades.

- **1900s:** With the turn of the century came the demise of the Victorian Age and the dawn of the Edwardian Age. While some brides still chose the long, elaborate wedding veils of the former, others decided to wear the large, wide-brimmed hats that were in style at the time.

- **1910s:** By this time, the "Gibson Girl" was firmly entrenched in the American psyche. She was the personification of beauty, and veil styles reflected it. Whether simple or fussy, the veil or hat a bride wore was arranged to show off the high, pompadour hairstyle that was piled on top of her head.

- **1920s:** While wedding dresses became shorter and simpler, following the "flapper" trend, wedding veils exploded. Puffy, fluffy, and billowing, veils of this decade were often held in place with jeweled or beaded headbands or tiaras or were decorated with feathers or flowers.

- **1930s:** The Depression affected wedding veils, as it affected everything else. Ostentatious weddings were out and simplicity ruled. Plain, white, long veils that matched the cut-on-the-bias dresses of the day replaced the frivolous veils of the '20s.

- **1940s:** As World War II loomed, American women gave up a lot when it came to fashion. The materials that went into women's stockings and wedding veils were now being used to make things such as parachutes. Brides made sacrifices even on their big day, forgoing veils and marrying in smart hats and two-piece suits.

- **1950s:** Peace reigned again and brides wanted their lavish weddings back. Inspired by Elizabeth Taylor in the film *Father of the Bride,* they chose full, long, lace veils attached to Juliet caps, paired with form-fitting, satin gowns. An all-white ensemble was again the popular choice during the Eisenhower decade.

- **1960s:** The decade began with brides continuing the conservative tradition of big, puffy veils (often anchored by Jackie Kennedy–style pillbox hats). But by 1966, many brides were eschewing them altogether—their long, hippie hair served as the only "veil."

- **1970s:** Between couples "doing their own thing" and country-inspired designers such as Laura Ashley and Jessica McClintock, the '70s produced perhaps a most unsightly wedding style. Many brides were still refusing to wear veils, instead adorning both their bridesmaids and themselves in the dreaded Floppy Hats.

- **1980s:** Taffeta and shoulder pads were everywhere as the television show *Dynasty* inspired brides to go big with everything—including wedding veils. While there were scary trends, such as the veil attached to the back of a white cowboy hat, for the most part, brides wanted traditional long, white veils in this conservative decade.

- **1990s:** Brides became more casual and experimental. Vintage wedding wear became very popular, and trends such as medieval weddings, goth weddings, and pagan weddings shocked the establishment. A proper veil was whatever a bride decided it was; some brides even used bright colors or chose "ethnic" veils from India or Africa.

# Reception Wed-i-quette!

*For most people, there is a certain element of decorum to their nuptials, and guests are expected to at least* try *to be on their best behavior. Here are a few etiquette tips for those headed to a reception.*

## Do R.S.V.P.

Planning a wedding is hard. Planning a wedding when you don't know who's actually coming is next to impossible. Always R.S.V.P. by the requested date.

## Don't bring extra people.

When you R.S.V.P., you are telling the couple exactly how many heads to count. If you show up with someone extra, there probably won't be room for him or her—and you, the bride and groom, and your rogue guest will feel incredibly awkward. Stick to the numbers, and if you have any changes, contact the bride as soon as possible.

## Do get a gift.

Coming to a wedding empty-handed is just rude. You can certainly choose to give a monetary gift in a card, which is even preferred by some couples. (If you gave a gift at the shower, you might not need to give a wedding gift, but different people have different beliefs about this. Ask your mother.)

## Don't give your gift to the bride and groom.

As you greet the happy couple in the receiving line, don't hand them a wedding gift. They're going to be too busy shaking hands to deal with it, and you'll slow up the line. There's usually a table nearby for gifts and cards, so put it there, and then pay your respects.

## Do accept that you probably won't get a lot of face time.

Unless the wedding is very small, a bride and groom's schedule at their reception is packed. Between greeting and visiting with guests, cutting cake, and posing for pictures, many don't even get to eat. You probably won't see much of your good friends, and you might not even get to say goodbye. Just know that your presence is what's important, and that they're grateful you're there.

## Don't be the drunk guy/girl with the microphone.

More than a few receptions have been nearly ruined by an awkward, unexpected speech by a drunk partygoer. If you've been selected to give a speech at a reception, curb your drinking until you're finished speaking. If you're the one getting married, make sure whoever is in charge of the microphone (usually the DJ or bandleader) has strict instructions not to hand the mic to just anyone.

## Don't make a fuss if you can't eat the filet.

If you have dietary restrictions, and you know the bride extremely well, you might be able to ask for an amended meal, depending on the size of the wedding. But don't even think about fussing to her (or the groom) about not being able to eat the food. Find what you can eat or wait until you get home—it's not about you right now.

## Do let the bride and groom have the first dance.

Sure, you're dying to get out on the floor, and the romance of the day might make you yearn to slow dance with your own partner. But leave the first dance to the bride and groom, or you'll look awfully silly out there.

## Don't take the flower arrangements.

Unless someone who would know (like the bride) has specifically told you that you can, do not take the flower arrangements when you leave the party. Many florists loan their vases out and charge a hefty sum if they're not returned. Taking your centerpiece could cost the couple a lot of money.

# The Best of Times, the Worst of Times

❧ ❧ ❧ ❧ ❧

*There are the best wedding ideas...
and then there are the worst.*

## Best Celebrity Wedding

On September 12, 1953, Jacqueline Lee Bouvier and then-Senator John F. Kennedy were married. More than 800 guests poured into St. Mary's Roman Catholic Church in Newport, Rhode Island, to witness the union. Kennedy family friend Archbishop Cushing presided over the nuptials with the assistance of no less than four priests, including the former president of Notre Dame and the head of the Christopher Society. Renowned Boston tenor soloist Luigi Vena sang "Ave Maria."

The bride wore an ivory silk gown with a fitted bodice, a bouffant skirt, and a taffeta train of 50 yards of ivory silk. She accessorized with a pearl choker and a diamond bracelet, and she donned an heirloom lace veil that had been worn by her grandmother, Lee.

Following the ceremony, the soon-to-be 35th President and First Lady of the United States fled to Hammersmith Farm, the Bouvier family's 300-acre oceanfront estate, where more than 1,200 guests crowded the terrace for the reception. The receiving line reportedly took over two hours. Meyer Davis and his orchestra played under a huge canopy, and the bride and groom had their first dance to "I Married an Angel." The wedding cake, four feet tall with five tiers, had been ordered by Joseph Kennedy and was served with a luncheon of creamed chicken, fruit, and ice cream sculpted in the shape of roses. As the couple departed in the late afternoon, guests showered them with paper rose petals. It was truly a fairy tale of a day.

## Worst Celebrity Wedding

They said it wouldn't last... and it didn't. The date was September 18, 2005. Already a couple twists into her downward spiral, former pop darling of chastity Britney Spears married former pizza delivery boy and back-up dancer Kevin Federline. It was the kind of cash-bar event where guests noshed on chicken wings and ribs, the bride changed from her Monique Lhuillier gown into sweats, and the groomsmen sported matching warm-up suits embroidered with the word "Pimps."

*Worst Celebrity Wedding Runner-up:* Oh, *Britney.* Nine months before marrying Federline, a baseball-capped Britney pledged her eternal love to childhood pal Jason Alexander in a quickie Vegas wedding, reportedly after a two-day drinking bender. The marriage was annulled shortly thereafter.

## Best Wedding Ring Recovery

While he was working on a boat at Wellington Harbor, New Zealand ecologist Aleki Taumoepeau felt his wedding ring slip off his finger, and he helplessly watched it sink into the water. Thinking fast, Taumoepeau recorded his GPS coordinates and returned with diving equipment. The initial search was unsuccessful. But Taumoepeau refused  to give up. Sixteen months after losing his "precious," he dove again and found it gleaming on the sea floor. One heck of a treasure hunt!

## Worst Theme Wedding

Didn't they read Stephen King's *It*? When Roadkill Racoon and Reddish Raddish (aka Carol Banner and Morgan Nilsen) decided to tie the knot in 2006, they weren't just clowning around. Nope, they dove in oversized feet first and staged a full-on clown-themed wedding that no doubt frightened small children and coulrophobics alike. The event was held at the famed Alberta Street Clown House in Portland.

With a pageboy hat, bowtie, and clown make-up, the groom looked like an out-of-work mime from the Depression era. The bride was attired in a flashy red dress, striped knee socks, and a big red Bozo nose. Their painted faces were threatened by the prevalent rain, but nothing could dampen their spirits. Guests partook in a bicycle parade and a roll in the mud wrestling pit. Yes, a mud wrestling pit.

# Best Marriage Proposal

North Carolina romantic Graham McGowan plotted the perfect proposal for his live-in love, Kristen. She was a snow globe fan, and throughout their relationship, he had made a habit of buying her a new snow globe to mark romantic occasions. He located a company specializing in snow globe kits and contacted another company that manufactured the wind-up music parts. He also scored some scrap diamond slivers from a jeweler's eBay auction. With all of the pieces in place, Graham assembled his ultimate proposal prop.

On the anniversary of their first date, Graham took Kristen to her favorite park and gave her a gift. When she opened it, she found a snow globe with a woman seated on a picnic table and a man on bended knee nearby. Written on the globe's base was, "Marry me Kristen." As Kristen looked up, she saw Graham holding a ring, reenacting the globe's scene. When she shook the globe, diamond flakes swirled like glitter and showered upon the figurine couple.

# Worst Father/Daughter Dance Song

Imagine a beautiful wedding. The Mr. and Mrs. were announced as husband and wife at the reception, and they chose Marvin Gaye's sexy "Let's Get It On" for their first dance, which, of course, induced a couple catcalls from the crowd. After a moment, it was announced that members of the bride and groom's families were welcome to join in on the dance floor. Well, apparently the eager father of the bride misheard or misunderstood. He bolted onto the floor and cut in for the father/daughter dance. So there they were: The bride and her father slow dancing to "Let's Get It On." The groom didn't really know what to do, so his mom joined him, and they also danced to the rest of the sensual song. Hmm, can you say awkward?

- *The Macedonian Greeks were so disdainful of the native Egyptian population that it was considered more honorable to marry one's own sister than to marry an Egyptian woman. The practice of marrying one's sibling was fairly common and had been borrowed from the royal families of Egypt.*

# Fast Facts

- *Where you get married makes a huge difference in the cost. In the elegant suburbs of Long Island, New York, wedding tabs routinely reach $50,000.*

- *Everyone's curious about wedding cakes: Cable channel WeTV's show* Amazing Wedding Cakes *nabbed more than one million viewers with its 2009 season premiere.*

- *Wedding gown accessories, like the veil and headpiece, cost, on average, $50 to $500.*

- *Brides try on an average of 13 dresses before they choose their favorite.*

- *If the bride and groom see a rainbow, they will certainly have good luck.*

- *In Victorian times, "pull charms" were baked into the wedding cake. The charms were different shapes—such as a heart, a flower, or a ring—and bridesmaids pulled them out of the cake via ribbons before the cake was cut. Each charm meant something different; for example, if you pulled the ring charm, you were next to wed.*

- *More than 115,000 weddings are performed in Las Vegas every year.*

- *Most weddings take place between May and October. (To cut costs, some couples have their nuptials outside these months.)*

- *Most bridal salons or retailers usually require a 50 percent deposit on custom-ordered gowns. Be sure it's the dress you want: Deposits are usually nonrefundable.*

- *This may only work for Catholic brides: Place a statue of the Virgin Mary in the window the week before the wedding, and the wedding day will be sunny and shining with good fortune.*

# I Do . . . Not

*Notable Women Who Never Married*

Who said it's every little girl's lifelong dream to get married? Several women have found solace outside the confines of marriage. Girl power at its finest, the list of women to evade the altar includes everyone from nuclear physicists and women's rights activists to haute couture fashion designers and media moguls. They're a group as eclectic as they are iconic and legendary not only for what they do, but also who they choose *not* to do it with.

## Early Lifelong Bachelorettes

Even in the days of yore when it was practically mandated that every woman marry, several ladies chose to go against the grain. Among the first and most remarkable was Joan of Arc, who chose sainthood and war heroism over nuptials and newlywed bliss. She scoured battlefields instead of dishes and made it quite obvious that God was the only man for her. Considered the national heroine of France, Joan of Arc proved that behind every good man (or in this case, an army of them) is an even better woman—but not always vice versa.

And she wasn't the only historical figure to choose valor over vows. Perhaps among the most influential and noteworthy was Elizabeth I of England. Better known as Queen Elizabeth, she reigned over an entire nation without, despite many attempts to force her hand, the matrimonial backing of a man. Elizabeth I was courted by several suitors, and while speculations on her non-nuptial lifestyle are still debated, it was quite clear she was nowhere near as concerned with marriage as the population surrounding her, which is the same sentiment shared by many other of her eminent successors.

## Making Changes Without Marriage

Civil and women's rights activist, Susan B. Anthony and the celebrated nuclear physicist, Lise Meitner were two others that booed the thought of marriage. Not to mention the inspirational revolutionary, Helen Keller; the iconic fashion pioneer, Coco Chanel; and the Nobel Peace Prize recipient, Jane Addams—none of them ever heard the wedding bells chime. (Probably because they were too busy making a difference—duh!)

There were also a number of critically acclaimed authors, hailed for their abilities to evoke passion and spark debate through their literary works, who chose a pen and paper over the companionship of a man. Still found in every classroom, library, and literary timeline around the world, Jane Austen, Emily Dickinson, and Louisa May Alcott, as well as two of the Brontë sisters, Emily and Anne, never took the plunge.

## Staying Single Shakes Some Heads

Not taking "the plunge," however, can sometimes cause just as much of a splash as taking it would, especially in this day in age. With the media at an all-time explosive high, women such as former Secretary of State Condoleezza Rice and Academy Award–winning actress Diane Keaton are sometimes thrown unwanted scrutiny for their choice not to marry. But no one—*no one*—has been debated about over her choice not to marry more than Oprah Winfrey. The woman practically wrote the book on how to be a success, and she did it all without taking vows.

After years of being the face of daytime TV, Oprah has been known to shine the light on the topic of herself. Almost laughingly, she can joke about how, even after countless awards, innumerable life-changing interviews, and incalculable donations, there are still people who view her as incomplete because she never towed the line and took a husband. It's all right Oprah, even if you never marry, there are about a billion reasons you'll never be left wanting. Go ahead with your bad self!

# Powerful or Powerless?

❧ ❧ ❧ ❧ ❧

*We've moved into the techno age, and weddings are no exception. You've seen video slideshows and PowerPoint presentations at the rehearsal dinner, the reception, and even at the wedding ceremony itself. Whether this is good or bad just depends on whom you ask.*

## Surprise Slides

If you've seen the movie *27 Dresses*, you know that PowerPoint and video slideshows can be dangerous! In the film, the bride's sister is asked to create a presentation for the rehearsal dinner, highlighting similarities between the bride and groom. Feeling that the bride has been less than honest with her future husband, the sister lets loose with every secret the bride has kept. Needless to say, the sisters fight, the groom calls off the wedding, and the rehearsal dinner ends up being, well, awkward.

Sure, this could happen in real life, but chances are it wouldn't. So don't worry. First of all, according to one bridal consultant, many couples are creating their own slideshows. There is no shortage of professionals out there who can do the job, but many couples choose to do it themselves. Today's generation of brides and grooms have grown up in the technology age; they know how to do just about everything on a computer. They already have the baby photos and vacation shots, and chances are, those photos are already stored on their computers. Add a little downloadable music and *voila*! Presentation accomplished.

## Yay or Nay

Most people who have attended a wedding over the last year or two have probably seen a wedding PowerPoint presentation. After all, they're becoming more and more common. Some couples choose to show it at the rehearsal dinner, but most wait for the reception where more people can see it.

And brides and grooms seem to really like the idea. After all, this is their day, and the PowerPoint presentation is all about them. Likewise, grandparents love it. An informal poll shows that guests are lukewarm about the idea, however. While most feel that it is in perfectly good taste, many can't even remember whether there was one at the last wedding they attended. Big impression? Not so much. One guest suggested that if you look around the room, it's mostly close family and friends who are watching. Of course, in a large room, it's hard to position a screen where everyone can see it clearly. So is it worth it?

It's really a personal preference. Do you want to share these memories with your guests? Do you have enough good pictures of each of you to make it worthwhile? Do you have the time—and know-how—to create it yourself? If not, do you have the funds in your budget to pay someone else to create it?

## Taking the PowerPoint Plunge

Video slideshows are generally short—or at least they should be—so everyone can give you their full attention. Usually the background is music, rather than someone speaking, so realize that your guests will probably continue to talk, clink, and chew while the presentation is going on.

Just be careful to avoid photos that are in poor taste—no risqué or compromising poses. No drunken party shots. No captions with double entendres. And don't bore—or confuse—your guests with inside jokes that leave them feeling left out and uninterested. In short, be sure it's tasteful.

According to wedding planners, it's best to avoid launching this type of presentation at the church. Some may, in fact, have rules about the inclusion of secular elements in the service. Even if they don't, most people expect the ceremony to be more solemn, and the two don't mesh very well.

And on a final note . . . while browsing Web sites, you might discover that there are PowerPoint templates available for the best man to use at the reception to toast the happy couple. Imagine that: the best man, an open bar, and a large screen. Choose wisely.

# Take Me Out to the...Wedding

*What better way to celebrate your love for each other than celebrating the love for your favorite team?*

A wedding with a baseball theme has endless possibilities. Some couples hold the actual nuptials at the ballpark, while others just have the reception at an onsite restaurant or banquet hall.

## Play Ball!

Most ballparks offer wedding and/or reception options during the off-season or when the team is playing an away game. But if your team isn't nearby or the venue won't work for you, don't worry. A baseball-themed wedding can be held just about anywhere by adding baseball-related touches to the festivities.

## Equipment and Uniforms

A baseball mitt is a perfect substitute for the traditional pillow the ring bearer carries down the aisle. And instead of a guest book, wedding-goers can sign a baseball bat or the back of a jersey.

Decorations for the reception are limitless. The tables can be named for favorite players or stadiums rather than the usual table numbers. Centerpieces may include flowers or pennants in team colors and can be as simple or elaborate as the bride and groom wish—vintage baseball cards add a more elegant touch. One bride filled a large vase with mini baseballs and added baseball-shape flowers, such as white carnations, for a fun and sporty look. For a sweeter twist, glass vases can be filled with chocolate baseballs or cracker-jacks (flowers optional).

Bridesmaids may wear dresses in one of the team colors and carry bouquets of flowers in the second team color. For a more subtle or traditional look, the dresses can be simpler with just a color-coordinated sash or flowers. In a super casual setting groomsmen can wear baseball hats and ushers can wear jerseys— these touches sometimes work best for an outdoor wedding or just the reception.

When it comes to food, for dessert, a stadium-shape cake shows true team spirit. But keeping it simple with a traditional cake garnished with team-colored buttercream flowers works, too. Perched on top: a miniature bridal couple sporting baseball hats (and veil, of course). If there's a groom's cake, it can be decorated like a baseball. And don't forget—cupcakes are always in style.

### Pinch Hitter

For the sports lovers whose idea of a dream wedding is more *Cinderella* than *Bad News Bears,* team spirit can always be shown in other ways. Baseball stadiums are a common setting for engagement photos. Baseball-themed bridal showers, engagement parties, or bachelor/bachelorette parties are also sporty options.

### For the Love of the Game

Longtime Cubs fans Jennifer Moran and Michael Blair went the whole nine yards—or innings—by holding their wedding and reception at Wrigley Field in Chicago, Illinois. It was a perfect fit for the couple because they didn't have a regular church. The bride, who said she is a bit of a tomboy, walked in to the musical theme from *The Natural.* The wedding began at 1:20—the time of a typical home game—and the ring bearer wore a Cubs jersey with the word "Batboy" on the back. Guests went home with baseballs personalized with the couple's names and wedding date, after dining on, what else, hot dogs, Italian beef, corn on the cob, and little sundaes served in miniature Cubs batting helmets.

# Outdoor Wedding Pitfalls (and How to Avoid Them)

*If you're planning to have your nuptials outside,
here are a few pitfalls to beware of and hopefully avoid.*

## Blow Ye Winds

Wind is a common issue for outdoor weddings—think of it as the silent killer. Hairstyles that were perfectly coiffed can be reduced to Crazy Town 'dos in a matter of minutes, chiffon gowns can be whipped to and fro, and entire tents can (and have) been uprooted from the ground. If you're going outdoors for your wedding, make sure you secure everything—hair, tents, skirts, and decorations— against Mother Nature's gale-force winds.

## Bugs

You can't really prepare for a plague of locusts, but you can at least try to guard against mosquitoes, gnats, and other annoying insects by lighting citronella candles and discreetly placing bug zapper lights around the wedding site. Even better, research the bug history of the area; some insects hatch in huge numbers every certain number of years—try to plan around their schedule because they don't really care about yours.

## Did He Say, "I Do"? What Did He Say?

The rushing river and the crashing waterfall look gorgeous, yes, but they're also really *loud*. When you pick a spot for your ceremony, make sure you're taking into account the acoustics of the place. If there's a busy playground, busy street, or active volcano nearby (you think we're kidding), your vows could be drowned out for your guests. Consider getting lapel microphones from your band or DJ to help make sure everyone can hear what's going on.

## Mmm... Tastes Like Salmonella

If the temperature where your outdoor wedding is going to take place is warmer than it is inside a refrigerator, there are important food considerations. If your caterer has experience with outdoor events, they'll take care of refrigeration and food temperature issues, but you should double-check everything. Deviled eggs and chicken salad don't last long under a blazing sun, and nobody likes to eat cold meatloaf. Either choose foods that can sit out for a period of time, like cold cut sandwiches and cold sides, or make sure you've got the proper equipment to keep your food delicious.

## What Permit, Officer?

Nothing spoils a party like a cease and desist order from a parks and recreation officer or other authority figure. If your wedding is out-side—and not in your own backyard—chances are good you'll need a permit. Make sure you know (and get in writing) the rules about trash pickup, decorations, and alcohol consumption so that there aren't any big surprises on your big day.

## Rain, Rain, Go Away

What if it rains? That's usually the first question couples ask them-selves when planning a wedding outdoors, and it's the first ques-tion for a reason—it's a huge consideration. Always have a Plan B if you're getting married outside. Whether that's a park building nearby, a tent large enough for everyone to seek shelter underneath, or some other location that can accommodate you and your guests, make sure you've got a Rain Day strategy in place from the start, even if the weather report predicts sunny skies.

## In the Dark

Once you've picked your spot, determine if you'll need to bring in your own power generator or if the site has electricity—if it doesn't, make arrangements immediately. And while you're doing that, deter-mine how many port-a-potties you'll need, if any, and reserve those, too. A wedding without lights, sound, or toilets doesn't sound like much fun, even if it's in Fiji.

# Stolen Brides, Artistic Pride

❧  ❧  ❧  ❧  ❧

*In 1954, MGM released a film that is considered one of the greatest musicals ever made, as well as a pioneering work in the field of choreography.* Seven Brides for Seven Brothers *is one of those wonderful movies in which all the stars seemed aligned.*

## DIY Dance Moves

The *Seven Brides for Seven Brothers* director, Stanley Donen, had already directed or codirected such classics as *On the Town* (1949), *Royal Wedding* (1951), and *Singin' in the Rain* (1952). Its male lead, Howard Keel, was a ruggedly handsome basso cantante (the lowest vocal range of all voice types) who had already made a name for himself on Broadway in such hits as *Oklahoma!* The film's lovely leading lady, Jane Powell, had been a musical star at both Universal and MGM studios since she was in her mid-teens. With a fabulous score by Gene de Paul and Saul Chaplin, the project—which was about a family of 19th-century frontiersmen in Oregon, who are searching for suitable female mates—looked like a winner from the get-go.

Perhaps the one thing that elevates *Seven Brides* to a classic, however, is Donen's decision to bring on Michael Kidd as choreographer. Kidd had already won several Tony awards for his work on Broadway, and his numbers for *Seven Brides* were groundbreaking and stunningly energetic. Kidd built his dancers' moves around the everyday lives and work of the backwoodsmen they were playing. As the men chopped wood and raised barns, they balanced perilously on suspended boards, jumped backward and forward over self-held axes, juggled hammers, and danced on rolling logs. Interviewed years later, Kidd explained his method of choreography as "human behavior and people's manners, stylized into musical rhythmic forms." *Seven Brides for Seven Brothers* was nominated for Best Picture but lost the Oscar to *On the Waterfront* in 1955.

## You Can't Hurry Love

In this GCI era, it's fun and exciting to witness this incredibly talented cast kickin' it old school and doing it the hard way, but there is no denying that other aspects of the film can be disturbing to our post-feminist sensibilities. *Seven Brides* was based on a short story by Stephen Vincent Benet called "The Sobbin' Women," which in turn was based on a legendary episode in Roman history called The Rape of the Sabine Women. The lead character of *Seven Brides*, Adam Pontipee, comes by his bride, Milly, honestly, even though they marry after knowing each other only a few hours. It's only after Adam's six younger brothers witness his marital bliss that things start to get a little dicey. The brothers want brides too, see, but they are more than a little rough around the edges. Milly tries to teach them manners and the proper way to dance with ladies, but disaster strikes at the barn raising, when the boys go after six women who already have beaus. Fought off by the jealous boyfriends, the Pontipee brothers return to their cabin in defeat.

Now, here's where it really gets politically incorrect: Adam sings about the book he has read on the Sabine women to his brothers and orders them to go back into town and abduct the six women. His brothers obey him, even going so far as to cause an avalanche so that the women can't be rescued by the townspeople. Back at the cabin, the women are not actually raped, of course —let's remember this was a "family" musical in 1954—but they are darn angry about being kidnapped. Milly is angry, too, and she insists that the boys sleep in the barn while the women live in the cabin. Adam stomps off in a huff and stays away for months, until he is informed that Milly has given birth to a child. Now the father of a daughter himself, Adam suddenly realizes the emotional turmoil the women's relatives must be going through over their kidnappings, but it's too late—the women are now in love with the brothers. A shotgun wedding for six couples ends this entertaining, if slightly disturbing, movie.

# Five Memorable Fictional Weddings from TV Land

*People love watching their beloved television characters get hitched. Living vicariously perhaps? If anything, those episodes tend to be highly entertaining. Some are deeply sentimental, with the viewer gripping tissues. Other TV weddings are virtual train wrecks to hilarious effect.*

## Rhoda and Joe: October 28, 1974

Almost 25 years before the ladies of *Sex and the City* defined single New York women looking for love, Rhoda Morgenstern (Valerie Harper) was the poster girl for her generation's single gals. Well, until she got married. During the monumental hour-long, eighth episode of *Rhoda,* the popular spin-off of *The Mary Tyler Moore Show,* Rhoda wed Joe Gerard (David Groh). However, the writers soon found it challenging to devise creative situations for a happily married couple, so Rhoda and Joe separated by season three and subsequently divorced.

**Where are they now?** Well, since the show was canceled during its fifth season, Rhoda and Joe no longer have writer's block keeping them apart. One could see them reuniting. Meanwhile, Rhoda will have to find a way to one-up her nemesis, Phyllis Lindstrom, as Phyllis (Cloris Leachman) most recently appeared on *Dancing with the Stars.*

## Luke and Laura: November 16, 1981

Thirty million viewers watched daytime television's original super-couple marry, making that pivotal *General Hospital* episode the highest-rated soap opera hour in history. Despite the offensive fact that Luke (Anthony Geary) once raped Laura (Genie Francis), couch potatoes were enamored by the pair's romance. Talk about "through good times and bad"! They bore two children, plus Laura's illegitimate child, and the family endured multiple kidnappings, a life-saving bone marrow transplant, a fire, Laura's stint in an asylum, and a divorce—among countless other melodramas. On November 16, 2006, on what would have been their 25th wedding anniversary, Luke and Laura exchanged vows again. Bummer to later learn the remarriage was invalid because Luke was still technically married to another woman. Details, details.

**Where are they now?** Perhaps the couple is still living in fictional Port Charles, and Luke is suffering from amnesia while Laura learns she has an evil twin.

## Zack and Kelly: October 7, 1994

After four seasons of *Saved by the Bell*, Zack's (Mark-Paul Gosselaar) wink-wink camera quips and well-moussed coif ultimately beat out Slater's dimples and ballet moves to win the heart of perky Kelly Kapowski (Tiffani Amber Thiessen). Following high school graduation, Zack and Kelly eloped to Las Vegas, bringing Screech and the gang along, of course. Hi-jinks ensued, and vows were exchanged.

**Where are they now?** After graduating from Cal U, the couple may have settled down near Bayside High. Since Jessie was always the one with the brains, good-hearted Kelly probably passed up a career in favor of motherhood. Meanwhile, Zack climbs the corporate ladder of computer and cell phone sales.

Actually, their "true" whereabouts may soon be revealed. As of press time, talk show host Jimmy Fallon has been actively campaigning for a *Saved by the Bell* reunion!

## David and Donna: May 17, 2000

*Beverly Hills 90210*'s Donna Martin (Tori Spelling) didn't quite remain a virgin until marriage as she had always promised. They just couldn't wait any longer (mainly due to May sweeps). But close enough. In the series finale, the Peach Pit crew capped off ten years of drama, hook-ups, and heartbreak by marrying perpetual good girl Donna to David Silver (Brian Austin Green) of the perpetually smarmy facial hair and hoop earrings. Ending things on a doubly hopeful note, Kelly Taylor ( Jennie Garth) caught the bouquet and reconciled with bad boy Dylan McKay (Luke Perry).

*Where are they now?* Unfortunately, fans have since learned in the far inferior *90210* reboot that neither couple is actually living happily ever after. David and Donna are in Japan where he is producing music—that's hopefully better than his Vanilla Ice sounds of the '90s. Donna is a thriving fashion designer (ok, sure, just go with it). But their marriage is on the rocks. Kelly and Dylan are also on the outs but still share a bond in their tousled-haired son, Sammy. In fact, judging by that kid's blond mop, Dyl might want to have a paternity test done to ensure that Sammy shouldn't actually be answering to the super-cute alliterated moniker of Sammy Sanders, à la Steve Sanders (Ian Ziering).

## Ross and Emily: May 7, 1998

The day a wedding crashed across the pond... Sweetheart, when your husband-to-be utters another woman's name during your wedding vows, it does not bode well for the marriage. To Rachel Green's surprise (and delight) and Emily's parents' horror, Ross Gellar (David Schwimmer) memorably said, "I take thee, *Rachel...*" Start backpedaling, Ross; backpedal like Lance Armstrong in quicksand. Unsurprisingly, the marriage did not last long. The weekend was not a total loss, though. It marked the first hook-up of Monica and Chandler—who would have their own memorable wedding three years later.

*Where are they now?* Emily, who was never more fun than a barrel of monkeys, probably found herself a stiff-lipped British chap her parents approved of and settled down. The series ended with Rachel and her baby daddy, Ross, professing their love. One could see thrice-divorced Ross rebuffing the need to make it legal this time. He probably lives contentedly with Rachel and baby Emma in a chic New York apartment with Joey across the hall.

## Honorable Mentions:

Kevin and Scotty on *Brothers and Sisters,* Joe and Helen on *Wings,* Niles and Daphne on *Frasier,* Charlotte and Harry on *Sex and the City*, Bobby and Lindsay (at Fenway Park, no less) on *The Practice*

Weddings Through the Years

# Bouquet Breakdown

*The color and scent of flowers create a festive look,*
*along with memories that will last a lifetime.*

## Ancient Times:

- Ancient Greeks are credited with introducing the idea of wedding flowers around the 5th century B.C. Flowers and plants, such as ivy, were used to create a crown for the bride to wear, which represented a gift of nature. The ivy stood for everlasting and unbreakable love—and had the bonus of warding off evil spirits. Evil spirits being a concern in early times, brides of Ancient Rome also carried herbs under their veils to ward them off, as well as to express fidelity and fertility.

- Bridesmaids of old were given the task of creating these floral arrangements for the bride as a token of thanks. But it might be the bridesmaids who deserved the appreciation. Instead of flowers, they carried bouquets of strong smelling herbs, such as garlic and rosemary, to ward off evil spirits.

## 17th Century:

- The language of flowers is credited to the people of Turkey back in the 1600s. Couples used certain types and colors of flowers to send messages. It was only natural to continue that symbolism on the wedding day by mixing certain flowers in the bouquet.

## Victorian Times:

- Symbolism went a step further by the early 1800s, when lovers sent one flower to convey a message. Unfortunately, otherwise beautiful flowers got a bad rap by being assigned a negative message—which meant there was no place for them in the bridal bouquet!

- The marriage of Queen Victoria to Prince Albert marked the replacement of herbs with fresh flowers. However, dill, known as the herb of lust, was still often tucked into floral arrangements and consumed by the bride and groom.

### Late 19th Century:

- A small circular bouquet called a posy was all the rage in the late 1800s. It was followed by a variation known as a *biedermeier,* which originated in Switzerland. This was a tightly formed bouquet that was carefully arranged in concentric circles of colored flowers. One ring would be made up of one type of flower, and the next ring, another. Orange and lemon peels were often included for their pleasing fragrance.

### 1900s:

- Arm sheafs were favorites of brides around the turn of the century. Popularized by actress Sarah Bernhardt, these bouquets looked just like the sheaf of flowers presented to the actress after an outstanding performance. Instead of being held in front of the bride, this natural-looking arrangement would be cradled in her arms, or draped over a single arm with the stems showing.

- Composite-flower bouquets were an ingenious creation by florists. Unable to obtain fresh flowers from around the world the way we do today, florists created their own "roses" by using petals of the gladioli. Known as galleria, they were sometimes used as part of a bridal bouquet but were more often worn separately as a corsage or adornment on a bridal hat.

### 1910s:

- So began the start of a long-running trend: the shower bouquet. If you can't picture what it looked like, consider that another name for it is a cascading bouquet. Think of it as the hanging plant of bouquets, with flowers and vines trailing down.

### 1920–30s:

- The cascading bouquet was very popular for the next two decades, reaching its peak by the late 1930s. In an effort to make a few changes to what brides already knew and liked, the bouquet became larger and more exaggerated. Some were so large that they nearly concealed the bride. These bouquets were decorated with ribbons, which were incorporated right into the floral design. Long streamers tied with "lover's knots" flowed from the bouquet. These small knots ran the length of the ribbon, and small buds and foliage were inserted. When brides threw the bouquet, the lucky girl who caught it untied one of these knots and made a wish that was supposed to come true. For a more rustic look, some brides added large turkey feathers that were tucked around the edges.

## 1940s:

- As the war effort spread across the country, cascading bouquets were suddenly too showy. Most brides gave up the bouquet altogether in favor of a simple corsage pinned to her suit or dress.

## 1980–90s:

- The shower bouquet made a bit of a comeback in the '80s as people tried to emulate Princess Diana and her cascading bouquet. Variations of this style continued into the '90s and peaked with the teardrop bouquet, which featured an elegant overflow of flowers forming a teardrop shape over the bride's clasped hands.

## 2000s:

- The start of a new millennium marked a trend toward anything and everything in terms of wedding flowers. Some brides choose to carry traditional bouquets; others carry original creations with unexpected elements.

- One modern tradition has the bride giving a single flower to her mother as she walks down the aisle and another flower to her new mother-in-law on her way back out.

- The idea of dogs bearing flowers on their collar or leash has become popular among canine-loving couples that include their pets in the ceremony.

# Wedding Chatter

"If you want to be happily married; And keep love in the loving cup; Whenever you're wrong, admit it; Whenever you're right, shut up."

—Guest Sarge

"When you realize you want to spend the rest of your life with somebody, you want the rest of your life to start as soon as possible."

—Billy Crystal, *When Harry Met Sally*

"Gravitation is not responsible for people falling in love."

—Albert Einstein

"The secret of a happy marriage remains a secret."

—Henny Youngman

"Nobody will ever win the battle of the sexes. There's too much fraternizing with the enemy."

—Henry Kissinger

"Biochemically, love is just like eating large amounts of chocolate."

—Al Pacino, *The Devil's Advocate*

"A woman has got to love a bad man once or twice in her life to be thankful for a good one."

—Mae West

"One of the best things about marriage is that it gets young people to bed at a decent hour."

—M. M. Musselman

"The market for wedding dresses is more often than not led by emotion and aspiration rather than rational decisions and financial constraints."

—Claire Birks

"A good wife always forgives her husband when she's wrong."

—Milton Berle

# Murphy's Law of Weddings

*Bride Gina Bailey encountered the Murphy's Law of weddings.*
*Everything that could go wrong... did.*

After two years of planning the perfect wedding, Gina felt pretty
confident that everything was under control. But a month before the
wedding, it all started to fall apart.

## One Disaster...

First, the wedding ring was lost. A new ring had to be ordered with
just three weeks to go. Then, the caterer canceled, and a construction crew working in the area filled up all the hotel rooms for the
wedding weekend. And that was just the beginning.

Two weeks before the wedding, the new ring hadn't arrived, and
Gina learned it hadn't been ordered yet. She was also told that the
reception could no longer be held outside due to "circumstances."
The church didn't allow dancing, so that was out, and no other place
was available for the reception. After that, neither the photographer
nor the videographer (who had already been booked) returned her
calls. And Gina didn't get her wedding dress back from being altered
in time for it to be cleaned and pressed.

## ...After Another

The day before the wedding, there was a mix-up with the tuxes.
And one of the groomsmen arrived—but his luggage didn't. Then,
as the wedding day dawned, the cake cutter was lost, and the serv-
ers didn't show up. One of the hairdressers canceled. Several streets
were blocked off for a town festival, including the one on which the
church was located. The groom's grandmother arrived late, and the
flower girl ran around yelling during the ceremony. Oh, and the cake
almost fell over. To top it off: Gina's ring arrived two sizes too big.
But you know what? Gina said it was the happiest day of her life.

## Weddings 'Round the World
# Chase Away the Evil Spirits

*While most weddings are full of good cheer, Norwegian weddings go a little further. The wedding couple takes steps to chase away evil spirits on this special day. Not a bad way to begin.*

### Norsk Nuptials

Norwegian food is known for its lack of color and taste—everything is white. But the country itself is beautiful, and each region brings a tradition of colorful clothing and designs that make a Norwegian wedding one to remember.

### The More the Merrier

Weddings in Norway are usually much smaller than weddings in the United States. Guests are primarily close family and friends. Norwegian weddings also include a procession to the church. In the old days, a fiddle player led the way, followed by the bride and groom, then her parents, the bridesmaids, the flower girl and ring bearer, and finally the guests.

### Wedding off Evil

In a traditional Norwegian wedding, the groom—and his groomsmen—wear a *bunad,* which is a woolen suit of short pants worn with stockings and a white silk shirt, a vest, and a topcoat. Colorful designs specific to the groom's birthplace (or ancestry) embellish the plain material and make it unique.

The bride's look is a more elegant one: a white or silver gown. Instead of a veil, she wears a silver or gold crown with silk ribbons. But most importantly, small spoon-shape bangles hang over the crown, and they make a musical sound when the bride moves her head from side to side. It's the sound created by these melodious bangles that chases away the evil spirits. What a responsibility!

The bridesmaid gowns are purposefully chosen to be very similar to the bride's wedding dress but in a different color. This is another way to trick the evil spirits—so they are unable to identify the wedding couple.

## Let Them Eat Cake

Music is an integral part of the Norwegian ceremony. "Come To The Wedding" is one traditional song played at most Norwegian weddings. The bride and bridesmaids typically dance at the actual wedding ceremony—also to chase away the evil spirits.

But the reception is still a big part of the day. Besides the food and music, it is a time for toasts—from just about everybody involved. A traditional wedding cake, called a *kransekake*, is often served, but many times other cakes accompany it as well. The kransekake is a white-tiered cake made of almond paste in the shape of rings that decrease in size as they approach the top. One bride's traditional Norwegian wedding served a chocolate sour cream cake, flanked by two kransekake. Each was decorated by placing a small bouquet of flowers in the top and tiny Norwegian flags in the rings. The couple saved the top ring to cut on their first anniversary and found it to be tastier than most frozen cakes.

Guests often bring additional cakes for the cake table, too. And these extra cakes are a good idea, because after a night of dining and dancing, a traditional Norwegian wedding should be capped off with *nattmat*, or night food: hot dogs, soup, and sandwiches, followed by more cake.

# Old Weddings' Tale

*Did you know it's bad luck to spot a lizard on the way
to your wedding ceremony? Find out why superstitions are still
a powerful part of wedding lore.*

Weddings are nothing if not surrounded by superstition. Whether it's
on the way to the wedding, during the ceremony, or after the fact,
any number of omens or actions can bring bad luck.

## Saturday Superstition

Although now a universally popular day for ceremonies, there was
a time when Saturday weddings were scandalous. Why? Several
superstitions imply a Saturday marriage means an early death for the
bride or groom.

Saturday isn't the only risky calendar date. The early church
prohibited couples to marry during certain religious seasons, such as
Lent. Ignore the antiquated ruling—even today—and it's believed
bad luck will befall you. Hence, the popular saying in Great Britain,
"Marry in Lent, live to repent."

Ancient Romans refused to marry in May, which was the month
when sacrifices were made to the dead. Later, England's Queen
Victoria even refused to allow her children to wed in May.

## Black Cat, Good Luck

It's long been purported that a cat—black or any other hue—can
bring good luck to a marriage. If a cat sneezes in the home of the
bride on the eve (or some sources say on the actual day) of her wedding, a blanket of good luck will cover her wedding day.

And, to be on the safe side, a bride should always personally feed
the household cat before leaving for the church on her wedding day.
The act is believed to bring lasting happiness to her married life.

Don't have a cat? Request one on your gift registry. At one time in England, it was believed that a bride who received a black cat on her wedding day would have the best of luck.

Of course, wedding superstitions don't always involve animals of the feline persuasion. It's unlucky if a pig crosses the path of a bride on her wedding day, and if she spots a lizard on the way to her wedding, she might as well go back home.

## Save the Soul with Rice

As long as people have been getting married, they've been avoiding supernatural spirits and their ethereal intents. In fact, to prevent trouble with the spirit world, guests began throwing rice when newly betrothed couples departed. The idea was that the tiny grains would assuage the injured feelings of spirits who really didn't like to see mortals happy.

Rice also played an important role for the groom. It was used as a charm to keep the groom's soul in his body. Turns out the souls of grooms had a penchant for running away from impending marital responsibilities.

In recent years, however, tossing this grain fell out of favor—largely because of an oft-repeated myth that the uncooked rice would be eaten by birds that would then explode as the rice expanded in their tiny bellies. According to the USA Rice Federation, however, uncooked rice is a harmless food for birds. Still, an increasing number of couples opt to have guests toss birdseed, release butterflies, or blow bubbles. There's no word on whether tiny bubbles cause bad luck.

- *Considered by the Ming dynasty to be the color of good luck, a traditional Chinese bride dons a red dress, red shoes, and a red silk veil. She may change clothing one or more times throughout the day.*

# Strike Up the Band!

*Here are some of today's intriguing acts, all available for booking.*

**The Steel Drum Guy, Chicagoland:** With a long list of corporate clients, a set of steel drums, and a dream, this one-man band has a song catalog that goes from here to "Margaritaville."

**Harlem Renaissance Orchestra, New York City:** This 16-piece orchestra has played everywhere from Lincoln Center to the Discovery Channel—you couldn't ask for a more authentic, Big Band sound.

**Jeff Brewer's Tribute to Billy Joel, Toronto, Ontario:** For a piano- and guitar-playing Billy Joel impersonator who really takes it all the way, you'll find what you're looking for in Canada's Jeff Brewer. He takes requests!

**The Upbeat Beatles Tribute Band, United Kingdom:** If you happen to be planning a wedding across the pond (or just really, really want a legit, British Fab Four), these are the guys for you. The band focuses on the upbeat Beatles tunes everyone loves, and they play more than 80 weddings a year.

**Pig Farmer, Savannah, Missouri:** With a brand of music they call "Punk-a-billy," this band will bring country and rock 'n' roll to the party. That, and a band name that will definitely get people talking.

**Red Rock Swing Band, Woodbury, Minnesota:** From 1940s swing music to show tunes, from polka to waltzes, this 17-piece band (including a female vocalist) will transport you to another era while keeping your toes tapping all night.

**Robert McCallion: Bagpipes for All Occasions, Fort Worth, Texas:** Texas is a long way from Scotland, but that doesn't stop McCallion from providing the winsome sound of the bagpipes wherever it's needed. (Don't worry, you can still do the Macarena—this bagpiper says he'll play *any* song you throw at him.)

# Quiz

*True or False?*

*Were these celebrity unions a match made in heaven or marriages from hell?*

1. Britney Spears was married to Kevin Federline for just two days.

2. Bill and Hillary Clinton have been married longer than George and Laura Bush.

3. Carmen Electra and Dennis Rodman's Vegas wedding lasted only two weeks before they decided to call it quits.

4. Paul Newman and Joanne Woodward met on a movie set while he was married to Jackie Witte. His first marriage lasted nine years. His marriage to Joanne lasted twice that: 18 years.

5. Alan Alda and his wife Arlene have been married more than 50 years.

6. Jennifer Lopez and Ben Affleck, referred to by the media as "Bennifer," were only married for ten months.

7. Tom Hanks has been married as many times as he has been nominated for an Oscar.

8. Drew Barrymore had two marriages that each lasted under two years.

9. Funnyman Bob Hope and comedienne Lucille Ball both had long marriages to their respective spouses.

10. Nicky Hilton was married for three years.

*Answers on the next page.*

## Answers:

**1.** False. Britney and Kevin were married for two years (and had two children).

**2.** True. In spite of Bill's infidelity, the Clinton marriage has lasted 34 years. The Bushes have been married 32 years.

**3.** True. After two weeks, Rodman called foul, claiming he was too drunk to realize what was going on when he tied the knot.

**4.** False. Paul's first marriage did last nine years, but he and Joanne were married almost 51 years until Paul died of lung cancer in September 2008.

**5.** True. The former *M*A*S*H* star may have been a lady's man on the hit TV series, but in real life, he's more of a one-woman man.

**6.** False. Jennifer Lopez and Ben Affleck were never married, although the couple was in the media spotlight over the course of the two years they dated.

**7.** False. Tom has actually been married as many times as he has *won* an Oscar, however, and that amount is two. (He was nominated for three.)

**8.** True. Drew was married to Jeremy Thomas for 11 months in 1994–95. Six years later, she tried it again with comedian Tom Green, but that marriage didn't fare much better. The couple divorced 15 months later.

**9.** True. Bob Hope and wife Delores were married for 69 years, until his death in 2003. Lucille Ball was married to Gary Morton for 26 years, separated only by her death in 1989.

**10.** False. And false again. This nickname is apparently unlucky in love. The first Nicky Hilton (born Conrad Hilton Jr.) was married only 205 days to actress Elizabeth Taylor in 1950. The second Nicky, his great-niece, married boyfriend Todd Andrew Meister in 2004 and had the marriage annulled three months later.

# Biggest. Weddings. Ever.

*Even if you've never planned a wedding,*
*you can guess that they're going to cost a little money—*
*or a lot of money.*

A wedding is essentially a big party, and the bigger the party, the bigger the checks you have to cut. For these billionaires, money was pretty much no object, so their weddings were beyond extravagant. And you thought you spent too much on the DJ...

## The Champagne's Covered

In 2005, Delphine Arnault, daughter of billionaire Bernard Arnault, got married. Mr. Arnault is the luxury titan in charge of—among a lot of other things—LVMH, the company that provides the world with the Louis Vuitton, Moet, Dior, and Hennessy labels. The wedding was held in the gorgeous French Bordeaux region, in a cathedral festooned with more than 5,000 white roses. Delphine wore a John Galliano–designed dress that took more than 1,300 hours to make. When it was time for the party, everyone headed to Arnault's nearby winery, where bottles of his bubbly can go for around $100,000. Famous faces filled the guest list, and *Harper's Bazaar* magazine called the affair "the wedding of the year." Hmm, you think?

## Party Like It's 1468

Though it's hard to figure how much the wedding of Margaret of York and Charles the Bold of Burgundy cost, we can assume it was a lot. Back in the 15th century, these two lovebirds married against the wishes of their governments (King Louis XI feared an alliance with the Burgundians) and threw a huge party to celebrate. Bloody jousts and duels were held for days, starring the most famous knights in England, and a pageant was held that included a parade through Bruges, which is reenacted every year to this day during the height of tourist season. The bride wore a crown so dusted with bling that it's now on display in the treasury of Germany's Aachen Cathedral.

## You're Married!

Three guesses as to who had one of the most extravagant weddings in recent memory? Donald Trump, of course! When Trump married Melania Knauss (his third wife) in 2005, he pulled out all the stops. Tony Bennett and Billy Joel were brought in to perform for the event, set against a backdrop of 10,000 flowers and a 200-pound Grand Marnier cake. Approximately 400 guests with Tiffany & Co. embossed invitations entered an 11,000-square-foot ballroom, replete with 17 chandeliers and 24-carat-gold embellishments. The affair was held at Trump's Mar-a-Lago resort in Palm Beach, Florida, and guests included A-listers such as Katie Couric, Heidi Klum, and Bill and Hillary Clinton. It's no surprise the wedding was big: After all, The Donald popped the question with a 15-carat, $1.5-million engagement ring.

## What, No Circus?

Andrei Melnichenko, who owns one of the biggest banks in Russia, spared no expense when he wed former Miss Yugoslavia, Aleksandra Kokotovic, in France in 2005. Apparently, the banker had a Russian chapel dismantled and rebuilt for the ceremony, though some say that's just a rumor. It's not so far-fetched when you consider that Melnichenko hired Christina Aguilera to sing three songs for a whopping $2 million—Whitney Houston and Enrique Iglesias also performed. Russian president Vladimir Putin was in attendance, as well as many other celebrity guests, who enjoyed food prepared by world-class chef Alain Ducasse. The whole affair was said to cost around $40 million.

## Can't Buy Me Love—but You Can Try!

When you're a billionaire steel king, you can afford to drop some serious cash. That's what L. N. Mittal did for his daughter, Vanisha, in 2004, when she married investment banker Amit Bhatia. The price tag for one of the most extravagant weddings in history is placed at somewhere between $60 and $78 million. That money went toward goodie bags filled with jewels for guests, who stayed in a five-star hotel in Paris during the festivities. There was a party at Versailles, another party in a King Louis XIV–era chateau, and another party at a wooden castle erected just for the event. Kylie Minogue performed, and the wine tab alone came in at around $1.5 million. Even the invitations for the event were massive and luxurious—they came to guests in silver boxes and were more than 20 pages long.

## The 21st Century's Big Kahuna

Of all the lavish weddings in the last century, one topped them all. In 1981, the sheikh of Dubai planned his son's wedding to Princess Salama, and nobody had seen anything like it. The party lasted seven days and the 20,000 guests (yep, 20,000) watched the marriage take place in a stadium built expressly for the rites. The entire city of Dubai celebrated the nuptials in the month before the event itself, and all in all, the price tag came in at about $100 million by today's standards. *Guinness World Records* claims this wedding holds the record for being the most lavish, but we're sure as time marches on, someone will find a way—and the means—to top it, too.

- *A 2007 bouquet boasted a combination of red and white gemstone flowers that included 90 gemstones, nine diamonds, and one star-shape ruby. At the whopping price of $125,000, it made its way into the* Vietnamese Guinness Book of Records *as the most expensive wedding bouquet.*

# Mr. and Mrs. Tiny Tim

*In the beginning, singer Tiny Tim was largely ignored or mocked—
surely, no one who heard him would ever have guessed how
famous he would become.*

## Tiptoeing Troubadour

Throughout the 1950s and early 1960s, Tiny Tim (real name:
Herbert Khaury) was a novelty act with a cult following in New
York and on East Coast college campuses. Born in Manhattan to a
Lebanese father and a Polish-Jewish mother, he became fascinated
with the music of the early 20th century at an early age and grew up
to be a musical archivist with an encyclopedic knowledge of vaude-
ville tunes and long-forgotten musicians. Though he was a baritone,
Tim would often sing songs like "You Are My Sunshine" and "On the
Old Front Porch" in a falsetto voice while accompanying himself on
a ukulele. Most of the time, he was ridiculed.

In the late '60s, however, booking agents began to take a second look at Tiny Tim. With his long, curly hair and enormous nose,
he looked like a wild hippie, even if he wasn't one. He was freakish

in an era when it paid to be a freak.
Soon, he was appearing on *Rowan
and Martin's Laugh-In, The
Ed Sullivan Show, The Jackie
Gleason Show,* and Johnny
Carson's *Tonight Show.* For
someone who had been denied
the spotlight for so long, Tim
seemed unfazed by his sudden
popularity. He always appeared
perfectly calm and comfortable
when chatting with his celebrity
hosts and didn't mind the

nervous laughter from the audience that often accompanied his songs.

Tiny Tim's first album, *God Bless Tiny Tim,* was released in 1968, and the single "Tiptoe Through the Tulips" became a big hit, charting at number 17 on *Billboard.* With music by Joe Burke and lyrics by Al Dubin, the song was originally published in 1926. Tim's strange and—some thought—beautiful version of this "old-timey" song propelled him to even greater heights, and soon, he was commanding $50,000 a week in Las Vegas. But Tim wasn't satisfied. He wanted to pull off the publicity stunt to end all publicity stunts—and he did.

## The Beginning of the End

In September 1969, Tim announced his engagement to 17-year-old "Miss Vicki" (real name: Victoria Budinger) on the *Tonight Show.* Johnny Carson—whether on a whim or by design is not really known—immediately offered to host the wedding live on TV. Tim had met Vicki at Wanamaker's Department Store in Philadelphia a few months before, when the young fan asked him to sign a book of his poetry for her. Neither seemed to care that he was more than twice her age. For months, Johnny Carson talked up their impending nuptials on his show, and finally, on December 17, 1969, the big night arrived. Though Carson had hoped the odd wedding would give him a ratings boost, he was shocked and delighted when over 40 million viewers tuned in to see Tiny Tim wed Miss Vicki, making it the highest rated *Tonight Show* episode to date.

It was all downhill from there for Tiny Tim's career, as well as his relationship with Miss Vicki. He was overexposed, and the public was tired of his shtick. Though he and Vicki had daughter Tulip Victoria in 1971, they mostly lived apart, divorcing in 1977. But Tiny Tim carried on with his vintage act until the end; he died onstage on November 30, 1996, singing "Tiptoe Through the Tulips."

Vicki Budinger found it hard to stay out of the spotlight after her marriage to Tim. She posed nude in *Oui* magazine in 1975, and in 2002, known as Victoria Lombardi, she got unwanted publicity as the girlfriend of Rabbi Fred Neulander of Congregation M'Kor Shalom in Cherry Hill, New Jersey—he was convicted of murdering his wife. She finally married her high school sweetheart, Jon Benson, in 2006, and now lives with him in Savannah, Tennessee.

# What Happens in Vegas...
# Should Be Shared with Friends

*For couples that love Las Vegas and plan to tie the knot in the near future, there are several ways to combine the two.*

Couples can easily have a destination wedding in Las Vegas. Or they can plan a Vegas-style wedding in their own hometown. Couples can even elope and then share the fun of Vegas at a reception back home.

## Viva Las Vegas

In Sin City, there's a wedding package for every taste and budget. Couples can get married in a helicopter, at the top of the Eiffel Tower (the one at Paris Las Vegas), or on the Treasure Island Pirate Ship. They can choose a theme wedding, a candlelight ceremony, or they can even be married by an Elvis impersonator.

Never mind the fun and excitement, one reason couples elope to Las Vegas is because it's just so easy. Even the Marriage License Bureau stays open from 8:00 A.M. until midnight seven days a week—including holidays. For $55 in cash, anyone over 18 years of age can get a marriage license in minutes. And there's no shortage of wedding chapels to choose from. Most of the major hotels have chapels—couples can find them all over the strip and in downtown Las Vegas.

And if the whole marriage idea is completely spur of the moment, there's no cause for worry. Brides can rent a wedding dress in Vegas. But no matter what, a delicious wedding cake from a Las Vegas favorite—Freed's Bakery—is a must.

## Bringing Sin City Home

For couples whose destination isn't really Vegas, or if couples want to bring the fun back home, a casino-style reception is something that wedding guests will never forget.

For a Las Vegas theme, the bridesmaids can wear dresses in touches of black, red, and green, while the groomsmen can wear coordinating cummerbunds and bow ties. The bride may choose to wear a wedding gown that reflects the glitz and glamour of Las Vegas, but any style is fine.

## The Vegas Scene

Las Vegas–style music is sure to be a big part of the fun. A DJ or band can play some of the old Rat Pack favorites. "Luck Be a Lady," "The Lady Is a Tramp," "Fly Me to the Moon," and other songs by Frank Sinatra, Sammy Davis Jr., Dean Martin, and, of course, Elvis Presley are good for starters. And for the younger crowd, songs from modern day Vegas headliners are hard to beat.

Table decorations can also reflect a casino theme. Black, red, and green are colorful accents, with scattered poker confetti on all of the tables. Place cards can be made out of Las Vegas postcards or made into a slot machine shape. They can even be on the back of playing cards. The cherry on top? Naming the tables after well-known Las Vegas casinos!

## Setting the Vegas Table

Instead of a sit-down dinner, treat your guests to a Las Vegas buffet. Any food does the trick as long as there's a cake! A traditional cake with a Las Vegas–related cake topper would certainly fit the occasion. Novelty dice with the wedding date or a tiny bride and groom set in a Las Vegas "moment" usually go far with guests. The groom's cake can be shaped like poker chips or the famous "Welcome To Fabulous Las Vegas" sign.

And at the end of the night, everyone goes home with something to remember. With chocolate playing cards, chocolate poker chips, and chocolate coins, who needs the real thing?

# Bachelor and Bachelorette Parties: Far and Away Fun

❧ ❧ ❧ ❧ ❧

*In the 2009 movie* The Hangover, *a groom and his three buddies take off for a pre-wedding fling in Las Vegas with disastrous results. The film's hijinks are hilarious but, fortunately, are not the norm in bachelor parties. Destination parties for both brides and grooms are, however, a growing trend.*

## How to Do It up, Destination Style

Both men and women are marrying at a slightly older age than they did a couple decades ago. So, at the average ages of 27 and 25, today's bridal couple is more likely to be able to afford a more extravagant getaway. And since the partygoers are expected to pay their own way, they might be a bit more financially stable as well.

With that thought in mind, it's a good idea for the maid of honor and best man (with help from the bride and groom) to consider that aspect as they plan the bachelor or bachelorette shindig. What is affordable in terms of travel, hotel, and food expenses? If the bridal couple—or their parents—has a cabin or condo somewhere fun, that always helps keep costs down. If not, are guests willing to share rooms? Is there a place within driving distance or are cheap flights available? Remember that airfare is usually cheapest at least two or three months ahead of time.

Travel agents and Web sites can also be a big help in planning destination bachelor or bachelorette parties. They can suggest places

to go, activities to do, and come up with special rates for the whole group. While the maid of honor or best man usually does the planning for this event, it is perfectly acceptable for each guest to pay his or her own way.

## Plan in Advance!

The movies tend to show the bridal party having their last fling the night before the wedding, leaving the partygoers tired and hungover on their wedding day. Most destination parties typically take place three to four weeks before the big day. That provides a nice break in the wedding planning but leaves enough time to finish last-minute details and to recover from the festivities.

## Picking a Place to Party

Some women love to get crazy for this last fling. Las Vegas is a popular destination (even for grooms) mainly because there is so much to do: gambling, club-hopping, sunbathing, and even shopping are all big draws. However, Miami, New York, or a bachelorette cruise might just fit the bill, too. For the bride-to-be who is not so much a party girl, a spa weekend, wine tasting, or overnight shopping trip might be more appropriate. And if the other participants can't afford a destination, it might be better to keep it close to home. Ask the bride: Is the place more important or the number of people who are able to join in the fun?

The same is true for the groom-to-be. Vegas might sound good, but is it okay with the bride? If the groom is uncomfortable with a strip club, find something else to do. Men looking for something exciting, but less exotic, are choosing white-water rafting, deep-sea fishing, and destinations that involve sports or other activities. Skiing, rock climbing, and other extreme sports are exhilarating choices that are a bit tamer. Just don't come back home with a broken leg before the big day! And for the guy who loves a round of golf with his best buddies, there are plenty of places to go for a golf vacation: Arizona, Florida, Pebble Beach, or Myrtle Beach.

## Surprise!

Some brides and grooms have even had surprise bachelor or bachelorette parties and claim they've had a great time. It's generally, however, a good idea to ask ahead of time and plan accordingly.

And for the bride and groom who are just not that interested in having a "last night of freedom," why not have a coed bash? It just might be double the fun.

# The Continuous Circle of Love

*We think of engagement and wedding rings as symbols of eternal love. The use of rings dates back thousands of years, but their meaning and makeup has changed over time.*

- **Ancient Egypt:** About 4,800 years ago, the first recorded exchange of wedding rings took place in ancient Egypt. When a groom placed a ring on his bride's finger, it demonstrated his confidence in her ability to take care of their home.

- **2nd Century B.C.:** Brides in ancient Rome were given a gold ring, but there was a catch—they were only allowed to wear it in public since it was too valuable to wear while doing household chores. These brides also had a second ring made of iron to wear around the house.

- **860 B.C.:** Christians started to exchange rings in wedding ceremonies. The bands were usually very ornate, engraved with doves, lyres, and two linked hands. The Church felt these rings were "heathenish," however, and discouraged their use.

- **13th Century:** Wedding and engagement rings became noticeably simpler—more a symbol of a couple's union than a piece of jewelry. The symbol was deemed so important that if a groom couldn't afford to buy a ring, he rented one for the ceremony.

- **16th Century:** It had long been common practice to wear a wedding ring on the third finger of the left hand, but this tradition was formalized in *The Book of Common Prayer,* written by the son of King Henry VIII.

- **17th Century:** Silver became the metal of choice in England and France for the popular poesy (or posy) rings of the time. The wedding ring was inscribed with a poesy, or love poem, either inside or out.

- **19th Century:** Plain gold bands were very common in the 1800s. Other rings of this time period were set with pearls or small diamonds, and some even used turquoise to symbolize the forget-me-not flower.

- **Early 1900s:** Delicate designs were the rage in the Edwardian era. Rings were made of platinum—or gold set with silver or platinum—to better show off the center diamond.

- **1910s:** Old-mine and old-European cut diamonds were the most popular gemstone. The high crown of this cut sparkled beautifully in the candlelight.

- **1920s:** Art deco was the trend for these "modern" brides, and rings took on the look of the times. Geometric designs and colored stones ruled the day.

- **1930s:** Wedding bands were narrow, in keeping with the economics of the Depression era, but the widespread choice of 18kt or 14kt gold for the rings illustrated how important they were to a new bride or groom.

- **1940s:** Platinum was needed for the war effort, so brides substituted silver for their wedding bands. Jewelry hoarding was not uncommon.

- **1950s:** Before 1940, only about 15 percent of grooms wore wedding bands, but by the Korean War, that number had jumped to 70 percent.

- **1960s:** Platinum, silver, and white gold took a backseat to yellow gold. This popular metal was usually set with diamonds for a simple ring that really sparkled.

- **1970s:** Free love was the order of the day, and a classic ring like your mother had just wouldn't do. Nugget and antique finishes became very popular because of their more rustic, natural look. They may have been expensive, but they didn't look it.

- **1980s:** Artisan rings lost their popularity, and brides turned to cathedral or dome mountings for their rings. The diamond was often set up high on a band that was a quarter to three-eighths of an inch wide, with smaller baguettes on the side.

- **1990s:** The '90s brought a renewed interest in white gold—often with yellow gold accents.

- **2000s:** Whether it's the generation or the economy, today's brides are returning to a simpler look. Diamond solitaires (usually .5 to 1 carat) are the most popular engagement ring style. Today's brides like the look of a silver ring and are usually choosing white gold as the metal. Sterling can tarnish, and the cost of platinum is out of reach for many newly engaged couples.

- *In a custom of the 17th century, the bride passed pieces of wedding cake through her ring. She then gave a piece to the unmarried girls who slept with it under their pillows, hoping to dream of their future husbands. The practice ended when brides decided it might be bad luck to remove their rings so soon after the wedding.*

- *In a wedding ceremony, the ring bearer carries the wedding rings from the entrance of the church to the bride, groom, and ceremony officiant. Typically, the ring bearer is a nephew or young brother (or a niece or a young sister) of the bride or groom but can also be any relative or child of a relative or friend.*

# Sound the Trumpets: Royal Weddings!

*The term "royal" often describes things gone badly: a royal disaster,*
*a royal pain in the bum, and most WWE Royal Rumbles. However,*
*when it comes to fascinating wedding stories, the castle-and-moat*
*crowd knows how to live it up.*

## Albert/George and Liz

One girl who knew how to play hard to get was Lady Elizabeth
Bowes-Lyon, aka the woman who would later be called Britain's
Queen Mother. She rejected two marriage proposals from Prince
Albert, Duke of York, before relenting. Whether Prince Albert
sported a unique, um . . . namesake piercing that scared her away,
only she would know.

On April 23, 1923, Albert and Elizabeth declared their love at
London's historic Westminster Abbey. By all accounts, the wedding
was lovely and fit for royalty. However, it was only through an unpre
dictable fluke that the couple would ascend to the apex of the mon-
archy. See, second-born son Albert was not necessarily destined for
the crown, as his big bro Edward VIII had dibs. However, Edward
surrendered the throne for—what else—a wedding! In a royal
scandal that set tongues wagging, Edward sought to wed American
Socialite Wallis Simpson. The controversy? She was already married at the time to her second husband, Ernest Simpson. By 1937,
Edward got his way and made it legal with his divorcee. But it cost
him his kingship. Which is how Queen Elizabeth came to be. And as
for Prince Albert, it was after his coronation that he would be known
as King George VI.

## Phil and Liz 2.0

King George and Queen Elizabeth's daughter, Elizabeth II, was only
eight years old when she met her then-13-year-old future hubby,
Philip Mountbatten. Twelve years later, Philip and Elizabeth decided
to tie the knot.

The problem was that Philip neglected to ask Elizabeth's father's permission first. Granted, anyone might be intimidated approaching the king of England for his daughter's hand. So the couple kept their engagement on the down-low for many months. When George learned of their plans, he was initially furious. Fortunately, the young couple soon gained papa's blessing. They were married at Westminster Abbey on November 20, 1947. The bride wore a white satin gown that sparkled with ten thousand crystals and pearls. To construct the silk, a virtual sweatshop of silkworms was required at Lullingstone Castle. Elizabeth also gripped a stunning waterfall bouquet of orchids, with a sprig of myrtle as a wink to Queen Victoria—who famously utilized Greek mythology's "herb of love" in her 1840 bridal bouquet. A tiara, a double strand of pearls, and a 15-foot train topped off the ensemble.

It was a multi-royal affair—the shah of Iran, the king and queen of Denmark, the king and queen of Yugoslavia, the king of Romania, and the king of Norway all attended the lavish event. The ceremony was presided over by the Archbishop of Canterbury. A total of 91 choristers, including the Choir of HM Chapels Royal and the Abbey Choir, provided breathtaking musical accompaniment from the crowded organ loft. It was the first royal wedding to feature the trumpet fanfares after the signing of the register. Of note: Among the 2,500 gifts showered upon the couple was a piece of crocheted lace inscribed with *Jai Hind,* meaning, "Victory for India." The gift-giver: Mahatma Gandhi.

The couple formed a strong lifetime partnership and went on to govern a nation. In fact, Elizabeth II became the first queen to celebrate a 60th wedding anniversary milestone with her man.

## Chuck and Di

At the young age of 19, bride-to-be Lady Diana Spencer reportedly chose the largest engagement ring on display, a white-gold sapphire ornamented by 14 diamonds. Six months later, she would be marrying her regal eagle. Even though the marriage ended in a Greek tragedy, the wedding was the stuff of fairy tales.

Like Cinderella, Diana rode a glass coach to join her Prince Charming. Of course, instead of an ugly stepsister, she would have to contend with a minimally attractive mistress. But at the time, the wedding seemed nothing short of magical. It was July 29, 1981, and the streets of London were lined with gawkers and well-wishers, while an additional 750 million were glued to the tube. Accompanied by her father, Diana waved to the admirers during the procession to St. Paul's Cathedral.

Westminster Abbey had been the go-to venue for royal weddings since King Henry I sealed the deal with Princess Matilda of Scotland in 1100. Bucking tradition, His Royal Highness Prince Charles selected the Christopher Wren–designed Cathedral instead. What was traditional, however, was the bride's "something old, new, borrowed, blue" preparation. Queen Mary's antique Carrickmacross lace stood in for the "old"; the gown, of course, checked "new" off the list; she "borrowed" a family heirloom tiara; and the "blue" was represented by a tiny blue bow secretly sewn inside the gown.

All eyes were on the girlish yet poised bride as she took three and a half minutes to promenade down the red-carpeted aisle. She wore a Victorian-style gown, designed by British husband-and-wife designers David and Elizabeth Emanuel. It was made of ivory silk and adorned by 10,000 pearls and mother-of-pearl sequins. The puffed sleeves and 25-foot train ensured that the dress would be memorable. During the ceremony, Charles slipped a Welsh gold wedding band onto Diana's finger, and before long, it was on to the reception.

On the Buckingham Palace balcony, the newlyweds treated fans to a kiss before settling in for a royal wedding feast. They nibbled on brill in lobster sauce, chicken breasts in lamb mousse, and strawberries with Cornish cream. Then the groom, clad in his naval uniform, whipped out his sword to cut the five-tiered wedding cake.

# The Birth of the Tuxedo

*They say no one pays attention to the groom at a wedding, but if he wore jeans and a T-shirt, you can bet everyone would notice!*

### Starting with the Suit

The tuxedo is *de rigueur* at formal weddings and has been for as long as anyone today can remember, but few know of the tuxedo's long and interesting history.

The progenitor of the tuxedo came from the fashion-obsessed imagination of Beau Brummell, born George Bryan Brummell on June 7, 1778. While still in his teens, Brummell became close friends with the prince regent (later to become King George IV), and for a time, he made a name for himself in the Tenth Light Dragoons, but gambling and partying were his only real interests. An inheritance left by his father made this lifestyle possible, and Brummell was determined to be the most stylish man in England while he pursued his debauchery. He was also set on influencing men to give up the loose, flowing 18th-century menswear and adopt a look composed of long, sleek lines, full-length trousers, and elaborate cravats (the forerunners to neckties). When Brummell appeared at a formal affair in a black-and-white ensemble that we would now call a "suit," he created a sensation and changed men's clothing forever.

### Turning Tuxedo

Black tie as we know it today was created in 1860, when London tailor Henry Poole & Co whipped up a short-jacketed black suit for the prince of Wales as an alternative to the more formal white tie. The prince introduced this new style to American friend James Potter, a wealthy New York businessman visiting London. Potter was soon back home strutting through the Tuxedo Park Club in his new get-up, and the tuxedo was born.

# *Fast Facts: Gowns*

- *The average amount spent on a bridal gown in 2009 was $1,075.*

- *If you're looking to save money, avoid custom alterations. Changing the shape of the neckline or altering a sleeve on your gown can cost up to $300 per adjustment.*

- *Older brides tend to spend more money on their wedding gowns than younger brides.*

- *Brides begin shopping/researching their wedding gowns almost immediately after they're engaged; grooms typically get their tuxedos five to six months after their bride's dress has been purchased.*

- *If you can attend a bridal shop sample sale, you might find a gown that will save you big bucks. At these events, buyers attempting to get rid of inventory often cut prices by as much as 80 percent. (Wedding dress samples are usually made in a size eight, so if that's what you wear, you're in luck.)*

- *The wedding gown will account for more than 6 percent of a couple's total wedding budget.*

- *National wedding dress retailer David's Bridal accounts for 20 percent of all bridal-gown sales, and that percentage is increasing.*

- *Renting a gown is becoming a popular option for brides who don't have much of a budget. Some online retailers will rent gowns starting at around 90 dollars and often throw in the veil for free.*

- *Seventy-three percent of women say their favorite part of attending weddings is checking out the bride's dress.*

- *Where you get married may play a part in your choice of gown: Churches may not allow bare shoulders or may require that a wedding gown fit various other criteria.*

# Sharing Your Wedding with the Animals

*We love our pets. With 39 percent of all U.S. households owning
a dog and 34 percent owning cats, it's no surprise that
Fido and Fluffy have made their way into the wedding festivities.
Now the other animals want to have their day.*

## Horsing Around

When Sandra Elor and David Williams invited 70 guests to their
nuptials in Harrow, Ontario, they told them it was a garden wedding. But even the couple's parents were unprepared for what came
next. Instead of wearing the traditional tux, the groom entered in full
dressage—atop a beautiful black gelding named Lazaar. And Sandra
followed on a sweet Arabian mare named Freespirit, riding side-
saddle of course.

The horses behaved throughout the ceremony, standing quietly
while the couple said their vows. It was when the pair leaned over
for their first official kiss that Lazaar tried to get in on the act. But
when he tried to kiss Freespirit, she nipped him. No harm was done,
and the rest of the day proceeded happily.

Including horses in their wedding wasn't much of a stretch for
Sandra and David, who are both horse lovers and equestrians. Plus,
fortunately, both horses had been in horse shows and were experienced around crowds. A few friends came early and helped by bath-
ing the horses, braiding their manes and even polishing their hooves.
The wedding was actually planned in three short days, but with the
help of these animal friends, the couple—and their guests—will
have memories to last a lifetime.

## Who Invited . . . the Llamas?

Another animal that seems to be quite popular at weddings these
days is the llama. Who would have thought? But at least two wedding couples out there had llamas added to their special day.

When one English bride married a man of Peruvian descent in the English countryside, the groom's sister-in-law decided the wedding needed a touch of Peru. So she arranged for a pair of llamas to make an appearance. Adorned with flowers and colorful blankets, they were quite a hit.

A bride and groom who got hooked on the beasts of burden after sharing an early date at a llama trekking center had llamas at their wedding as well. The bride's parents planned the addition, surprising the newlyweds as they emerged from the ceremony. The pictures turned out great, but did anyone think to add two more for dinner?

And if you like llamas yourself—or just want to surprise someone, too—there are several llama ranches that have animals available for weddings and other special events. Just check the Internet.

## Polly Wants to Party

Besides the normal dog, cat, horse, and llama weddings, bridal couples have been known to include other favorite pets as well. Lovebirds are sometimes included in cages, and doves are often released at weddings. But how do you include your pet parrot?

Parrots can be trained to do a variety of things, and one of the most popular "tricks" is having the parrot fly to the altar and deliver the wedding rings to the couple. It's spectacular.

Another possibility is to have the parrot speak. You probably don't want to risk including your parrot if it swears like a sailor. And be sure it won't spew risqué or bigoted phrases—or worse, private information that would insult or embarrass any of the guests. But if your parrot is well behaved, and you decide to include it, consider having it say, "You may kiss the bride" or doing a toast at the reception.

As with dogs or cats in the wedding party, it's a good idea to have a handler committed to tending your parrot throughout the day. And if he's going to be loose, keep him away from the food and keep this in mind—he may drop little "surprises" on your guests!

And finally, watch out for uninvited animal guests. One couple that didn't include any pets of their own found their wedding reception featured on YouTube—when a large iguana jumped onto a table and proceeded to eat the wedding cake.

# Double Your Pleasure, Get Married Together

*When two sisters recently got engaged—to brothers—
they did the only logical thing: They decided to get married in
a double wedding. Why not? It's a great way to save
on expenses and double the fun.*

## Make It a Double

Double weddings aren't common these days, so it takes a little extra planning—and most importantly, communication—to make it work, but with a little effort, it turns into one big fabulous wedding. And sisters aren't the only ones who can have a double wedding. Any two couples can share their special day as long as all four people buy into the idea. If there are serious doubts, it's better not to take the plunge, but after listing the pros and cons, couples may be surprised to find that it's an idea that's hard to pass up.

Like the buy-one-get-one-free sale of weddings, a double wedding is an unbelievable value. There are two schools of thought: One is that by sharing the church, reception hall, photographer, flowers, food, and music, couples can save almost half the cost. On the other hand, sharing all those costs allows couples to splurge on some of the aspects that are most important to them.

## Double Date

When brides are sisters, there are a couple of ways to go. Sometimes the father of the bride walks both brides down the aisle at the same time—one daughter on each arm. Some brides choose to have the father walk one bride down the aisle and then go back for the other bride.

In the old days, etiquette dictated that the eldest bride (whether sisters or friends) was always the first to walk down the aisle, say her vows and walk back down the aisle with her new husband. Today, things are a little looser, and it's up to the brides to decide who does what and when.

## Double Feature

If the wedding is outdoors, the chairs can be set up in any manner. If it's in a church, there are factors to take into consideration, such as the presence of one or two aisles and the size of the altar area. These logistics affect how the wedding proceeds.

If the church has two side aisles, each bride—and her wedding party—enter separately, either alternating with each other or at the same time. If there is only a center aisle it's best for one whole wedding party to precede the other; however, both brides might want to enter after all the bridesmaids have walked.

And speaking of bridesmaids, it's best if each bride has no more than three attendants, unless any or all of them are shared as well. Their dresses don't have to be the same, but they tend to be the same general style or color family. And the brides? They still choose the dresses of their dreams. They don't have to match in any way as long as the brides have seen each other's dress and agree that they work together. Most brides want to shop for that special dress together anyway.

## Double Space

Reception seating can be a challenge at a double wedding. A long table with the brides seated next to each other and their wedding parties to either side is one option, but separate long or round tables can also be done. There really are no rules—couples just do whatever feels right to them.

Don't forget the cake! There are many options. Some couples have one large cake with two smaller groom's cakes of different flavors. Or there can be two matching cakes that are placed on the same table or on opposite sides of the room. It's fun when both couples cut their cakes and share that first bite at the same time.

But what about gifts? Do all the guests have to bring two? Not unless they're friends with both couples. If you're a guest of only one couple, you're off the hook!

# This Ain't Your Grandma's Wedding Cake

❧ ❧ ❧ ❧ ❧

*One more wedding tradition has inevitably fallen victim to pomp,*
*circumstance, and apparently, bridal wizardry.*

## Alterna-cakes

Among the most well-known cake alternatives are cupcakes and candy bars. Arguably rivaling the traditional wedding cake, cupcake towers and candy bar buffets have really become household names in the wedding world. Working their way up the popularity ladder, these customized creations have proven it time and time again: What they lack in tradition, they gain in delightful designs. Because both choices can be dipped, dolloped, shellacked, sprinkled, and stacked any way a bride sees fit, they are easily taking over the market of goodies miniature in size but powerful in taste.

## Kreme Is the New Cake

Not to be outdone by the more popular wedding cake alternatives, places like Baskin-Robbins and Krispy Kreme Doughnuts have also jumped on board the wedding dessert bandwagon. Each has started customizing dishes for couples looking for something original and nontraditional. Krispy Kreme will refine, ruffle, and raise up rows of doughnuts in the name of "holey" matrimony, while Baskin-Robbins likes to give their newlyweds-to-be the option of choosing their favorite flavors to be merged and quaffed into a giant ice cream creation . . . giving ice sculptures and "cold feet" reassurance that it's super cool to be a part of wedded bliss. (What? Too much?)

## Sweet Snack Cakes

While chilled cream cakes and ice sculptures give couples a reason to freeze their assets, stacking their favorites in tiers is yet another alternative that will leave their guests with full bellies and warm hearts. Everything from fruit-packed pastries to mousse-filled toasting flutes—and even pancakes and pork pies (yes, pancakes and pork pies!)—have been displayed in reception halls across America. Not only can this cut down on service charges, but it also allows newlyweds the opportunity to have more than one choice. One of the most popular "tier"-ing choices is a combination of prepackaged confectioneries, such as Twinkies, Ding Dongs, and Sno Balls, assembled and stacked on cake plates and platters. These are obviously done by a bride looking to be the "Hostess with the Most-est!"

## Cultural Confections

Aiming to please isn't the only reason people are leaning toward wedding cake alternatives. More often than not, dessert options are decided by someone's preferences, culture, heritage, or beliefs. Thus, many couples will look to other parts of the world for inspiration. For instance, while many Americans revel in the fruitcake as a holiday gag gift, places such as the British Isles, the Caribbean, Ireland, and Scotland revere it as a wedding-day "must have."

Couples looking for something different might look to Europe where France venerates its caramel covered, cream-filled pastry towers *(croquembouche)* or Lithuania, where *sakotis*—a cookielike dessert shaped into a Christmas tree—are nothing short of blue ribbons. Even newlyweds who don't have a sweet tooth can look for inspiration in Korea, where they cover ground steamed rice in red bean powder, or Japan and India, where they use "dummy cakes." While guests might not like eating cardboard, the money saved will leave at least two people smiling!

Bottom line, wedding cakes and all their alternatives really don't have specific rules to follow. In fact, since everyone knows calories don't count when someone's getting married (or that's what we tell ourselves at least), it may even be encouraged to go for broke and try them all!

## Flinging Flowers

*Overzealous luck-seekers are distracted by
flowers tossed in self-defense.*

### It's Tradition

Nuptial lore asserts that the unwed woman who catches the bouquet will be the next to marry, but the origins of this practice are a bit more sinister. Intrigued? Let's head to medieval Europe for some (albeit disturbing) answers.

### Distracting the Desperate

In the early 14th century, brides didn't keep their wedding gowns for posterity; instead, after the wedding, the dress was torn to shreds—with the bride still wearing it. Single women chased the bride, yanking the dress to shreds because the bits of fabric were good luck to the oh-so-desperate-to-wed. As the bride attempted to escape with her new husband, she threw the wedding bouquet to distract mad-with-envy throngs.

A century or two later, brides wanted to keep attendees' paws off their increasingly couture creations, so gown-tearing fell out of fashion. Still, tossing the bouquet remained a winsome tradition. Why? Flowers are a symbol of fertility.

### Better Safe than Sorry

Today, the modern bouquet-throwing tradition sometimes has disastrous effects. In July 2009, a couple in Italy actually caused an aircraft to fall out of the sky during the process. It seems the bouquet became tangled in the ultra-light's tail rotor.

It's no wonder some brides opt to skip the bouquet toss—and the risk of a stampede. Instead, they award a small, token bouquet to each bridesmaid or pass a singular flower from the bouquet to each single woman at the reception.

But where's the sport in that?

# Meant for Each Other

*The Chinese have an enduring history of special wedding superstitions and practices.*

## About Last Night

In ancient China, some of the most popular wedding rituals took place the night before the big day. The "installation of the bridal bed" was a big to-do for the groom. As implied, a newly purchased bed was installed. The bed was scattered with lotus seeds, dates, pomegranates, and peanuts, and children were invited to scramble for items on the bed as an omen of offspring to come.

## Slumber Party

For her part, the bride spent the night with her girlfriends in a secluded part of the house, called the "cock loft." True story, and no, it's not a loft full of male chickens. There she could vent about her troubles and would probably receive tips to prepare for marriage. At Western sleepover parties, fixing each other's hair is a mainstay, and the ancient Chinese had their own version. Both bride and groom would separately perform a four-part combing ritual. The first comb-through marked "from beginning 'til the end." The second combing represented "harmony from now 'til old age." The third signified "sons and grandsons." The fourth would bring "good wealth and a long lasting marriage."

## Here Comes the Groom

To claim his beloved, the groom would lead a parade to the bride's home. Firecrackers and drums both announced his upcoming arrival and warded away evil spirits. The bride's attendants would not surrender the bride until they were appeased with packets of money from the groom's party.

# The Much-Married Tommy Manville

*Thomas Franklyn Manville Jr.—flamboyant Manhattan socialite and heir to the Johns-Manville asbestos fortune—earned minor celebrity and a place in* Guinness World Records *for being the American man married the most times in the 20th century.*

Manville appeared to revel in his reputation and frequently made self-deprecating comments that made for memorable sound bites...

## "I propose to anybody.... Sort of an introduction."

During his lifetime (1894–1967), Manville racked up 13 marriages to 11 different women. Why the hankering to get hitched? Well, part of his marriage compulsion may have been motivated by financial gain. You see, when Tommy's wealthy father died, his father's will set up a trust for Tommy—but he was only entitled to withdraw from the interest. However, the will reportedly stipulated that Tommy would receive a million dollars from the principal when he married. The loophole? It didn't specify that only the first marriage was eligible for the payout!

## "I've only had lunch with her once or twice, [but].... I think this could be one of the richest experiences of my life."

The above statement was made while Manville was still married to his eighth wife. He was referring to a brunette nightclub singer named Ruth Webb. Ruth managed to avoid becoming wife number nine, but perhaps Manville regretted that he went another route....

## "I'm done with blondes."

Manville's love of women and reciting marital vows was only matched by his passion for fast cars. In fact, as a parting favor, Manville typically gifted each wife with an automobile on their way out. Other than that, Manville barely had to tap into his $20 million bank account while freeing himself from his first eight marriages. But wifey number nine, blond bombshell Anita Frances Roddy-Eden, caused quite a headache. When they wed in 1952, the dancer was 30 years Manville's junior. And she didn't age much in the 12 days they were married. She hauled the eccentric playboy to court and took the stand with accusations of "extreme mental cruelty." Among her claims: Manville drank excessively, and when she questioned his morning gin consumption, he threatened to kill her with a gun. Plus, he allegedly hung photos of his previous wives around the house and constantly talked about his exes. She even said that while they were still married, he tried proposing to her twin sister, Juanita Patino, the ex-wife of a Bolivian tin tycoon. A bit of a sassy character herself, Roddy-Eden Manville remarked that if they were unable to come to terms with a satisfactory settlement, "I am still his wife, and I am going to be the widow Manville!"

## "She cried, and the judge wiped her tears with my checkbook."

Ultimately, Roddy-Eden Manville walked away with $260,000—a sizable sum at the time and significantly more than any of her predecessors received. She went on to pen and publish a biography entitled *The Many Wives and Lives of Tommy Manville*.

## "When I meet a beautiful girl, the first thing I say is will you marry me? The second thing I say is how do you do?"

Over the years, Manville's notoriety made its mark on popular culture. Anita's book inspired a campy musical by Jackie Curtis called *Lucky Wonderful: 13 Musicals About Tommy Manville*. Manville is also referenced in Irving Berlin's song "What Chance Have I With Love." Furthermore, it is widely believed that Manville was the basis for Gary Cooper's serial marrying character in the 1938 movie *Bluebeard's Eighth Wife*.

# 'Til Death Do Us Part...
# or Not Even Then?

*There are a couple varieties of ghost weddings...*

## Haunted Honeymoon

In the movie *Clue,* Madeline Kahn's character, Mrs. White, proclaims "Life after death is as improbable as sex after marriage." One wonders how Mrs. White would have felt about marriage after death. For centuries, many Chinese romantics have participated in afterlife marriages known as *minghun.* If a young man dies after the age of 12 and was never married, his parents may choose to arrange an afterlife wedding.

The Western world has dubbed these practices "Ghost Weddings." However, in China and other parts of the world, afterlife marriages are not considered morbid. In accordance with Confucian values of loyalty to family, an afterlife marriage is often viewed as natural (supernatural) parental responsibility. Many Chinese believe that an unmarried life is an incomplete or unhappy one—contrary to what some divorced or cynical Americans may feel. Therefore, an afterlife marriage ensures that the departed will not navigate the afterlife alone or incomplete—an eternal honeymoon if you will.

The ritual may also be a superstitious preventative measure. After all, if a soul is unhappy in his afterlife, he may be more inclined to haunt his old stomping grounds. Like any afterlife philosophy or funeral tradition, it's debatable if the benefit is for the deceased or for the peace of mind of the living.

## You Can't Take It with You

In the post-mortal marital ritual of *minghun,* a bride corpse is laid to rest beside the deceased male, in separate coffins or together. A ceremony is performed, often with music, flowers, wine, and other standard wedding components. Gifts are also exchanged. (Unfortunately, though, Crate & Barrel has yet to expand their registry options to include beyond this plane.) Depending on the wealth of the families, gifts may include actual household items, valuables, and even the act of physically burning fake money. Less extravagant gifts include constructed replicates of automobiles or home items. Families too poor to afford a corpse bride may create a womanly figure of straw and bury it beside their loved one.

## Grave Consequences

Though increasingly popular, *minghun* is officially deemed occultist by the Chinese government and is not sanctioned. Technically, it is illegal to purchase a dead body for, uh ... personal use ... in China. The Communist Party has denounced the practice. Families discreetly make the arrangements and exchange the cash. A bride corpse can usually fetch the *yuan* equivalent of anywhere between 500 to 5,000 U.S. dollars.

In fact, in the last five years, there has been an inadequate supply for the increasing corpse bride demand, and China has experienced a wave of grave-robbing crimes. To compensate for the shortage of natural deaths in 2009, one criminal gang in south China even resorted to murdering young women for the purpose of selling their corpses for ghost weddings.

## Ghost at a Wedding

Then there is the "ghost wedding," where an unexpected spirit makes its presence known. The *Queen Mary* cruise ship is well regarded as a haunted vessel, which may be why some brave, curious, or macabre couples choose to host their weddings in the historic ballroom.

## Prohibition, Criminal Convictions, near Demolition

When built in 1902, the Landmark Center in St. Paul was originally the Federal Court Building and Post Office of the upper Midwest. It housed many high profile gangster trials in the 1930s, including Ma Barker's son "Doc," Alvin "Creepy" Karpis, and John Dillinger's main girl, Evelyn Frechette. It was also the site where gangster Jack Peifer, of the Barker/Karpis gang, was sentenced to 30 years in prison. Peifer had worked previously as a bellhop and carnival employee before taking up a life of crime; he graduated from running a speakeasy and money laundering to first-class kidnapping. His kidnapping of banker Edward Bremer marked him as a high priority target since Bremer Sr. was a personal friend of President Roosevelt. Unable to face his prison term, Peifer committed suicide in his jail cell by swallowing potassium cyanide.

What does this have to do with weddings? As time passed, the Landmark Center deteriorated until it was virtually abandoned and poised for the wrecking ball. In the 1970s, it was renovated into a beautiful center for the arts and special events, such as weddings. It is thought that the ghost of Jack Peifer still likes to haunt the building where his fate was sealed. More than one wedding reception has experienced happenings it could not account for: shot glasses mysteriously shattering on their own or alcohol bottles tipping over or going missing.

Is a ghost just a convenient scapegoat for excessively boozy wedding guests? Maybe. But in addition to Peifer's spirit loving spirits, he also has a well-known fondness for women. In the women's bathrooms throughout the building, stall doors reportedly open and shut on their own. One woman claimed to witness a menacing male presence in the second floor restroom that suddenly disappeared.

## I Want to Believe

In other spirit sightings, Landmark Center employee Woodrow Keljik recounted the story of two visitors who saw a transparent man wearing a bellhop uniform ride in the elevator and then vanish. However, it was the 2001 wedding of Joseph and Kimberly Arrigoni that produced actual proof of Peifer's spooky presence. When the happy couple sorted through their wedding photos months after their event at the Landmark Center, they noticed something peculiar in one of the shots. The photo showed the bridal party posing on the stairway near the second floor balcony, and blurred in the background behind the ring bearer stood a fuzzy, scruffy figure that they didn't recognize. Apparently, the Peifer apparition had decided to crash the wedding! The *St. Paul Pioneer Press* declared the Arrigonis' photo to be legitimate and declared it the "first photographic evidence" of the Landmark Center haunting.

# Wedding Chatter

"Love is friendship plus sex and minus reason."

—Mason Cooley

"I'm so in love, every time I look at you my soul gets dizzy."

—Jesse Tyler

"In Hollywood, brides keep the bouquets and throw away the groom."

—Groucho Marx

"Marriage is not just spiritual communion, it is also remembering to take out the trash."

—Dr. Joyce Brothers

"Better to have loved a short man than never to have loved a tall."

—David Chambless

"Love is a game that two can play and both win."

—Eva Gabor

"Sometimes it's a form of love just to talk to somebody that you have nothing in common with and still be fascinated by their presence."

—David Byrne

"Grief can take care of itself, but to get the full value out of joy, you must have someone to divide it with."

—Mark Twain

"Heaven will be no heaven to me if I do not meet my wife there."

—Andrew Jackson

"We are all a little weird and life's a little weird, and when we find someone whose weirdness is compatible with ours, we join up with them and fall in mutual weirdness and call it love."

—Author Unknown

# Marriage by Proxy

❧ ❧ ❧ ❧ ❧

*What is a proxy marriage? Do both parties have to be in the same country or on the same continent? Can anyone do it, or is it just for those serving in the military?*

## He/She Does

The reason there are so many questions about proxy marriage is because the laws vary so widely from country to country, and here in the United States, from state to state. In the United States, only five states allow marriage by proxy: California, Colorado, Kansas, Montana, and Texas. In a proxy marriage, either the bride or groom is not physically present for the ceremony, and someone stands in for that missing person based upon a power of attorney.

Historically speaking, probably the most famous proxy marriage was that of Napoleon Bonaparte to Archduchess Marie Louise in 1810. But proxy marriages still make headlines today: Cosmonaut Yuri Malenchenko was orbiting the earth in a space station on August 10, 2003, when he married Ekaterina Dmitriev, who looked radiant in a long, white gown at NASA's Johnson Space Center in Houston, Texas. A close pal stood in for Yuri as his agent, and the couple blew kisses to each other via video link.

## They Do

A double proxy marriage is one in which two representatives stand in for both parties. Double proxy marriages are much harder to obtain and are only legal in Montana. Even there, laws vary from county to county, and in many Montana counties, at least one party must physically be there to pick up the marriage license. In the United States, proxy marriages are most often obtained by those serving in the military and are exceedingly rare amongst the general populace. In California, proxy marriages are available only to members of the military currently on active duty.

# Quiz

*Match these actors with the wedding movie
in which they starred*

### Bring on the Brides

1. *Corpse Bride*
2. *The Bride of Frankenstein*
3. *The Princess Bride*
4. *Bride Wars*

a. Boris Karloff and Elsa
   Lanchester
b. Robin Wright Penn and
   Cary Elwes
c. Johnny Depp and Helena
   Bonham Carter
d. Kate Hudson and Anne
   Hathaway

### Wedding Checklist

1. *The Wedding Date*
2. *The Wedding Planner*
3. *The Wedding Singer*

a. Jennifer Lopez and Matthew
   McConaughey
b. Adam Sandler and Drew
   Barrymore
c. Debra Messing and Dermot
   Mulroney

### A Wedding Story

1. *The Proposal*
2. *Meet the Parents*
3. *Honeymoon in Vegas*

a. Ben Stiller and Teri Polo
b. Sandra Bullock and Ryan
   Reynolds
c. Nicolas Cage and Sarah
   Jessica Parker

### Wedding Themes

1. *My Best Friend's Wedding*
2. *My Big Fat Greek Wedding*
3. *How to Marry a Millionaire*

a. Marilyn Monroe and
   Betty Grable
b. Nia Vardelos and John Corbett
c. Julia Roberts and Dermot
   Mulroney

*Answers: Bring on the Brides—1. c; 2. a; 3. b; 4. d; Wedding Checklist—1. c; 2. a; 3. b; A Wedding Story—1. b; 2. a; 3. c; Wedding Themes—1. c; 2. b; 3. a*

233

# Delightfully Wacky...
# or Downright Tacky?

*When it comes to their big day, people like to set themselves apart. In some cases, their enthusiasm results in clever and innovative scenarios. Other times, these unique ideas turn out just plain tacky!*

## Over the Hills and Far Away

High times! The first documented wedding at the world's highest summit belonged to bride Moni Mulepati and groom Pem Dorjee in 2005. The Nepalese climbing enthusiasts exchanged vows atop Mount Everest as part of the Rotary Centennial Everest Expedition. Forty-five other climbers witnessed the couple remove their oxygen masks to tie the knot at 29,035 feet. Even scarier than the hazardous weather conditions was the anticipated reaction of their families. See, Nepalese culture favors arranged marriages in accordance with a strict caste system. The bride hailed from the Newar community, while the groom was from traditionally incompatible Sherpa. Yet the sky was the limit for these two lovebirds as they bucked convention and secretly eloped. Ultimately, in a happier ending than the Montagues and Capulets ever experienced, the newlyweds were welcomed into the bride's home on their wedding night.

*Verdict:* Delightfully wacky.

## Working Class Hero

Couples have utilized a variety of transportation methods to make it to the altar on time. Limo, decked-out Escalade, shuttle bus, horse-drawn carriage, vintage Coupe de Ville, tractor... *tractor*? One may expect tractor-pull weddings to crop up in rural Kentucky or the town in *Footloose.* Yet, according the *Huashang Daily,* one couple in China got creative by plowing down the aisle in his and her tractors. Since the groom sells heavy machinery for a living, the tractor presence seemed apropos. However, it looked less appropriate when the formally dressed bride, along with two bridesmaids, were lifted in the rickety tractor shovel to meet up with the groom and two best men waiting in a separate tractor.

*Verdict:* Downright tacky.

## Rocket Man

Brooklyn couple Noah Fulmor and Erin Finnegan met at a science fiction club in 2000. Nine years later, these die-hard sci-fi fans voyaged to the Kennedy Space Center in Cape Canaveral, Florida, to make history as the first couple to have a "weightless" wedding.

The feat was facilitated by Zero Gravity Corporation or ZERO-G. The nuptials took place above the Gulf of Mexico in the 90-foot-long, padded "floating zone," in a specially modified Boeing 727–200 aircraft. Richard Garriott, ZERO-G cofounder and the son of an astronaut, officiated the ceremony.

In order to beam up friends and family to attend their Space Oddity, the couple reportedly shelled out $5,200 per guest. The wedding party wore blue flight suits. The bride wore planet-shape earrings and a futuristic white satin pantsuit—the pants ballooned out during weightlessness. Her updo was kept in place with wires.

To replicate zero gravity without actually going into space, the pilot executed parabolic flight maneuvers. The plane climbed and descended sharply several times during the one-hour flight. The disorientation made locking lips comically challenging.

"The physics of the first kiss were off," the over-the-moon groom admitted. He added, "Weightlessness is probably the best metaphor for love that one can experience."

The newlyweds visited Space Mountain (Disney World) for their honeymoon.

*Verdict:* Delightfully wacky.

## Dirty Deeds Done Dirt Cheap

There are so many tacky weddings out there, there's naturally an entire Web site devoted to them. It's called, well, tackyweddings. com. Alas, in a quest to crown the tackiest of them all, one must sort through cringe-worthy wedding cakes and scroll down many, many leather and lace biker wedding photos, including one of a bride wearing a white thong with a "JUST MARRIED" sign on her back as her Harley drives off into the sunset.

Yet the downright tackiest recent wedding has to be the 99 Cent Only Store wedding. The extreme-value retail chain claims that about 3,000 hopeful couples vied for the opportunity to wed in a Sunset Boulevard 99 Cent Only Store on 9/9/09 for only 99 cents. They selected . . . wait for it . . . nine numerology-fan (or bargain-hunting) couples. Each couple was allowed to invite nine friends to the store-held ceremony and reception. Ironically, guests were instructed to purchase gifts from Nordstrom registries. *Kidding!*

With a budget of $99.99, self-proclaimed Discount Store Diva Kathy Jacobs designed the wedding decor, exclusively using items carried in the 99 Cent Only stores, including dinnerware, place cards, and candles. This dollar store MacGyver even created a wedding gown using 99 Cent Only T-shirts, embroidered tablecloths, and silk flowers. She said it was inspired by Chanel No. 9. Seriously.

*Verdict:* Um, the MackDaddy of tacky!

## Start Me Up

Second Life is a three-dimensional virtual universe where people create avatars (computerized images of themselves—usually flattering replications). Since its inception in 2003, escapists have logged in to Second Life to participate in virtual everyday experiences. They can shop, work, attend higher education classes, travel to exotic locales, and socialize with other avatars from around the world. They can even get married.

Avatars in love! Matthew Fishman, a 3D graphic designer and performance artist, was distinguished as Second Life's "most talented avatar" by *America's Got Talent* in 2007. Naturally, he met his future bride, Shava Nerad, in the Second Life world. They courted online and decided to seal their love with a Second Life wedding in front of all of their virtual friends. In the computer-generated wedding, Fishman's avatar, dubbed Tuna Oddfellow and uncannily resembling Skeletor in a top hat, took his bride in his arms against the backdrop of a flawless blue sky. In her self-penned virtual vows, Nerad professed, "In this life and the next I am yours." The virtual wedding, while not legally binding, led to a real-life engagement!

*Verdict:* It's a toss-up!

# Quiz

*Match the celebrity couple to songs played at their wedding.*

### Soulful Tastes
1. Mariska Hargitay & Peter Hermann
2. Taye Diggs & Idina Menzel
3. William H. Macy & Felicity Huffman
4. Bethany Joy Lenz & Michael Galeotti
5. Melissa Etheridge & Tammy Lynn Michaels

a. "Ain't No Mountain High Enough"
b. "My Girl"
c. "Overjoyed"
d. "Son of a Preacher Man"
e. "I Feel Good"

### Sentimental Tastes
1. David Arquette & Courteney Cox
2. Rob Thomas & Marisol Maldonado
3. Britney Spears & Kevin Federline
4. Adam Sandler & Jackie Titone
5. Charlie Sheen & Denise Richards

a. "I'll Be"
b. "Open Arms"
c. *Life Is Beautiful* theme
d. "Lights (City by the Bay)"
e. "Maybe I'm Amazed"

### Rocker and Unconventional Tastes
1. Bob Guiney & Rebecca Budig
2. Andrew Firestone & Ivana Bozilovic
3. Brad Pitt & Jennifer Aniston
4. Debra Messing & Daniel Zelman
5. Melissa Joan Hart & Mark Wilkerson

a. "Whole Lotta Love"
b. "Oops ... I Did it Again"
c. "Livin' on a Prayer"
d. "Never Tear Us Apart"
e. "Thunder Road"

*Answers: Soulful Tastes—1. a; 2. c; 3. e; 4. d; 5. b; Sentimental Tastes—1. e; 2. a; 3. d; 4. c; 5. b; Rocker and Unconventional Tastes—1. e; 2. c; 3. a; 4. b; 5. d*

# DIY: Vows

*In the late '60s, it seemed as if love was redefined
every day. Hippies held "love-ins," protesters urged fellow Americans
to "make love, not war," and four millionaire musicians assured us
that "love is all you need." But universal love was not
the only kind of love undergoing a big change.*

## Rewriting the Words of Love

During this time, couples all over the United States—and the
world—were questioning the meaning of romantic love and the
importance it should have in men's and women's lives. Was romantic
love a selfish desire when so many people were being killed in the
controversial Vietnam War? Were women betraying feminism when
they fell in love with and married men? Could traditional marriage
still work in the Space Age?

As the equality of the sexes became an accepted idea, the concept of marriage changed, along with the marriage ceremony. One of
those changes concerned the couple's vows. Rather than simply following the lead of a clergyman, many couples wanted to have more
control—they wanted to write their own vows. Some liberal religions
were open to the idea and allowed the bride and groom to "do their
own thing," but the practice was forbidden in many mainstream
Protestant churches, in the Catholic Church, and in Orthodox and
Conservative Judaism.

The solution? A civil ceremony. Secular officiants tended to be
more flexible about giving couples the freedom to write their own
vows, to use nonreligious verse, or to drop certain aspects of traditional vows that they found offensive (for example, the bride promis-
ing to "obey" her groom).

## Doing Their Own Thing

Though the trend of couples reciting untraditional vows or writing
their own had already become popular by the late '60s, the practice

exploded with the release of the blockbuster movie *Love Story* in 1970. The tale of rich boy Oliver Barrett IV (Ryan O'Neal) and poor girl Jenny Cavalleri (Ali MacGraw) was felt by many to be a return to "old-fashioned romance." But Oliver and Jenny weren't *that* old-fashioned. In fact, they were atheists who didn't want "the God bit" to be part of their wedding ceremony. Instead, Jenny recited lines from Elizabeth Barrett's *Sonnets from the Portuguese* and Oliver responded with lines from Walt Whitman's *Song of the Open Road.* Though the scene is rather cringe-worthy when viewed today—the couple comes across as a little too self-satisfied perhaps—it perfectly captured the mood of the times and inspired many couples to dispense with traditional vows in favour of a "do-it-yourself" ceremony.

## TV Takes It Up

As the '70s went on, the representation of DIY vows in the mainstream media became hip to the point of cynicism. When TV's Rhoda Morgenstern (Valerie Harper) and her hunky, blue-collar groom, Joe Gerard (David Groh), promised faithfulness "as long as we both shall love," did anyone watching think the marriage was going to last more than a few years? Irony-free romance returned in a big way, however, in the '80s, when soap opera couples like Luke and Laura *(General Hospital)* and Steve and Betsy *(As the World Turns)* began writing their own from-the-heart, super-sincere vows. The exchange of self-written vows is now almost a requirement for such TV couples, not only on daytime soaps, but also on prime-time sudsers like *Grey's Anatomy.* And it's not just a trend for TV land!

Today's real-life couples also continue to take their vows into their own hands. And these days, instead of turning to poets, couples can go online—the Internet is full of tips and tricks (as well as wedding vow examples) on how to craft the perfect way to say, "I do."

# What Does Your Wedding Cake Flavor Say About You?

*From citrusy to savory, wedding cake has come
a long way from vanilla!*

## Have Your Cake...

When it comes to weddings, everything is symbolic. The wedding cake, and its increasingly varied flavors, is no exception. Where once wedding cakes were strictly vanilla, today the flavors range from pistachio to poppy seed and include distinctive tastes like peanut butter and espresso. And rather than repeating a single flavor throughout a tower of cake, a number of bakers report an increased interest in layered flavors. For example, while a cake's foundation may be vanilla, it's often topped by tiers reflecting more extravagant tastes such as tiramisu, blood orange, and caramel apple.

## ...And Eat It, Too

A nontraditional flavor can be a unique way to express a newly betrothed couple's personality. See what these flavors say about you:

- **Nutella:** You're a couple of big kids who like to have fun. For you, the hazelnut and chocolate flavors in the iconic Nutella spread are the most natural choices in the world for your wedding cake.

- **Orange cream:** A consummate optimist, you've found the love of your life. And, with your head firmly in the clouds, you're ready to celebrate—with a light, citrus-inspired cake, of course.

- **Tiramisu:** You're indulgent and complex, just like the layers of this decadent cake. And, with a generous dosing of espresso-laden wedding confection, you'll be ready for the reception dance of your dreams.

- **Coconut:** A lighthearted flavor, coconut is a welcome change for those tired of traditional vanilla. A coconut-flavored cake topped with a whimsical sprinkling of shaved coconut is as entertaining as the two of you are.

- **Pistachio:** It's easy being green, especially when your wedding cake is this delicious. This cake shows guests you have great taste—while advertising your penchant for a "green" lifestyle.

- **Peanut butter:** A richly flavored peanut butter cake topped with chocolate ganache is perfect for couples with a serious sweet tooth. So, if you're ready to share a love for sweets with your wedding guests, this selection is sure to please.

- **Chocolate mint:** If you choose this distinctive flavor combination, you clearly aren't concerned with what others may think of your tastes. In fact, you want your guests to expect the unexpected—even when it comes to something as traditional as wedding cake.

- **Chai spice cake:** Perfect for a fall wedding, this luxuriantly spiced cake is as beautiful as it is comforting. Knowing the two of you, you'll want extra servings to enjoy after the honeymoon.

- **Blood orange:** As a couple, you are as exotic as this deeply hued fruit, and a blood orange cake is a fitting tribute to your outgoing personalities. But, as much as you like being the center of attention on the big day, you can't wait to say farewell to an adoring crowd and enjoy your honeymoon in an equally exotic locale.

- **Pineapple:** At a warm-weather wedding, whether you're saying "I do" on the beach—or only wish you were—serving pineapple wedding cake will paint a tropical picture for your taste buds.

- **Caramel apple:** Laced with fresh apples and topped with caramel-flavored icing, this is one wedding cake guests won't soon forget. With just one bite, everyone will be reminiscing about caramel apples, which are a favorite autumn treat.

- **Guava:** A light and carefree taste of the tropics, this fruit-infused cake signals to all that your thoughts are already on the honeymoon destination...an island near the equator, of course.

- **Lemon poppy seed:** An ideal selection for a spring wedding, this bright flavor is as sunny and optimistic about the future as you are. After all, the two of you are proof that you can have your cake... and eat it, too.

# On the "Threshold" of Tradition

*Why does the groom carry the bride over the threshold?*
*It's all in the good luck that follows.*

### Avoiding Evil

The centuries-old origins of this practice range from the mystical to just plain bizarre. In ancient times, it was thought that the spirits of the dead could attach themselves to the living—and brides were particularly at risk. To make matters worse, these spirits congregated near doorways, so when a bride walked across the threshold, they entered through her feet. These bodiless interlopers were believed to doom newly minted couples to a tragic end. The spirits wreaked havoc on the bride, causing everything from physical ailments to mental illness. To prevent this kind of relationship carnage, grooms played it safe by carrying their brides over thresholds. It stands to reason: If a bride's feet never touched the threshold, then she couldn't be possessed by wayward spirits.

In the Roman Empire, grooms carried brides over thresholds for luck. If a bride tripped while stepping across the threshold into her new home, bad luck rained down on the marriage and abode. Carrying the bride through the doorway eliminated this danger.

Lifting a bride over the threshold also eliminated fodder for the rumor mill. If a bride rushed across the threshold of her own volition, she may have seemed too enthusiastic to offer her virginity. By carrying her across the threshold, a groom could avoid scandal and his betrothed could appear reluctant and demure.

### Or Avoiding Escape

Perhaps the most disturbing origin of this now-symbolic gesture is the role it played in medieval times, when brides were often kidnapped. Carrying a bride across the threshold prevented her from escaping of her own volition.

# Wedding Dress Styles

*From Cinderella ball gowns to sexy sheaths,
the wondrous white gown is truly "laced" with history.*

- **1840–1900: Great White Way:** American brides traded in their "Sunday best" for white wedding dresses that followed the fashion of Queen Victoria's 1840 trailblazer: a heavily decorated, white satin gown, complete with 18-foot train, lace veil, and orange blossoms. In the northern states, where orange blossoms were hard to come by, women used wax flowers instead. And every bride had to have a veil, even if it was just sewn onto the back of a bonnet.

- **1900s: Modest Proposal:** Stiff, buttoned-up morals meant stiff, buttoned-up brides. Think corseted white gowns with high necks, long sleeves, and floor-length skirts that left everything to the imagination. Veils fell to the waist, topped by a wreath of flowers or a hat (the bigger and fancier, the better). But all of this ended with the dawn of World War I and the rise of more practical fashion. Corsets gave way to reveal a natural waist, and skirts (gasp!) showed ankles for the first time, as women opted for more functional, less decorative ensembles.

- **1920s: Flapper Chic:** Coco Chanel's knee-length wedding gown—with full-length veil and train—became the dress du jour for freewheeling flapper brides, who showed off their fashionable bobs in complementary headpieces, such as Juliet caps, cloche hats, and headbands worn low across the forehead. And white wasn't a must—modern girls often opted for pastel pinks and blues or off-white shades. By the end of the decade, as the flapper reputation turned from on-trend to outlaw, bridal gowns adapted a longer, leaner look with Grecian styles cut in white satin, lamé, and velvet.

- **1930s: Star Struck:** Simple, unadorned, floor-length silk dresses echoed the somber spirit of the Great Depression. But the 1930s also saw the rise of Hollywood glamour, and down-on-their-luck audiences swooned for cinematic endings, which often included an elegant wedding. When the economy rebounded, a new era of wedding dress emerged, modeled after the sleek, satin styles reflected on-screen—now easier than ever to get with the advent of inexpensive, synthetic fabrics.

- **1940s: Ration Fashion:** Wartime rationing limited the use of fabrics—especially silk, which was used in parachutes. So while wealthy brides could still walk the aisle in fancy, new white gowns, the majority of American women wore their best suits—or borrowed a white gown from someone married in more prosperous times.

- **1950s: Cinderella Style:** Postwar prosperity heralded a modern reincarnation of the elaborate 19th-century princess gown. Ultra-femme silhouettes featured tightly molded bodices, super-cinched waists, and scooped necklines with cocktail-length ballerina skirts and short, bouffant bridal veils.

- **1960s: Hippie Chick:** The end of the decade saw counterculture brides bucking tradition in favor of short hemlines, caftans, eyelet dresses, Mexican wedding gowns, peasant smocks—and in 1967, a cutting-edge paper wedding dress debuted. But styles also hinted to the nostalgic, with romantic flower motifs and childlike Peter Pan collars, long, cuffed sleeves, and pintucked or buttoned bodices.

- **1970s: Flower Power:** Though the sexually liberated woman could—and did—wear everything from mod miniskirts to pants to skin-revealing suits, most brides opted for *Little House on the Prairie*–type getups: high-waisted, long-sleeved gowns, fresh wildflowers, lots of gingham, long veils, and wide-brimmed hats.

- **1980s: Princess Bride:** Lady Diana Spencer's 1981 white taffeta ball gown—featuring thousands of sequins and pearls, puffed sleeves, antique lace, and a 25-foot train—and jeweled tiara launched a new breed of bride that became the icon of the decade.

- **1990s: Dressed Down:** The overdone big hair, big veil, and big dress of the '80s gave way to the simple, unadorned elegance of the 1990s, epitomized by the long, sleek, satin slip dress Carolyn Bessette wore to wed John F. Kennedy Jr. in 1996. Unfussy A-lines, sheaths, and shorter hemlines also came into vogue.

- **Today: Ab Fab:** From retro to rebel, today's style is virtually anything goes—although experts agree the consistent "thread" in modern bridal gowns is a focus less on adornment and more on figure-conscious styles that show off the bride's buff gym body.

- *Traditionally, in Spain, brides wore black—more specifically a black silk dress and black lace veil.*

- *When Grace Kelly wed Prince Ranier in 1956, her dress featured 125-year-old rose point lace.*

# Long Road to Love

*Paving the way for the acceptance of interracial marriage
hasn't always been easy . . .*

## Love for the Lonely

Until 1662, interracial marriage was legal in every British colony in
North America. It's not hard to imagine why: The white women of
England and Western Europe were very wary of the long, dangerous journey to the Colonies and even more frightened of what they
might find once they arrived, yet the white male settlers were lonely
and needed mates. Many were more than happy to take Native
American brides or to satisfy their lusts with African American slave
mistresses. Who was going to stop them? Colonial men were all in
the same boat, so to speak, and political and religious leaders feared
anarchy if natural desires were not satisfied.

## The Law Intervenes

As the decades went on and more Caucasian women arrived on the
American shore, however, laws began to change. Colonial leaders
no longer saw any "excuse" for white men to carry on with women
of other races. In 1662, lawmakers in Virginia doubled the fine for
fornication between white men and black women. In 1664, interracial marriage was banned completely in Maryland. And by 1750,
every southern colony, along with Massachusetts and Pennsylvania,
had outlawed the practice—though those who were already married when laws were passed were rarely hunted down and forced
to separate. When interracial marriages were nullified, most of the
white men involved in them simply chose to keep on living with their
partners, whether their relationships were recognized by law or not.

Though the word "miscegenation" is rarely used anymore, from
1863 on, it was a term used to describe marriage, cohabitation, or sex
between members of different races. Originally coined during the
Civil War in an attempt to vilify the Abolitionist movement and scare

the public about the results of outlawing slavery, the word "miscegenation" was widely known, but often, it was not the actual legal term used to prosecute those who broke such laws. Instead, the parties would be charged with the more generic sounding "felony adultery" or "felony fornication." Thus, local authorities could prosecute people for engaging in interracial sex and/or marriage without raising too many questions outside their own communities. Federal anti-miscegenation amendments were proposed in the U.S. Congress in 1871, 1912, and 1928, but no nationwide law against interracial marriage was ever passed.

## A Loving Change

Religious institutions began to speak out about the issue in the mid-20th century. The Presbyterian Church, the Unitarian Universalist Association, and the Roman Catholic Church all expressed disgust at anti-miscegenation laws and support for interracial couples who wanted to marry, and these weighty opinions seemed to finally turn the tide. In the 1950s, anti-miscegenation laws finally began to be struck down. Arizona, California, Colorado, Idaho, Indiana, Maryland, Montana, Nebraska, Nevada, North Dakota, Oregon, South Dakota, Utah, and Wyoming all legalized interracial marriage within just a little over a decade.

Many other states clung tenaciously to their anti-miscegenation laws, however, and it took a federal ruling to legalize interracial marriage everywhere in America. Richard Perry Loving, a white man, and his wife Mildred Loving, a black woman, filed suit against the state of Virginia for denying their marriage that had taken place in the District of Columbia and for prosecuting them under Virginia's anti-miscegenation law. In 1967, after the Supreme Court's decision in the Lovings' favor in the case of *Loving v. Virginia,* interracial couples were suddenly free to marry not only in Virginia but in Alabama, Arkansas, Delaware, Florida, Georgia, Kentucky, Louisiana, Mississippi, Missouri, North Carolina, Oklahoma, South Carolina, Tennessee, Texas, and West Virginia. The battle for love and justice that had lasted hundreds of years was finally over.

# Henry VIII: Serial Groom

*He may have gained a little weight over time and become
a little, well, psycho. But hey, the marriage market was tough
back in the 16th century.*

- **Catherine of Aragon:** Catherine was the daughter of King Ferdinand II of Aragon and Queen Isabella I of Castile. Though a devout and humble Catholic, she was raised to think of herself as a princess worthy of respect. And she needed all the self-esteem she could handle when she married King Henry VIII of England in 1509. It certainly helped her to stay strong when her husband decided he wanted an annulment because she had only borne him a daughter—the future Queen Mary I—not the son and heir he wanted. Catherine fought as hard as she could to remain queen, but in the end (1533), her husband made history by breaking with the Roman Catholic Church, founding the Church of England, divorcing Catherine, and marrying the object of his obsessive desire, Anne Boleyn.

- **Anne Boleyn:** Henry and Anne were married in January of 1533, and the pope wasn't too happy about it. He excommunicated both Henry and the Archbishop of Canterbury, who had performed the wedding. By the time Anne was crowned Queen of England on June 1, she was already pregnant with Henry's child. But both were disappointed when she gave birth to a girl, the future Queen Elizabeth I, on September 7. Now it was Anne who Henry wanted to get rid of, and he did. Charged with adultery and treason—but almost certainly innocent—she was found guilty and beheaded on May 19, 1536.

- **Jane Seymour:** Henry's wedding etiquette could have used some work: He announced his engagement to Jane in 1536—the day after Anne was executed. Yeah, kinda tacky—but why should Henry care what anyone thought? Without the pope breathing down his neck, he was in charge now. Jane annoyed Henry with her continued attachment to the Catholic faith, but she made up for it by bearing him a son and heir, the future King Edward VI. Jane died shortly after giving birth, on October 24, 1537, and was the only one of Henry's wives to be given a Queen's funeral.

- **Anne of Cleves:** This Anne was a German noblewoman, and this marriage was conceived purely for political reasons. And things didn't go well: Henry was simply not physically attracted to Anne, and there may have been some hygiene and grooming issues as well. In her portrait by the famous artist Hans Holbein the Younger, which now hangs in the Louvre, Anne really doesn't look so bad. But for whatever reason, the chemistry just wasn't there, and the marriage—which lasted from January 6 to July 9 in 1540, was never consummated. Strangely, she and Henry remained friends after the annulment, and she never returned to Germany.

- **Catherine Howard:** Henry called Catherine "the rose without a thorn" because of her free and easy manner, but that trait is exactly what wound up getting her in a lot of trouble. By the time the two married, on July 28, 1540, Henry was an obese, middle-aged man with a really gross ulcer on one of his thighs. She wasn't blessed with much intelligence, nor was she much of an actress, so the 19-year-old Catherine just couldn't fake attraction to him. Pretty soon she was fooling around with Thomas Culpeper, one of Henry's pals at court. Unlike Anne Boleyn, she was almost certainly guilty of adultery, but of course she did not deserve her brutal fate. She was beheaded on February 13, 1542.

- **Catherine Parr:** Married to Henry in 1543, she was the last Catherine and Henry's last Queen. And she was far more mature and savvy than her predecessors. Catherine did not have any children by Henry, but she was friendly with his children from his previous marriages. She'd had two husbands before Henry and would have one husband after him, but until Henry died in 1547, she kept him happy—and she kept herself alive.

# Grease Is the Word

*A wedding based on this 1970s movie (set in the '50s) will never be considered an elegant affair, but it can certainly be fun.*

There are several wedding-day words or phrases that everyone is waiting to hear. No matter what the theme, these usually include "I do," followed by "I now pronounce you man and wife," and finally, "You may kiss the bride." But when the bride and groom are fans of the John Travolta and Olivia Newton-John movie classic *Grease,* what will be going through everyone's minds is "Grease is the woooord..."

## Go Greased Lightnin'!

For the bridal couple looking for a retro theme, lively music, and a good time, *Grease* may just be the word! There are a lot of possibilities for couples looking to use this theme for their wedding.

Wedding invitations can be shaped like a film reel, movie ticket, record, or even a vintage car. If this is too casual for the wedding itself, the idea can be used for a bridal shower, bachelorette, or bachelor party.

## The Threads

Wedding dresses are such a personal choice that the bride needs to decide how far she wants to go when tying the theme to the dress she wears on the big day. One version is to find a regular wedding gown in a style reflective of the '50s or early '60s. It would still tie in with the event, but it would be less apt to inspire future children to shout, "What were you wearing?!" For brides who like the *Grease* idea but love a more modern, designer look, Caroline Herrera's spring 2009 line featured a polka dot dress that could fit the bill nicely. More daring brides (or bridesmaids) might have their dress resemble a bridal version of the poodle skirt or encompass splashes of pink.

John Travolta and his buddies sported the leather jacket look, but some grooms and groomsmen find that to be a bit much. Suits in popular '50s styles are always an option.

## How to Make the Bash a Blast

The reception is where the wedding party and guests alike can let their hair down and have fun with this theme. The hall can resemble a sock hop with brightly colored streamers, balloons, and even old records and movie posters. Table decorations can be fun with everyday items that relate to the *Grease* theme: flowers in old glass Coca-Cola bottles, milkshake glasses, vinyl records, or even saddle shoes.

A jukebox, DJ, or live band playing songs from the movie, as well as songs of the times, should get everyone in the dance mood. *Grease* tunes are familiar and extremely danceable! And food? A '50s-era punch and cake reception might bring a touch of elegance to the event. But to do it right, what *Grease* theme would be complete without diner food? Hamburgers, fries, cherry Cokes, and root beer floats are definite crowd-pleasers. To top it off: Make the cake in the shape of an old car or a giant sundae.

## Two Kids Real Gone

Phil Yates and Anita Lane of Grantham, England, were fans of "oldies" music and decided they wanted to use the *Grease* movie theme to create a unique atmosphere for their 2008 wedding. The unusual affair was the talk of the town, even among those who didn't attend. The Yates event included a pink limousine for the "pink ladies" of the wedding party as well as a "greased lightning" car for the men!

# The Pros and Cons of Destination Weddings

*Destination weddings have become very popular in recent years, but a couple thinking of having one needs to consider both the pros and the cons of this nontraditional type of ceremony.*

## Pros:

- *It bonds the couple.* Planning and executing a destination wedding can be a delightful bonding time for a bride and groom. It's a way for the couple to dream together, be creative together, and learn and grow together. Making this truly unique experience for themselves and their guests should bring the two even closer to one another.

- *It gives the couple breathing space.* Sometimes being so close to one's "real life" makes the wedding experience a stressful one. There are brides who will work until 5:00 P.M. on Friday and get married on Saturday morning! A destination wedding is a multi-day event that forces even the most Type-A bride or groom to turn off the Blackberry, let their hair down, and relax.

- *It creates a wonderful memory for the couple's guests.* While the couple is getting married, the guests will be enjoying much more than just another country club chicken dinner. They will be soaking in the beautiful sights, treating themselves to luxuries they're unable to find back home, and perhaps having romantic interludes of their own. The wedding couple can be sure that no matter what happens, guests will remember their wedding for years to come.

- *It is surprisingly economical.* The average destination wedding costs 40 percent less than the average traditional wedding in one's hometown. Choice of destination is key, however: A couple wanting to save money will do well to pass up Britain or Europe and look into Mexico or the Caribbean. Planning ahead is essential when it comes to getting the best group deals on airfare and hotels.

- *It affords the couple more freedom and choices.* The closer the couple is to their hometown, the more cooks there will be to spoil the broth. Mom insists on inviting the Smiths. Dad tries to allocate funds. The bridesmaids stage a dress rebellion. Move the wedding a thousand miles away, and it's likely these very same people will want no part of the planning.

## Cons:

- *It can cause resentment in the couple's guests.* If guests are expected to pay their own way, it's likely that some who are invited will have to pass for financial reasons. On the other hand, if the couple pays for the guests' airfare and hotel expenses, the guests may feel obligated to attend even if they'd rather not. It's a delicate situation.

- *It involves foreign countries and foreign laws.* Couples and their guests must be sure to do their research so that they will understand the traditions and laws of the country in which their destination wedding will be held. They must also familiarize themselves with customs laws so that there won't be problems reentering the United States. Failing to do these things can result in a dream turning into a nightmare.

- *It may make a religious wedding impossible or extremely difficult.* Weddings are fairly easy to obtain in foreign countries, but if a religious service is important to the couple, staying home may be the better choice. Catholic and Jewish weddings are particularly hard to move overseas, because many rabbis and priests insist on premarital counseling and ceremonies that are held in houses of worship.

- *It can cause strife in the couple's relationship.* The added burden of having to do all the planning themselves and not having as much support from parents and the wedding party can really take its toll.

## Weddings 'Round the World
# Spreading a Little Island Cheer

*If the bride or groom has an island heritage, Caribbean traditions are all the more meaningful. But adding a little island tradition to any couple's wedding can make their event just as fun.*

### Aruba, Jamaica...

Some couples take a trip to the islands to delve deep into their Caribbean culture and customs on their wedding day. And some couples, regardless of heritage, choose beach weddings or destination weddings because they love the laid-back atmosphere of a wedding by the sea. But if it's not possible to get to the islands for the big day, the islands can be brought to any wedding through the incorporation of Caribbean traditions.

### Spread the Word

Traditionally, guests are invited to a Caribbean wedding by word-of-mouth, and everyone is welcome. Since island villages tend to be small and rather intimate, this is usually manageable. However, hometowns are slightly bigger nowadays, so regular invitations might make more sense—that way the couple's friends and families remember the date but their "enemies" don't. The invitations can be embellished with a colorful accent to add Caribbean flair.

### Frolicking and Finery

According to Caribbean tradition, the wedding day begins with the priest ringing the church bells to proclaim the wedding. The bride and groom, dressed in their finery, walk together to the church, while guests and other members of the village (or for a stateside wedding, the wedding guests) line the streets to observe the procession.

Tropical decorations (think palm trees and hurricane glasses), vibrant colors, and Calypso music are a good way to set the mood for the evening. One mother of the bride hired a steel drum band for the whole experience. She had a reggae group play soft music before the ceremony as guests arrived. Later, the group moved to the reception where they picked up the beat for dancing late into the night. Whether it's the music or the company, it's not unusual for a Caribbean wedding to continue all night long.

A traditional American wedding gown is perfectly acceptable for a traditional island wedding. However, if the bride insists on a Caribbean touch, a dash of color can be added, or she can choose a white silk sarong. Toe rings and flip-flops are the order of the day; some brides even choose to go barefoot. After all, what better way to dance the night away? Plus, comfort is key when joining the Congo line or doing the limbo.

Tropical flowers are just the thing for the bridal bouquet. Hibiscus, orchids, and bird of paradise flowers are perfect for an exotic bouquet you'll remember long after the wedding is over.

Bridesmaids and groomsmen are optional in an island wedding; traditionally, there is no best man. However, the bride's father—or both parents—still walk her down the aisle.

## The Feast

At the reception, traditional Caribbean food is the highlight. Spicy jerk chicken, curried shrimp and goat, conch fritters, and fried plantains are unique to most American weddings, but you'll find most, if not all, of this fare at a typical Caribbean wedding.

The traditional Caribbean wedding cake is a "black cake." The recipe is passed from mother to daughter, generation to generation. Each person tweaks it a bit based on her own tastes, but the basic ingredients include glazed cherries, prunes, and currants. Oh, and rum. All of the fruit is soaked in rum for three weeks to a year! And in case that doesn't add enough flavor, the cake is served with a hard rum sauce. Who could pass that up?

# Quiz

*Show what you know about weird, obscure,*
*or fun wedding facts with this wedding trivia quiz.*

**1.** In the Czech Republic, a prospective bride's future in-laws might place this in plain view to test her skill before granting their blessing:
a. Bed
b. Broom
c. Baby

**2.** In Nigerian culture, where does the bride-to-be go with her female relatives to learn how to be a wife?
a. Etiquette class
b. Brothel
c. Fattening room

**3.** According to the Scottish tradition of Creeling, what must the groom carry across the village on his back until his bride is satisfied with his strength?
a. His bride
b. Bagpipes
c. Basket of stones

**4.** What does the French wedding custom of *coupe de marriage* mean?
a. The couple toasts themselves with a two-handled cup
b. The groom's family bestows a new car upon the happy couple
c. Eloping

**5.** What celebrity wedding ceremony reportedly included the vows, "And when she's older, do you keep her still?" "I do."
a. Tom Cruise and Katie Holmes
b. Ashton Kutcher and Demi Moore
c. Donald Trump and Melania Knauss

**6.** What might French relatives bang outside of the newly-wed couple's room?
a. Drums
b. Pots and pans
c. Cowbells

Answers: 1. b; 2. c; 3. c; 4. a; 5. a; 6. b

# Fast Facts: The Cake

- On average, wedding cakes will run you anywhere from $3-$12 a slice.

- For that smooth, flawless frosting look, you'll want fondant, which is a thick, chewy form of sculptable frosting. It's a must if you want edible flowers, bows, etc., but watch out—that fondant will increase the price of your cake considerably.

- Queen Victoria and Prince Albert's wedding cake was nine feet around, weighed in at 300 pounds, was 14 inches high, and was actually served at the wedding breakfast.

- Originally, the wedding "cake" was just grains of wheat that were thrown on the happy couple as a symbol of fertility and prosperity.

- In 2004, chefs at the Mohegan Sun Hotel and Casino in Uncasville, Connecticut, baked a 15,032-pound wedding cake—it holds the record for largest wedding cake ever. (Nearly 5,000 pounds of the total weight was just frosting!)

- In the Middle Ages, couples would kiss over a pile of scones and bread—the taller the pile, the more luck they would have. But a French chef visiting London in the 16th century decided this tradition was in need of his help; he created an iced, multi-layered cake, instead, and the trend caught on.

- Careful of hidden costs: Most tiered wedding cakes must be delivered and assembled on site by the bakery—trust them, they're professionals—and delivery charges can be $50 to $100 or more, depending on travel logistics and cake size. (Some bakeries charge a cake-cutting fee, too.)

- Wedding cake toppers can be found on the cheap, but those who go all out can purchase Swarovski crystal cake toppers that can cost several hundred dollars or more.

# Tony n' Tina's Wedding

❧ ❧ ❧ ❧ ❧

*This interactive event draws guests into
its satirical, theatrical ceremony.*

## You're Invited!

Imagine going to a wedding, enjoying a
champagne toast, and dancing with the
bride and groom. Doesn't sound unusual,
right? For some theatergoers, it's not,
thanks to *Tony n' Tina's Wedding*.

*Tony n' Tina's Wedding* is an interactive
theater performance that offers ticketed
guests an inside look at a satirical Italian-
American wedding. The play is so popular,
in fact, that it's been running continually in
New York City—and more than 100 other
locations—since 1988. Traditional theater buffs, novice attendees,
and critics alike have given "two thumbs up" to this unique concept,
which creates a familiar environment where audiences can drink
champagne, eat a pasta dinner, and enjoy plenty of dancing.

## Take Part, or Sit Back and Enjoy Some Cake

During *Tony n' Tina's Wedding*, audiences not only get an up-close
view of the wedding and a seat at the subsequent reception, but
they interact with the wedding party as they act out their roles.
Theatergoers aren't forced to participate, but many find it easy to
become part of the experience, acting as if they are Tony's probation
officer or Tina's childhood Sunday school teacher.

Attendees are asked to dress in wedding-appropriate attire,
which ranges from formal to business casual. Those who ignore
the dress code won't have any problems being admitted. They will,
however, have to answer a few pointed questions from Tina's mom,
Mrs. Vitale.

The cast of *Tony n' Tina's Wedding* effuses all the energy and charm one might expect to encounter at a real-life tête-à-tête, which makes it little wonder the experiential comedy has become the second longest running off-Broadway show in history. While every performance is a repeat for the outrageous Vitale and Nunzio families, the boozing and brawling never seems to age. Still, it's all in good fun as raucous, but ultimately good-natured, family members celebrate the nuptials of an iconic couple.

The *Tony n' Tina* phenomenon has launched a number of variations on the theatrical wedding theme, including *Joey & Maria's Comedy Italian Wedding* and *Frankie & Gina's Comedy Wedding*, which have been met with varied levels of success.

## How Tony and Tina Got Hitched

The *Tony n' Tina's Wedding* concept grew out of characters created in the late 1970s by Hofstra University drama undergraduates Mark Nasser and Nancy Cassaro. Nasser and Cassaro, who call themselves the "original Tony n' Tina," used the characters as an improvisational vehicle to hone their acting skills. They spent years acting out the roles of an Italian boyfriend and girlfriend from Queens.

After graduating from the Long Island, New York–based Hofstra University, Nasser and Cassaro moved separately to New York. The two characters they created continued to grow and change, and Nasser and Cassaro toyed with the idea of putting on an interactive wedding where Tony and Tina could marry, surrounded by theater attendees who played their family and friends. In 1985, the duo planned three sample performances to test their interest in the idea. The actors invited real-life friends and family to the events. The interactive play was a hit, so producer Joe Corcoran started putting together a several-week run of the show. Word spread, causing *People* magazine, *The New York Times,* and *TIME* magazine, along with multiple other international media outlets, to take notice.

In February 1988, Corcoran and his brother, Dan, presented the first commercial production of *Tony n' Tina's Wedding*. The wedding took place at New York City's St. John's Church, then the audience walked with the cast across 7th Avenue to Waverly Place. The show had an 11-year run at that location and has been making history ever since.

# Wedding Chatter

"In my wedding, they, uh ... Well, in *my wife's* wedding, that I was allowed to go to ..."

—Craig Ferguson

"Marriage is the alliance of two people, one of whom never remembers birthdays and the other who never forgets them."

—Ogden Nash

"What do you have against honeymoons? It's basically sex with room service."

—Samantha Jones, *Sex and the City*

"I was the best man at the wedding. If I'm the best man, why is she marrying *him*?"

—Jerry Seinfeld

"Where there is love there is life."

—Mahatma Gandhi

"Love is an act of endless forgiveness, a tender look which becomes a habit."

—Peter Ustinov

"One's first love is always perfect until one meets one's second love."

—Elizabeth Aston

"Success in marriage does not come merely through finding the right mate, but through being the right mate."

—Barnett Brickner

"For two people in a marriage to live together day after day is unquestionably the one miracle the Vatican has overlooked."

—Bill Cosby

# Wedding Dress Shopping Done Right

*They say it's all about the dress. And if they're right,
then there are a few things the bride should keep in mind when
she starts the hunt for the perfect gown.*

The gown has always been important, but this is the information age, and brides are more informed than ever before. They used to read *Bride* magazine and talk with their friends. Today's brides search wedding and designer Web sites. They shop online—yes, even for a wedding gown. Some even make Internet phone calls to friends and relatives right from the bridal shop.

Lynne Kosterman, a bridal-gown consultant, has seen it all. Some brides come in wide-eyed and clueless about the whole dress shopping experience. Others are flanked with six bridesmaids, a mother, mother-in-law, camera, and computer. Here are some tips for everyone:

- Finding the right dress is a bit like trying a new hairdo, according to Kosterman. What looks really good on the model may not be the dress that's right for you. You might have an idea in your head—or ripped from a magazine—but keep an open mind. By all means, try on that dream dress, but don't stop with one. Try on a couple other styles to see what really looks best on you.

- On the other hand, don't try on too many. Fifteen is the maximum. By that time, you've hit pretty much every style. It's just a matter of finding the look, the fabric, and/or the detailing that works best for you.

- Don't wait until the last minute to look for your dress. It takes between three and six months for the salon to get the dress in— and then it still needs to be fitted.

- Be careful who you choose to take dress shopping with you. Take a couple trusted friends or family members. Someone who you know will tell you the truth. Don't take two friends who will be in competition with each other—leaving one to feel bad when you agree with the other. Don't take anyone who will be jealous and give you bad advice. And don't pit your mother and mother-in-law against each other before the wedding!

- Have an idea of what you want to spend ahead of time. And how much you are willing to go over. Yes, this is a once-in-a-lifetime event, but consider that you're only going to wear the dress one time. Do you want to take money out of savings for your dream dress? Are you willing to scrimp on something else, such as the flowers or the cake? Look at the price tags as well as the styles before you try them on. If you try on the most expensive dress first, nothing else is going to measure up. Do you really want to go over budget—or leave with your second choice?

- Don't buy the dress and then show it to your fiancé. One bride who did that was devastated when she showed her groom a picture (without telling him it was the one she picked) and he said he hated it. With the dress already purchased and altered, it was hers for better or worse. Either ask for his advice ahead of time, or surprise him on the day. Once he sees you on your wedding day, he's bound to think any dress is beautiful. Don't open yourself up to heartache!

- Don't go *too* sexy with your wedding gown. Save that for the honeymoon. Remember: Your grandparents and your boss are going to see you walk down the aisle in this dress.

- Don't wear dark lipstick while wedding dress shopping! Or at the fitting. Or even on your wedding day—until after the dress is on.

- Be sure to pay with a credit card in case there is any dispute. If you pay cash, you'll have no leverage if there's a problem.

- It's okay to buy a pair of jeans that are a little tight, hoping to wear them when you lose a little weight. Do not do this with your wedding gown. Sure, dresses can be altered, but they can usually only be made to fit one size larger. Also, imagine how you'll feel if it needs to be let out. It won't do much for your self-esteem on your big day. If you wait too long to discover it's too small, the alterations may be visible... or the dress may be so tight, you'll be uncomfortable your entire wedding day. And whatever you do, don't starve yourself in the days leading up to your wedding. This is a stressful time and you need all the fuel you can get.

- Think about the fabric. Sometimes brides focus on the look and don't consider how comfortable the material will be for dancing and sitting. If it's stiff or itchy, keep looking.

- Don't let your mother talk you into a style you don't want. Maybe she's projecting a style she'd like for herself. Maybe she wants you to keep up with her friend's daughter. Maybe she's more traditional than you are. Do listen to her opinion, however. Maybe, just maybe, she can see something in a dress that you can't see.

- Don't feel pressured to make a decision if you aren't feeling it. Some brides claim they know the instant they put on a dress that it's "the one." Some never feel that. Salesclerks want to be helpful; they want a happy bride. But they also want to make a sale. One bride—who was ready to move on to another store—realized that the clerk wasn't going to stop bringing in dresses until she found "the one." So the bride decided to love the next one she tried on—a puffy pink concoction. Then she had to convince the clerk that she wasn't prepared to put down a deposit quite yet.

So, yes, it may be all about the dress, but remember, the dress is only about you and making you feel beautiful on your wedding day. And your wedding day is only one day among the many that you'll share in your married life ahead.

# Honeymooning at Home

❧ ❧ ❧ ❧ ❧

*The reasoning behind a honeymoon in the good ol' U.S. of A. need not be economic (though the modest price tag sure doesn't hurt).*

## Vacationing Stateside

More couples than ever are deciding to stay within the 50 states during that special time immediately after their weddings. The United States is an especially wonderful place to honeymoon for those who love history. Couples can start at the very beginning in St. Augustine, Florida, with its beautiful Spanish fort, the Castillo de San Marcos, or move up the coast to Colonial Williamsburg in Virginia or Ben Franklin's Philadelphia, Pennsylvania. Following one particular historical figure across the country is a fun, new trend in honeymoons. A couple might follow George Armstrong Custer, for example, from the United States Military Academy at West Point, New York, to the First Battle of Bull Run in Manassas, Virginia, to the Battle of Little Bighorn in central Montana. Or perhaps they'd like to trace the same path as Laura Ingalls Wilder did in her long life, from the Big Woods of Wisconsin through Minnesota, South Dakota, and Kansas.

## Romantic Roaming

Southern cities like Charleston and Savannah give Rome and Paris a run for their money when it comes to old-fashioned romance. The American South's reputation for graciousness and hospitality is well deserved, and its natural beauty—especially in the spring, summer, and fall—can be absolutely breathtaking. The Southwest, too, offers gorgeous landscapes and fascinating history in states like Arizona and Nevada. The Grand Canyon and other lovely national parks offer endless amusement and education at very reasonable prices (but whatever the budget, at least one piece of turquoise jewelry for the bride is surely in order).

And for those who insist on the "exotic"? They need not leave the United States: There's always Hawaii.

# Fast Facts

- A honeymoon will run you about $4,500, depending on the trip.

- Every wedding dress needs alterations; the average bride will schedule between two and three fittings before her big day.

- These days, many engaged couples choose a bakery or specialty wedding cake store for their cake, but most supermarkets make wedding cakes, too. Supermarket cakes account for more than $280 million of wedding cake sales.

- Gamophobia is the fear of marriage.

- On average, an engagement ring runs around $4,411. Couples spend approximately $2,067 for his-and-hers wedding bands.

- Not so long ago, wedding cakes were predominately white cake with white frosting. These days, chocolate devil's food cakes are more popular, and fruit fillings such as pear, blood orange, coconut, and lime frequently top a bakery's most-wanted list.

- Accessories such as shoes and undergarments can cost about one-third of the price of the dress itself.

- It's common for couples in India and China to cut down on costs by displaying a fake wedding cake. Made of cardboard and wax, it's just for show, not for dessert, though the uppermost tier is sometimes the real thing.

- Roughly 46 percent of brides purchase their gowns on sale.

- Don't want to do things the traditional way? Cupcake tiers have become increasingly popular as alternatives to the wedding cake. Other couples serve towers of truffles, slices of tiramisu, or even "cakes" made by stacking doughnuts.

# The Common and the Covenant

*There is more than one way to be married!*

## Skipping the Ceremony-Thingy

Can you be married without the marriage license or the wedding? In about a dozen states in the United States, yes. While grounds vary from state to state, common law marriage typically declares couples legally wed if they live together, file joint tax returns, and willfully regard themselves as husband and wife in all traditional respects.

## Not Just Playing House: The Rules

A common law marriage abides by the same rules as traditional marriage. And common law couples must follow the same legal divorce procedures—including potentially being on the hook for alimony. The upside? Along with establishing a higher level of commitment to the relationship, they may receive spousal privileges such as tax and employer-benefit advantages; inheritance rights; and in the event of a life-or-death situation, visitation and decision-making powers.

## The Covenant Contract

While some perceive common law marriage as a shortcut to matrimony, covenant marriage lies at the other end of the spectrum. Fed up with trivialized weddings and quickie divorces? Well, covenant marriage advocates a truer interpretation of "'til death do us part." What constitutes a marriage as "covenant"? The couple is required to undergo premarital counseling to ascertain compatibility and clarify the gravity of the covenant agreement. The martial pact is super-highly binding. Once a covenant marriage is entered into, it's for the long haul. Only a very few allowances will dissolve the marriage.

## The Blame Game

No way out? Well, unlike traditional marriage, covenant marriage does not permit a no-fault divorce. Meaning: Start the finger pointing, because someone's gotta be unequivocally to blame. Divorce can be obtained—after first seeking mandatory counseling. But there must be proven "blame," with adultery, abandonment, abuse, or a felony criminal conviction as primary acceptable reasons.

## A Polarizing Practice

The movement has found minimal but steadfast support. For most covenant crusaders, entering into a near-iron-clad union demonstrates a well-intentioned show of devotion. However, the practice has also provoked some vocal detractors. According to dissenters, covenant marriage puts the "institutionalization" in the institution of marriage. Since acts of adultery and certain types of abuse may be difficult to prove in court, covenant critics fear that individuals (mostly women) will be trapped in a potentially harmful situation.

## Covenant Marriage: A Love Story

Perhaps the most famous poster couple for covenant marriage is former Arkansas governor and 2008 presidential hopeful Mike Huckabee and his wife Janet. Eighteen years old and unable to afford a proper ring at the time for his high school sweetheart, Mike proposed to Janet with a soda can pull-tab. After a year of marriage, the  couple was devastated when Janet was diagnosed with cancer of the spine. Doctors grimly reported that if she lived, she would likely be permanently wheelchair-bound. Well, Janet recovered her ability to walk, but she was told she likely would never bear children. Three children later, Mike and Janet renewed their lifelong commitment by upgrading to a covenant marriage on Valentine's Day 2005. On May 25, 2009, they celebrated their 35th wedding anniversary.

## Not Winning any Popularity Contests

Only a few states legally recognize and enforce the terms of covenant marriage. In 1997, the state of Louisiana blazed the trail and enacted the first covenant marriage law. And Arkansas and Arizona also hopped on board. Yet, in those three states combined, less than 5 percent of married couples go the covenant route.

# To Prenup or Not

❧ ❧ ❧ ❧ ❧

*Considering that half of marriages end in divorce, many practical couples are signing on the dotted line first. There are pros and cons to ponder when determining whether a prenup is right for you.*

## Pros Versus Cons

**Pro**: It's a good opportunity to have a mature discussion about finances. It's only responsible to be prepared for the worst and to have a fair arrangement in place.

**Con:** The road to marriage should be paved with romance and hope. It's pessimistic to go in planning for failure. Worse, it could be your first major premarital blow-up argument!

**Pro:** In case the marriage does not work out, your individual assets are protected. Many people are finding love at an older age or are entering into a second marriage. They may already own their own home and have substantial retirement savings. You don't want to walk into a marriage with an IRA and a condo and crawl out with a fragmented checking account and a cardboard box.

**Con:** If splitting up will leave your spouse empty-handed, there's always your life insurance policy.... Instead of calling a divorce lawyer, your spouse might dial a hitman!

**Pro:** A prenup isn't necessarily just about divvying up the goods; it can also be a tool to ensure an agreeable marriage. Beyond declaring who gets the goldfish, a prenup can cover everything from what religion hypothetical children will be raised under to how many times a week a couple will have sex. They can specify how much weight she can gain after the wedding or how much time he can spend watching football. While it varies as to how enforceable certain clauses are, prenups have gotten increasingly creative.

**Con:** If your apparent control freak fiancé is requiring you to weigh in every morning, perhaps this is not a match made in heaven.

**Pro:** All the celebrities are doing it. Case in point:

*Show Me the Money:* Tom Cruise and Katie Holmes's prenup reportedly states that she gets $3 million for every year they are married. If they split after 11 years, she'll get half of his wealth.

*Cheater, Cheater!:* Catherine Zeta-Jones's prenup with Michael Douglas allegedly stipulates that she will be compensated if he is unfaithful. She earns a $1.5 million "fling fee" for each proven extra-martial dalliance.

*Random Drug Testing?:* Before marrying reformed bad boy of country Keith Urban, Nicole Kidman reportedly arranged a prenup provision that he pays if he is caught abusing drugs.

**Con:** All the celebrities are doing it. Celebs are the last people to make good marital role models. See below.

## Better Safe Than Sorry

While starry-eyed couples enter marriage with the best of intentions, things don't always work out. Some famous cautionary tales:

Director James Cameron called "Cut" after only about a year and a half of marriage to actress Linda Hamilton. But during that time, he directed a little movie called *Titanic,* and its phenomenal success netted Hamilton about $50 million in the divorce.

It's not just the boys coughing up the dough. When Madonna's marriage to British director Guy Ritchie ended, *she* had to shell out $76 million!

Before Steven Spielberg wed actress Amy Irving, she signed a prenup—that was reportedly scribbled on a cocktail napkin. When the marriage went bust, she contested the pseudo-prenup and successfully raked in half of Spielberg's fortune, which was $100 million!

When Neil Diamond and Marcia Murphey called it quits after 25 years of marriage, her severance was $150 million.

When basketball superstar Michael Jordan split with former wife Juanita after nearly 18 years, she slam-dunked a settlement worth a whopping $168 million! But that record was broken by Tiger Woods's divorce. Tiger's former wife Elin reportedly walked away with something around $700 million! Ouch.

# Bachelor Parties and Bridal Showers

*Pre-wedding rituals for men and women . . .*

## Stag Night

The first bachelor parties date back to fifth-century Sparta, when soldiers would gorge themselves on food and drink the night before one of them got married. Instead of gifts, the men took up a collection and, at the end of the night, presented a bag of money to the groom—so he could still afford to party with his buddies after his wife took control of the household finances. (Strip clubs weren't part of these celebrations, but probably just because they weren't really around in ancient times.)

Bachelorette, or "hen," parties didn't come into fashion until the late 1960s and '70s, when liberated women decided they deserved to party just as hard as the guys.

## Shower Power

More traditional for brides-to-be is the shower, which many say can be traced to the Dutch. Hundreds of years ago in Holland, a maiden fell in love with a poor miller, but her father refused to allow the marriage—because clearly the broke-as-a-joke miller couldn't provide a "properly set up" home. Rallying to her defense, the bride's friends "showered" her with household items to help her get settled—and ultimately marry the miller.

England may be another point of origin for the bridal shower. A friend of the bride felt she couldn't afford a nice-enough gift to convey the magnitude of her happiness for the engaged couple. So she convinced the bride's other friends to pool their resources and shower the bride with several smaller gifts. A version of the story suggests the English girl had heard about the Dutch bride and took her cue from that.

# Memorable Movie Weddings

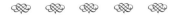

*People dream of finding "movie love." But having a movie wedding may not be the best idea—they never seem to go smoothly.*

## The Graduate

Mrs. Robinson: "Elaine, it's too late."

Elaine: "Not for me."

The most memorable scene in this movie is sans wedding: The iconic shot through Mrs. Robinson's (Anne Bancroft) stocking-covered leg as Benjamin Braddock (Dustin Hoffman) hedges, "Mrs. Robinson, you're trying to seduce me." Mrs. Robinson may have had her way with our confused new grad, but it's her daughter, Elaine, who becomes the true object of Ben's affection. At the end of the day—or literally, the end of the film—it's a climatic wedding scene that elicits major emotion. Depending on the viewer, the scene is either touching or hilarious (intentional or otherwise). It's the mother of all "speak now or forever hold your peace" scenes.

*Highlight:* Furious that Elaine is set to marry another, Ben tries to stop it, despite obstacles. First, his car runs out of gas. So a persistent Ben runs the rest of the way. Sweaty and disheveled, he bangs on the church glass screaming, "ELAINE!" And after showing off some self-defense moves and charging an aisle of people, he wields a giant cross to deter the upset throng, and he and Elaine make a run for it. Ben flags down a bus, and their escape is complete.

## Father of the Bride

George Banks: "I used to think a wedding was a simple affair. Boy and girl meet, they fall in love, he buys a ring, she buys a dress, they say 'I do.' I was wrong. That's getting married. A wedding is an entirely different proposition."

You've heard that the joy is in the journey, not the destination. When it comes to wedding movies, the drama and comedy are aplenty on the road to the altar, rather than at the event itself. The *Father of the Bride* remake follows the expensive, wonderful, expensive, romantic, expensive wedding planning process through all of its joys and frustrations. Good thing parents of the bride George and Nina Banks (Steve Martin and Diane Keaton) have wedding planner extraordinaire Franck Eggelhoffer (Martin Short) and his loyal executive assistant, Howard Weinstein (B. D. Wong), to navigate them through the countless decisions. Chic seafood or cheaper chicken? Can son Matt invite his friend, Cameron, if Cameron promises not to eat?

*Highlight:* George's supermarket meltdown that lands him in jail.

## My Big Fat Greek Wedding

Maria Portokalos: "Toula, on my wedding night, my mother, she said to me, 'Greek women, we may be lambs in the kitchen, but we are tigers in the bedroom.'"

Toula Portokalos: "Eww. Please let that be the end of your speech."

From *Miss Congeniality* to *She's All That*, makeover movies are a Hollywood mainstay. Toula (Nia Vardalos, who also penned the screenplay, based on her stand-up show) is crushing hardcore on Aidan . . . er, Ian. To everyone's surprise, he finds her shy, clumsy shtick adorable! Only in the movies, right? Ian willingly jumps through mega hoops to win over her large, loud family. And hey, Joey Fatone from N'Sync plays one of her cousins. Sadly, aforementioned hoop jumping does not include trimming Ian's mullet. Maybe Toula should have tried spraying Windex on it in his sleep.

*Highlight:* Watching Ian's super-straight parents interact with the rowdy Greeks. *Opa!*

## Four Weddings and a Funeral

Carrie: "Having a good night?"

Charles: "Yes. It's right up there with my father's funeral for sheer entertainment value."

Serial monogamist Charles (Hugh Grant) attends a few weddings— and one funeral, obviously—with his mates, including flatmate

Scarlett (Charlotte Coleman), gregarious Gareth (Simon Callow), straight-laced Matthew (John Hannah), bumbling Tom (James Fleet), and cynical Fiona (Kristin Scott Thomas). He meets and becomes infatuated with an American, Carrie (Andie MacDowell). Unfortunately, Carrie is already promised to Hamish, a Scottish bloke with quite possibly the worst teeth in all of Great Britain. Yet the charm of Charles's blinking and stammering prevails, and he and Carrie end up together.

*Highlight:* Of the four weddings, the most memorable is the first, with Mr. Bean as a new priest who botches the ceremony.

## Betsy's Wedding

Stevie Dee: "I could be whatever you need. I could do anything for the woman I love. I believe in saying what you feel. You are the blood in my veins; I would walk through fire for you. I will always be available; I belong to you."

This flick cracks the list if only for the opportunity to see *The Breakfast Club*'s Clare and Allison reunited post high school. This time around, Molly Ringwald plays Betsy, a woman with the same dreadful fashion sense as her *Pretty in Pink* character. Ally Sheedy plays cop older sister Connie, who embarks on a romance with shady mobster Stevie Dee (Anthony LaPaglia). Sharing the screen are the talents of patriarch Alan Alda and the late, great Madeline Kahn.

*Highlight:* Any scene with LaPaglia

## Honorable Mentions

*The Godfather:* Carlo (Gianni Russo) and Connie (Talia Shire)

*Old School:* Frank "the Tank" (Will Farrell) and Marissa (Perrey Reeves)

*Wedding Crashers:* Um, pick one.

*Honeymoon in Vegas:* Jack (Nicholas Cage, in Flying Elvis impersonator gear) and Betsy (Sarah Jessica Parker, in showgirl costume)

*My Best Friend's Wedding:* Michael (Dermot Mulroney) and Kimmy (Cameron Diaz)

*Steel Magnolias:* Jackson (Dylan McDermott, not to be confused with Dermot Mulroney) and Shelby (Julia Roberts)

# I Do? No, Thank You!

*Eternal bachelors around the world*

George Clooney is one of today's most recognized eligible bachelors. And like most eternal bachelors, he has one distinctive trait that separates him from a world of commonality: He's never found a girl who moved him enough to answer Beyoncé's call to "put a ring on it." Oddly enough, it's the same trait that can link the members of a list filled with philosophers, artists, political leaders, media personalities, and scientists. Whether they didn't see the point, were too focused on other goals, or simply weren't the marrying kind, one thing is for certain: The noteworthy men on this list are just as famous for what they did as for what they didn't—which is get hitched, of course!

## In Love with the Arts

While Clooney may be the most recognizable solo act today, he is by no means a pioneer of avoiding a wedding. Dating back to the 15th century, Michelangelo made it distinguishingly obvious that his work, which includes some of the most renowned masterpieces in history, was all the fulfillment he needed. Instead of marrying a woman who would bear him a great brood, Michelangelo painted, sculpted, engineered, and crafted his offspring all on his own, as he considered each piece one of his children.

This poetic attachment to art could also be the reason behind why men like Sir Joshua Reynolds, an influential painter who was among the founders of the Royal Academy, and Henri de Toulouse-Latrec, a provocative French post-impressionist, never married. One might even consider it to be a theme in the art world, as Vincent van Gogh—famed for his vibrantly colored, emotion-inducing works—also chose to never get on one knee for a lady. (This may or may not have also been affected by his bouts of anxiety, mental illness, and ear chopping—just a thought.)

# Married to the Job

Regardless of the reason, however, it seems many influential bachelors are often times more defined by their love of work, than their love of family. Take for instance, Sir Isaac Newton, considered by many to be one of the most influential men in history; Ludwig van Beethoven, a brilliant German composer and pianist; and Blaise Pascal, both a physicist and philosopher—they were all famous for throwing themselves into their work. Marriage must seem insignificant when compared to discovering gravity or composing, conducting, and performing some of the world's most powerful music…while deaf.

No matter what, there seems to be a definite correlation between a man's ability to plunge headfirst into work but not down the aisle. Even in the political world, where politicians are generally depicted with a picturesque family, there are a number of men who have vetoed marriage. President James Buchanan remains the only U.S. president to come out of Pennsylvania and the only one to never get married. But he's not the only man in the political sphere to shun marriage! Among some of the other politically involved men who populate Single Town are Ralph Nader, a political activist who's made a name for himself running for president, and Ed Koch, U.S. congressman and former mayor of New York City.

## Acting Alone

It seems every walk of life has a laundry list of bachelors, but none is more notable than the one George Clooney represents—the entertainment world. Fellow actor and multiple Academy Award winner Al Pacino ranks near the top of the list of men who have never married, and he and Clooney keep company with many others like them, from comedian and television host Bill Maher to filmmaker and actor John Waters. And don't forget '80s pop icon, Billy Idol. Apparently, for him, it was NOT "a nice day for a white wedding."

# No Longer a Human Sanctity

*"If you love (fill in the blank) so much, why don't you marry it?!"*

Suffering from a disorder commonly referred to as objectum-sexuality, or OS, Amy Wolfe of Pennsylvania found comfort in marrying an object rather than a human. Yes. Really.

## I Eija, Take Thee Wall . . .

OS was brought to the forefront in the late '70s when Eija-Riitta Berliner-Mauer, a woman from Liden, Sweden, married the Berlin Wall. Because people with OS often express strong feelings of love, passion, attraction, and commitment toward manmade structures, they find it natural to bind themselves eternally to them.

Berliner-Mauer even speaks of the Berlin Wall as any other woman would her own husband. Using terms like "we" and "our," she asserts that neither she nor her now "retired" husband (wall) like to travel and are still as much in love today as the first day they met.

## The Ride of Her Life

Wolfe, the most recent known OS case—who appropriately changed her surname to Weber, after the manufacturer of her main squeeze—began courting her love, an 80-foot gondola ride called 1001 Nachts, when she was 13 years old. Claiming she was instantaneously attracted to "him," her love for 1001 Nachts has motivated her to take him "for a spin" over 3,000 times and painstakingly make the 160-mile round trip to visit him at least ten times annually.

Against all odds (and several judgmental critics), Wolfe stands by her "man," declaring to share a relationship that is both physically and spiritually fulfilling. She doesn't even get angry when other people ride him!

# Love Weddings?

❧ ❧ ❧ ❧

*People are always going to fall in love and want to get married. And you, the budding "wedtrepreneur," can capitalize on that. Is one of these wedding industry roles right for you?*

## Caterer

Experience is key. Consider working for an established caterer or a hotel banquet service before going out on your own. If you're serious about your kitchen skills and have high culinary ambitions, attend a culinary school. You must learn to be not only a good cook (for hundreds of people), but a good planner, organizer, and supervisor.

Once you've put in your time learning the trade, gather your tools and start building your clientele. Depending on your start-up budget, you may need to rent certain items like dishes and linens, but you'll want to invest in the right cookware and serving items. Brides will expect you to offer tastings, sample menus, pricing sheets, and customizable options. A caterer needs a large van for delivering the food, and this can be tricky when you consider how and where the food needs to be prepared, stored, transported, and served. It's a competitive business, so you'll want to develop unique menus and learn the nuances of serving formal meals. Plan for the unexpected!

## Disc Jockey

You may already know you need to keep the music fresh, but being a wedding DJ isn't the same as spinnin' at a nightclub; it takes a wide variety of music for an array of age groups. It's important to know the sentimental father/daughter dance songs and the silly group dances like the Macarena, the Hokey Pokey, the YMCA, and the Chicken Dance.

Part of your job is to lure people onto the dance floor, so monitor the crowd for their reactions to each song. If the song is a dud, it's okay to fade it out and launch into something that will be more of a crowd-pleaser. This is where taking a course in radio production might be helpful. That way, you can learn about fading, mixing, lights, and other "board skills."

Finally, rehearse some funny stories or jokes. It's even better if they can be personal (but not embarrassing) stories about the couple or a member of the wedding party. You may think your job is just to click "play," but you will need to develop an energetic, entertaining personality in order to engage the crowd and aid transitions from toasts to dances to announcements.

## Photographer

If you are starting out as an amateur, take a photography course or get some on-site experience by tagging along with a professional. You'll need to invest in quality photographic equipment, too. Here are the basics: a quality camera, a good flash, lighting equipment, lots of batteries, and plenty of memory cards. There is no bigger nightmare for wedding photography than having your camera go dead or filling up a memory card—*before* the festivities end.

Plan to use a wide-angle lens for group and interior shots and a longer lens for candid and individual shots. If you can afford a second camera, it will save time to switch between cameras rather than changing lenses.

Showing up with a bag full of equipment isn't enough. You should prepare for the shoot in advance. Visit the venue ahead of time. You may even want to visit at the time of day when the wedding will take place so that you'll know how outside light will affect your shoot.

Also, help the couple make a list of the photos they want. This can be painstaking but will save a lot of miscommunication on the wedding day—as well as hurt feelings when the proofs are making the family rounds. You may want to give them a list of "stock poses" that are popular with most couples: close-up of rings, family groups, bride and groom kissing, etc.

## Coordinator/Consultant

A wedding coordinator helps a bride find the best people in all of the above categories (and more!) and coordinates the wedding vendors on her behalf. The coordinator may negotiate with any of these individuals for different terms or simply communicate changes in plans. He or she helps the bride avoid the pitfalls of wedding planning and helps her achieve her vision for the wedding day.

As a wedding coordinator, you are the "go to" person on the day of the event: marketer, mercenary, designer, decorator, director, stage manager, cheerleader, counselor, and confidante all rolled into one. Your role is so multifaceted and depends so much on the bride and groom's needs and lifestyle that an entire chapter could be written about the job of the wedding consultant alone.

## Best Practices

Regardless of which of these wedding-related gigs appeals to you, there are some common business practices you should adopt.

For example, determine how to organize and structure your business. Find out if any licenses or certifications are required or would give you added credibility. Find out what tax laws apply to you and deduct or save appropriately. Consult an attorney for help in drafting a contract that clients will sign to secure your services. Although you don't need a college degree for any of these wedding industry jobs, it would be wise to take a few business classes.

Set up an email account solely for your business and consider a Web site to help you launch your business. Make marketing materials: business cards, brochures, flyers. Take these to community bulletin boards, bridal shops—any place a bride might spot them.

Try to build relationships with other bridal industry businesses in your area. Word-of-mouth referrals are an easy (and inexpensive!) way to build business. Restaurants, hotels, dress shops, other wedding vendors, and the local chamber of commerce are all good contacts. If possible, try to partner with other businesses that provide similar services but don't directly compete with you. There's power in cross-promotion! Bridal shows and bridal publications are another wonderful way to display your business and reach brides en masse.

# Once Wasn't Enough

*These famous serial spouses married their way into infamy.*

When famous couples wed, their stories are as apt to end in infamy as they are with "happily ever after." Unless they give marriage another go-round, that is. These celebrity paramours managed to marry the same person twice—with a divorce in between.

But why would a celeb marry an ex-spouse again? It may depend on the reasons they divorced in the first place. Becoming older and "wiser" may have revealed new insight into problems that once plagued them as a couple. From this new, more sophisticated perspective, they value the good parts of the relationship and can make a commitment to managing conflict in a more healthful way. Or it could just be the amazing makeup sex.

## Richard Burton and Elizabeth Taylor

This couple tops the list of twice-married celebs. Movie-star-turned-fragrance-maven Elizabeth Taylor got married eight times, twice to Richard Burton. Sixteen months after their first divorce, they tied the knot again. That marriage was about as short-lived as the divorce, lasting less than a year.

## Don Johnson and Melanie Griffith

Melanie Griffith and Don Johnson said Las Vegas "I do's" when she was only 18 years old. The two divorced, and Melanie moved on to marry Steven Bauer. When drug and alcohol addiction overwhelmed her career, she and Bauer divorced—Melanie turned to Don for support. They reconciled, wed again, and—you guessed it—divorced again.

## Marshall Mathers and Kim Scott

Troubled shock-rapper Marshall Mathers (whose stage name is Eminem) married high school sweetheart Kim Scott after an on-again/off-again relationship that spanned a decade. The marriage came to an end after Scott attempted suicide and then sued her husband for depicting her violent death in one of his songs. As if that wasn't enough drama, they remarried five years later—but divorced within a year.

## Travis Barker and Shanna Moakler

Former Blink-182 drummer Travis Barker and beauty queen Shanna Moakler turned their volatile relationship into a reality television show on *Meet the Barkers*. The two filed for divorce in 2006 (it was finalized in 2008), but when Travis was injured in a plane crash, Shanna ran to his bedside. In subsequent interviews, Shanna revealed the fiery crash reignited their affections: "We would like to renew our vows and have another wedding. When you almost lose a loved one, it makes you appreciate things you took for granted." To date, however, official nuptials have yet to take place.

## Steven Crane and Lana Turner

Apparently, the postman isn't the only one who rings twice! Seven-times-wed actress Lana Turner wed second husband Steven Crane twice. Why? Their first marriage was annulled in a shocking paper-work snafu. Turns out, Crane's divorce from an earlier wife wasn't the real deal.

## Robert Wagner and Natalie Wood

Academy Award–winning actress Natalie Wood rose to fame as a teen, starring in plays and movies such as *Miracle on 34th Street*, *West Side Story*, and *Rebel Without a Cause*. Apparently, she found *Love with the Proper Stranger* twice in husband Robert Wagner. Although Wood—like many other Hollywood starlets—has multiple marriages to her credit, her last marriage didn't end in divorce but rather at the time of her accidental drowning at age 43.

# A Mardi Gras Wedding

*For some people, the wild freedom of Mardi Gras lends itself to a wedding celebration. They're both essentially big parties, after all.*

## What Mardi Gras Means

Though it falls on a different day each year, *Mardi Gras,* French for "Fat Tuesday," happens anywhere between February 3 and March 9. The day—and the party—gets its name because of its

proximity to the fasting that begins the next day, the first day of Lent. On "Fat Tuesday," Roman Catholics who observe what is called the "Carnival" tradition drink, make merry, and eat lots of high-calorie foods in preparation for Ash Wednesday and the days that follow, which are supposed to be more on the solemn, reflective, and restrictive side.

Mardi Gras traditions came to North America by way of a pair of French Catholic brothers, Pierre Le Moyne, Sieur d'Iberville and Jean-Baptiste Le Moyne, Sieur de Bienville, who arrived in what is now Louisiana in the late 1600s. They set up camp about 60 miles from where New Orleans is today, and years later, a full-on Mardi Gras tradition had begun among the French settlers in Mobile, Alabama, Biloxi, and New Orleans. When New Orleans was made the state capital in 1723, the Carnival party moved there and has come to be closely associated with New Orleans and the French Quarter, a section of the city with particularly rich Creole culture.

## Mardi Gras Style

Mardi Gras, New Orleans–style, is an explosion of color, but the official colors are gold, green, and purple. This goes back to tradition, but most revelers just like the way the colors look together. Any Mardi Gras–themed wedding should incorporate these colors: Bridesmaids can wear purple dresses with gold sashes, for example, and the guys can sport green cummerbunds and ties.

Beads, masks, and doubloons (large, colored coins) are must-have Mardi Gras accessories. Brides that have organized Mardi Gras–themed weddings have chosen to incorporate these festive touches in various ways, e.g., handing out beads to guests at the reception, using masks to serve as table numbers, giving doubloons as favors, and so forth.

## Dinner and Dessert, the Carnival Way

Creole cooking has a worldwide reputation. The flavors, techniques, and recipes that come from the area are like no other—it's no doubt your wedding guests will be thrilled to know they'll be eating Cajun-style on your big day. A dish such as jambalaya, a traditional Cajun stew made with crawfish and sausage, is great for feeding a big group, as well as shrimp Creole, gumbo, fried catfish, and dirty rice—all dishes made for Mardi Gras each year.

A place to truly exhibit the Carnival tradition is with your cake, however. The "king cake" is a presence at pre-Lent festivities around the world, and New Orleans is no different. King cake is a type of breadlike cake, similar to a cinnamon roll. It's usually braided and deep fried, like a donut. Within the cake is placed a charm, and tradition says that whoever finds the charm has to make the cake the next year. While you might want something a little more dramatic, elements of the king cake can be used, such as hiding charms throughout the cake; using gold, purple, and green sugars to dust the cake; and/or opting for a cinnamon flavor.

## Two Tickets to New Orleans, Please

While a Mardi Gras wedding nearly plans itself in terms of color scheme, menu, and general tone, you could choose to have your Mardi Gras wedding *at* Mardi Gras. Each year, hundreds of couples get married in "the Big Easy," and many of them choose to schedule their wedding during the city's biggest day of the year.

Packages are available through travel agencies, and some hotels offer newlywed specials. You can get married on a boat, in one of the hundreds of churches in the city, even on the fly during the parade. However the vows happen, you and your new spouse being stars at Mardi Gras is just one more reason to celebrate.

# Shining Light on Some Bright (and Dim) Situations

*Whether a person is willing to admit it or not,
the fact still remains that reality television is one of the most
successful forums ever brought into production. Though millions
would never say out loud that they give into this guilty pleasure,
there's no denying the popularity of something with millions of
viewers and growing numbers of cultlike, fanatical fans every week.
This most certainly rings true with wedding reality shows.*

From *Bridezillas* and *Platinum Weddings* to *Say Yes to the Dress* and *Bulging Brides,* here's a list of some of the more outrageous reasons people are tuning in to reality wedding TV:

- *Say Yes to the Dress:* Set in Manhattan's famed Kleinfeld Bridal Salon, this wedding wonder features 35,000 square feet of bridal dresses and hot messes. Between all the variables (i.e., differing consultant opinions, wide-ranging budgets, entourage sizes, and bride-to-be styles), *Say Yes to the Dress* is the ideal setup for beautiful gowns and crazy personalities to clash. While some stories will easily tug at one's heartstrings and end with big smiles, they are juxtaposed with just as many jerks and quirks…ahhh, bridal magic.

- *Bridezillas:* A true gem of wedded reality, this unfortunate display of brides-to-be often leaves viewers wondering why the soon-to-be grooms ever got down on one knee in the first place. Filled with raging "I'm pregnant with octuplets" hormones and fueled by a severe case of "It's all about me!" mentality, bridezillas are a breed all their own. While the first couple seasons all had happily-ever-after endings for the bridal brats and unhappily-ever-after endings for just about everyone else, the next few might just show the winds changing. Hmm, could Alice Cooper be right? Is it time for "No more Mr. Nice Guy"!?

- *Whose Wedding Is It Anyway?:* This reality show pairs wedding planners with prenuptial couples looking to create the wedding day of their dreams. With a wide range of budgets and per-  sonalities to mix and mingle, the show discloses what can only be described as a power struggle between the forces of good and evil. Of course, who is good and who is evil is strictly left up to the viewer, but one thing is for cer- tain: While there may be no definitive answer to who's right and who's wrong, there will always be strong rebuttals on both sides supporting their cause.

- *Platinum Weddings:* Talk about living in the lap of luxury—the brides featured on this show give definition to all things haute couture, creatively custom, and drop-dead dramatic. Because bud- gets are never an issue, the couples on this show only know one speed (warp) and one end result (over the top), and no matter how bad a person is with numbers, it doesn't take a math wizard to see just how lavish an event can become when money is no object.

- *Bulging Brides:* As its name would suggest, this reality show is all about brides trying to shape up, trim down, and *squeeeeze* in to look more fabulous than ever on their Mrs. debut. Like most ladies planning a wedding (heck, ladies in general), the girls featured on this show struggle with weight gain and willpower throughout the wedding planning process. So *Bulging Brides* teams them up with a personal trainer and nutritionist for six weeks of true grin-and- bear-it workouts, meal plans, and rules in hopes that they will look and feel just the way they always dreamed.

- *Four Weddings:* Get the score cards ready, ladies, for this series has four brides—along with their grooms and their entire wedding package—set up on the chopping block. Each bride is responsible for judging the other three brides' big days and concentrates on four main areas: the dress, the venue, the food, and the overall experience, with only one being crowned the top bride. And to the victor go the spoils: The bride with the best overall score wins a dream honeymoon for her and her new hubby to enjoy for free!

# Shower Games!

❦ ❦ ❦ ❦

*No bridal shower would be complete without at least one or two group activities. There are countless games to choose from, and you can put your own unique spin on each. Prizes for winners can include beauty products, tickets to a play or movie, or anything else that you'd like to win yourself!*

## Two Truths and a Lie

This game is great for a group of people who may not know each other very well. Each guest says her name and three things about herself. Two of the things she tells should be true and one should be false. The other guests then try to figure out what was untrue. There aren't prizes in this game; it's just a great icebreaker.

## The Bride/Groom Quiz

Most showers you'll attend will use this game in some form or another. The maid of honor and bridesmaids get together before the shower and create questions regarding the bride, her fiancé, or both. For example, "What is Tricia's favorite food?" "Where did Tricia meet John?" "When did Tricia and John get engaged?" Then at the shower, the quizzes are passed out to the guests. The person with the highest number of right answers wins.

## Bridal Bingo

This is a simple wedding twist on the tra-ditional bingo game. Each guest gets her own bingo card with words like "engage-ment ring," "honeymoon," or "union" in boxes on her card. The bride has these words on slips of paper in a fish bowl or hat and draws them one at a time, announcing to the group what she draws. Players mark off the words on their individual cards until someone has a bingo (five words in a consecutive line across, up, or in a diagonal row).

## Word Games

Any word game can be fitted to a shower: Crossword puzzles, word scrambles, acrostics, and "hangman"-type games using wedding-related words can all work well. (Tip: Try personalizing these games using words specific to you, your bridesmaids, your guests, and your wedding, e.g., the name of the bakery where you're getting your cake, your colors, your mother-in-law's home state, etc.)

## Bridal Pictionary

This game is played like traditional Pictionary, but with wedding-related words and phrases. The key is to get as creative as possible with the words and phrases that must be drawn and then guessed by the teams. Good examples of marriage-themed (and fairly challenging) words and phrases might be: bridezilla, runaway bride, tying the knot, to have and to hold, and commitment.

## Arts and Crafts

For the bride or bridal party that just can't get too excited about formal games, an arts and crafts table is a big hit. Set aside time at the shower, or just let guests drift to the table naturally, and encourage everyone to get creative. They can make an ornament for a "wedding tree" as a gift to the bride; they can make cards for mothers, aunts, or any other special woman in their lives; or you can provide lanyard- or jewelry-making supplies and let the guests keep their creations. Whatever they make, guests will talk about a shower that involves arts and crafts for a long time to come.

## Poetry in Motion/Marriage

Another idea for the bride who's not necessarily interested in formal games is a poetry reading. Each guest is asked to bring a verse or two that speaks to them regarding love, commitment, relationships, or marriage. Each guest then reads her verse aloud at the shower. This literary spin can make everyone feel like they've spent the afternoon using their heads as well as their hearts.

# Mrs. X

❧ ❧ ❧ ❧

*In many Western industrialized countries,*
*the matter of whether or not a woman should take her husband's*
*last name when she gets married is debatable.*
*(And you thought picking out bridesmaids dresses was tough.)*

## Father Knows Best?

For centuries, cultures far and wide have generally accepted that when a man and a woman get married, the woman assumes her husband's surname. The reasons for the custom are based in various (often unspoken) cultural beliefs, e.g., the importance of preserving the male bloodline, establishing the male as the dominant figure in the relationship, keeping things simple, etc.

Then feminism came along. Though there were women working for equal rights prior to this period, when women were granted the right to vote in 1920, the growing dialogue regarding male-female equality could not be quieted. One of the many conversations that sparked among women had to do with the custom of changing one's name. Women began to ask why they had to drop their identity in favor of their husband's just because they chose to marry.

## I Am What I Am: Not Changing Your Name

The reasons why some women choose not to take their husband's name after marriage are numerous. Some feel that they will lose a piece of themselves by surrendering the name they were born with; others believe their name won't sound or look particularly good, or might even be downright silly, i.e., "Jane Brown" becoming a "Jane Jaines." Some women simply prefer their name, while others are professionally recognized before they marry and worry that changing their name would be detrimental to the career they've worked so hard to build.

Options for these women have grown and become more acceptable over the years. A woman can choose to hyphenate her maiden name with her husband's. She may choose to adopt her husband's last name but make her maiden name her middle name and then go by the new, comprehensive full name. Some women stay with their maiden name professionally, but legally change their name for tax and medical purposes, for example. However it sounds good to you will do just fine, if you're not inclined to change your name when you wed.

## The Case for Change

There are strong cases for changing your name, however. If you and your husband choose to have children, having one name makes life a lot easier for them. Indeed, *your* life becomes a bit more complicated when you have two last names, too: It's hard for people to know how to list you alphabetically, and you'll find you'll have to spell and respell your name over the phone when doing business with people who don't know you personally. Other women have indicated that taking their husband's name is just trading one male name for another, so you might as well go with the flow, right?

It's important to point out that there are some women who can't wait to change their last names. Many marrying women look forward to the day they can go to the courthouse and sign their old name away. They may see it as an act of love and commitment to their new husbands, or maybe they actually dislike their maiden name.

## Alternative Ways of Solving the Name Game

There have been cases where a man, in a very progressive act, has taken his wife's name or at least adopted her maiden name as his middle name. Some couples will choose to use the husband's name but name a child after the wife's.

Over the past few decades, couples have also begun to combine both their names into a new name. Susan Alexander and Bill Ross might become the Rexes, for example, or perhaps the Andeross family. This allows both husband and wife to feel like a team in the whole name game, though it may be hard for families who feel a strong connection to their birth names. Like anything in marriage, it's a compromise.

# *Something Old: Saving the Top Tier*

*Most people have a few mysterious, unidentifiable things in their freezer. And if it belongs to a newlywed couple, you can be pretty sure that one of those tinfoil lumps is wedding cake.*

Saving the top tier of the wedding cake is a tradition that traces its roots to Europe in the late 19th century. 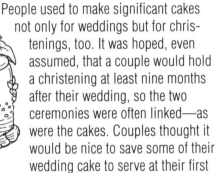 People used to make significant cakes not only for weddings but for christenings, too. It was hoped, even assumed, that a couple would hold a christening at least nine months after their wedding, so the two ceremonies were often linked—as were the cakes. Couples thought it would be nice to save some of their wedding cake to serve at their first christening, coming full circle on the whole "commitment" thing.

This trend resulted in the cakes themselves changing a bit; tiered wedding cakes became logical. The bottom tier was for the party, the middle tier was for giving away to guests, and the top tier was to save for later. It helped that wedding cakes back then were often brandy-soaked, fruitcakelike affairs that lent themselves to preserving for long periods of time.

## Times Change, Traditions Remain (for Better or Worse)

Over the past 100 years or so, the length of time between the wedding day and the christening or baptizing of a couple's first child has gradually gotten longer, so the two events have become less connected. People still save the top tier, but the reason for doing so has shifted. Nowadays, most couples want to save cake to enjoy on their one-year anniversary, simply as a reminder of their special day.

The question of whether or not this actually makes sense has been under debate over the past few years, however. It's a nice idea, but in reality, modern wedding cakes won't last in a freezer much longer than three months. Today's wedding cakes are made with buttercream, lots of eggs and sugar, chocolates, fruit fillings, and nuts—ingredients that simply don't freeze well in the long-term. It's not good news for the couple that wants to save their cake…but sometimes a frozen block of goo is a frozen block of goo—even if it has sentimental value.

## But I Love Stale, Waxy Cake!

If you still want to save your top tier (or just a slice) of your wedding cake, no one is going to stop you. You probably paid dearly for it, the trend is still popular, and it *is* cake, after all. If you do attempt it, however, there are important steps to take.

Well before your reception, find a plastic container big enough to fit the top tier with an airtight lid. Make sure your caterer or reception hall manager has this container and your instructions ready. As soon as the cake is cut, the top tier or slice should be put into the container, then put into a fridge as soon as possible—time is of the essence. Ideally, not much time would pass between that stage and the freezing stage, which involves wrapping the container itself in tinfoil and hoping for the best.

## Have Your Cake and Eat It Too

A memorable one-year wedding anniversary isn't going to hinge on whether or not you get to savor the exact cake you ate one year earlier. But if having that flavor is important to you, there are other ways you can create it.

Most bakers save recipes or use the same ones again and again, so ask your baker if he or she can create a fresh, mini-version of your wedding cake on your anniversary. (It is guaranteed to taste better than last year's.) You could also try baking your own version or, perhaps most fun of all, discovering a new dessert or kind of cake that becomes your yearly anniversary tradition.

# Kissing Cousins

❧ ❧ ❧ ❧

*Incest is best? Marriage between first cousins is legal in Europe, Canada, Mexico, and many of the United States. Yet the concept carries an unconventional—and icky—connotation in mainstream perception. Nonetheless, some independent-thinking historical, as well as modern, figures did not let mainstream perception stop them from romancing relatives.*

## The Tell-Tale Heart

Macabre writer-poet Edgar Allan Poe is best known for penning harrowing stories such as *The Pit and the Pendulum* and *The Fall of the House of Usher.* But in his private life, Poe fell in love with his cousin, Virginia Clemm. On May 16, 1836, a 27-year-old Edgar married 13-year-old Virginia in a small ceremony officiated by the Reverend Amasa Converse, a Presbyterian minister and the editor of the *Southern Religious Telegraph.* They remained together until Virginia succumbed to an agonizing death from tuberculosis in 1847. By all accounts, the relationship was loving and devoted. An unorthodox pairing, but sometimes the Tell-Tale Heart wants what the Tell-Tale Heart wants, to paraphrase Woody Allen (another mad genius known for his personal scandal of boundary-crossing familial love).

## The Theory of Relativity

The Father of Modern Physics, Albert Einstein, decided to keep it in the family when he took a second wife. He was still legally married to his first wife, Mileva, when he moved in with his cousin (first cousin maternally and second cousin paternally)—and eventual second wife—Elsa.

# Survival of the Fittest?

The offspring of related parents have a higher risk of birth defects. So it's interesting that the founder of evolution, Charles Darwin, plucked from his own family tree to propagate. He married his mother's brother's daughter, Emma Wedgwood. Together, the first cousins wed and furthered the species with ten children.

# Presumed Incestuous

More recently, screen siren Greta Scacchi charmed men in the early 1990s in Hollywood hits such as *Presumed Innocent* and *The Player.* But she really set tongues wagging several years later when she became romantically linked with her first cousin, Carlo Mantegazza. Far from a brief forbidden fling, the taboo couple cohabited and remained committed for over a decade, even raising a son together.

# Not a New Deal

More than one of the United States' most illustrious presidents had a cousinly connection to his First Lady. Anna Eleanor Roosevelt (Roosevelt was her maiden name) added a second Roosevelt to her surname when she married her fifth cousin, once removed. Franklin D. Roosevelt met his future bride when they were children but was reintroduced at a dinner hosted by Eleanor's uncle (Teddy Roosevelt). They wed on St. Patrick's Day 1905.

Back in the founding days, second president of the United States John Adams was married to his third cousin, Abigail Smith. Following in the family footsteps, Adams's grandson, also named John, married his first cousin, Mary Catherine Hellen. The ceremony was held at the White House.

# "Once Removed"... Huh?

"Removed" refers to the generational difference between an individual and his cousin. Cousins of the same generation aren't "removed." "Once removed" means the cousin is one generation away (i.e., from his parents' generation). "Twice removed" signifies two generations, etc. For example, FDR's fifth cousin, once removed, shared his great-great-great-great grandparents (hence, fifth cousin) and was one generation away (aka once removed).

# Smooching Siblings

On *Arrested Development,* George Michael Bluth—played by the always über-awkward Michael Cera—pines for his first cousin Maeby Funke. The reoccurring social taboo provided guffaw fodder for three seasons. But the line between character/art and actor/real life becomes murky when people portraying family on-screen spark romance off-screen. Ewww or hmmm? Dating coworkers is common in any trade. For TV actors, coworkers are often portraying relatives. Get your flow chart ready—this can get confusing.

Dave Annable and Emily VanCamp were cast as half-sibs on the appropriately titled *Brothers & Sisters.* The two performers displayed palpable chemistry. So much so that rumors emerged that the two were dating in RL (Real Life). Soapy art imitated complicated life when the writers crafted a twist to reveal that VanCamp's father was actually not patriarch/adulterer/fruit-shilling businessman William Walker. No longer fictional-blood relations, the two characters were free to follow their tingly feelings and ultimately marry. Too bad RL Annable and VanCamp cooled off a couple seasons ago!

Michael C. Hall, deliciously dichotomous as serial killer with a conscience Dexter Morgan on *Dexter,* had his own RL double life. He secretly dated his costar, Jennifer Carpenter, who plays Dexter's (adoptive) sister, for a year and a half before they tied the knot on New Year's Eve 2008 in Big Sur, California.

Peter Krause allegedly started seeing his costar and fictional sibling on the show *Parenthood,* played by spunky *Gilmore Girls* alum Lauren Graham. Coincidentally, Peter Krause also played Michael C. Hall's on-screen brother on the show *Six Feet Under.* No, the bros did not hook up in RL.

And we won't even get into the behind-the-scenes sexual shenanigans that the siblings (and mother!) of *The Brady Bunch* were rumored to indulge in!

- *Former New York mayor Rudy Giuliani fell in love with and married his second cousin Regina. After 14 years together, the Catholic Church annulled the marriage.*

# The Marriage Ref

*For Jerry Seinfeld's* The Marriage Ref *(NBC), the format is as such: A quirky couple explains their beef via video clip. Host and "referee" Tom Papa and three celebrity panelists discuss the merits of each side, ask questions, and then Papa makes his ruling.*

## Bring in the Big Guns

Seinfeld called in favors to many of his A-list buddies to ensure appealing panelists with various marital viewpoints and expertise, such as Kelly Ripa, mother of three and multiple full-time job-juggler; Gwyneth Paltrow, who has successfully stayed married to a rock star; Demi Moore, who has successfully stayed married to a hottie 15 years her junior; and Alec Baldwin. . . who had one of the ugliest celebrity divorces in recent history. Come to think of it, however, he probably is quite qualified to comment on bickering spouses. Other celeb guests have included Bette Midler, Martin Short, Matthew Broderick, Martha Stewart, and Madonna.

## Settling the Score

What about the couples trying to settle their disputes (or gain their 15 minutes of fame)? The probing issues so far: Can a husband have a stripper pole in his bedroom? Can a husband have a urinal in the bathroom? Can a wife floss in bed? Should a couple move to Hollywood or Amish country? Is wifey right to prefer a clean house over affection? Each issue gets a verdict—to the delight of one spouse and to the chagrin of another. However, with unkind reviews and declining ratings, the future of *The Marriage Ref* may be shaky. Hopefully the marriages they've weighed in on fare a bit better.

# Putting the "Death" in "'Til Death Do Us Part"

*Feeling like the traditional wedding is as empty as your immortal soul? Not to worry, Child of Darkness! Your wedding can reflect your dark, tragically romantic outlook on life!*

## Go-Go-Gothic

What's understood as the "Goth" subculture in the world today has deep cultural roots. The term comes from a Germanic tribe known as the Goths, who eventually splintered off into different groups, one of which (the Visigoths) was known for its barbarism and successful overthrow of the Roman Empire in the 6th century. Ever since that happened, there's been some nostalgia for the medieval era in which the Goths thrived, especially concerning the clothing, romantic ideals, and art of the period.

Then in the 18th century, Horace Walpole published a novel called *The Castle of Otranto: A Gothic Love Story,* a tale full of love, murder, long dresses, death, and candles, among other things. From then on, the term "Goth" in popular culture came to be associated with horror, morbidity, and romance, as well as a healthy dose of camp and self-parody. Walpole's story inspired many of today's Goth touchstones, including the film *The Hunger* (1983), anything written by Anne Rice or Edgar Allan Poe, the band Dead Can Dance, and wearing black from head to toe.

Today, the Goth scene includes subcultures of its own. The scene is varied, but if you spot a girl wearing all black with black-rimmed eyes who has more than three piercings, a shock of pink through her hair, and a playlist including Siouxsie and the Banshees, you're probably in the presence of a Goth chick.

## Bride of Frankenstein, Baby!

To a full-fledged Goth gal, even the idea of a traditional white wedding may turn her stomach. If she's likely to feel more beautiful and happy in black lace with a chain running between her lip and her ear, then so be it. She can also choose to make the ceremony itself a little darker.

The invitations are the first idea guests will get that the wedding they'll be attending will be unique, so if you're throwing a Goth wedding, start there. Using deep purple or inky black invitations is going to send a clear message. You might try to find other ways to inform your guests of the tone of the party by putting spider stickers on the invite or including lines such as, "Join us for the "Til Death Do Us Part' part…" Be sure to use a creepy or dramatic font.

## The Ceremony Is About to Begin…

Goth weddings often happen in cemeteries if the weather's nice. If the wedding takes place during the colder months—which is favorable, due to the barren trees and dark skies—any place with lots of stained glass and old stone is good, like a historical church or mansion. If there's a haunted house around, even better.

As far as colors go, black is always going to be the foundation color of a Goth wedding. In this sense, these weddings have it made: Everything looks great with black. Bright fuchsia flowers, crimson sashes on the bridesmaids, grey ties for the guys—it all works. The cake is another great place to insert Goth style into the festivities: Cakes in the shapes of coffins, crosses, or roses are big hits, especially when the cake itself is blood red velvet.

Those deep into the Goth subculture aren't often particularly religious people, so it's likely that if you attend the marriage ceremony of a Goth couple, you'll hear vows penned by the couple itself, rather than traditional text. There are exceptions, of course, but don't be surprised if you hear poetry in place of a sermon or an excerpt from a graphic novel instead of the Bible.

Of course, any Goth wedding should go heavy on the candles and the incense during the ceremony and definitely at the reception. Just watch those open flames while you dance the night away with the creatures of darkness.

# Daughters-in-Law in Distress

*The tale of two mothers-in-law, as portrayed in*
2005's Monster-in-Law:
*Viola Fields (dressed in white to attend her own son's wedding):*
*I cannot believe she compared me to Gertrude*
*[Viola's mother-in-law]!*
*Ruby: I know. That's just wrong.*
*Viola Fields: Thank you!*
*Ruby: You are far worse. I don't recall Gertrude ever trying to*
*poison you, and I believe she wore black to your wedding.*
*Viola Fields: Black. Yeah, she said she was in mourning...*

Ah, yes. The age-old skirmish of Mama Drama as it directly relates to the most infamous mother ever—the in-law. As one of the world's most ancient and perilous battles, the type of combative behavior displayed between in-laws has fallen victim to more tragic trials, tribulations, and—let's face it—sheer comic genius than any other counterpart. And it's no wonder why.

Made famous by characters like Viola Fields (played by Jane Fonda) and Marie Barone (played by Doris Roberts) in *Everybody Loves Raymond,* mothers-in-law are typically portrayed in some of the most unflattering lights known to man. While the "glass-half-full" people of society may want to give these sad pot-stirrers the benefit of the doubt, they will inevitably be forced to face the factual information at hand.

## Mother-in-Law Hell

And the information is nothing new. Dating back centuries, the battle between mothers and daughters-in-law is one of the longest running "clash of the Titans" perils ever, and when Dr. Phil aired an episode of MIL vs. DIL battles waging into wars, it became apparent that this was no longer just a laughing matter. In the episode, which aired February 19, 2010, Dr. Phil featured Patricia Bachkoff-Weber, founder of MotherInLawHell.com and the DILS (Daughter-in-Law Sisterhood), and she shed some light on why in-laws are responsible for nearly 25 percent of divorces in the United States. That's right, people, 25 percent!

Bachkoff-Weber, like so many other daughters-in-law in her position, started off with a decent enough relationship with her mother-in-law, but as time progressed, she began to see changes that were small at first but got bigger. Bachkoff-Weber disclosed how she started to feel like "the other woman" in her husband's life and was constantly forced into positions that tested where her husband's loyalty really lay: with her or his mommy.

Seeking help from friends, family, online, and in books, Bachkoff-Weber never seemed to get the answers she wanted. Hence, an online star was born. She began MotherInLawHell.com to provide an outlet for "other women" like her with a much-needed platform of release. When she appeared on Dr. Phil, she brought one of these women with her, named Robin. Robin shared the story of her mother-in-law and the blatant disregard she has for health, happiness, and, apparently, Robin's own general well-being. After years of battling a smoking addiction, Robin was finally able to kick the habit. But instead of having the full support of her MIL, Robin reported: "She said if I didn't start losing the weight that I had gained from [quitting] smoking, she was going to have me pick up smoking again so I would lose it." WOW.

## Let It All Out

If ever there was an argument for people being born with little to no shame, much less tact, this Web site could be the number one witness. MotherInLawHell.com is made up of tens of thousands of women forming the Daughter-in-Law Sisterhood. It's the reality check a person needs when she starts to feel her mother-in-law is out of control, but compared with everyone else's MIL stories, she really may not be thaaaat bad. And it's a forum to put an MIL on blast when she actually really is. It's a site that will make people laugh or perhaps make them cry. It easily provides people with advice, an encouraging virtual shoulder to lean on, and a safe place to vent.

## Weddings 'Round the World
# Italian Wedding Customs

*Many of the wedding customs we observe in the United States trace their roots to Italy. Perhaps you can incorporate some of these* buone *ideas into your own wedding plans...*

### Doing as the Romans Did

From aqueducts to art, we still "do as the Romans do" in many ways, including the way we celebrate marriage. Pre-wedding banquets, gifts for the bride and groom, and the ring as a symbol of union are all Roman customs that have continued to this day. Most weddings were held in June, since they were forbidden during Advent or Lent, and August was so hot and sticky it was considered unlucky. Nuts and wheat were thrown over the newlyweds after the ceremony as a symbol for fertility, and everyone ate until they were stuffed.

Most Roman weddings were arranged by the parents, however, and a dowry was paid by the bride's father to the groom. A pig was sacrificed before the meal, and a parade from the church to the bride's new house ended in the bride smearing the doorposts with oil and fat. After that, she took to the bed, since ancient Romans were pretty clear that marriage was there for procreation.

### Italian Weddings Today

Of course, Italian wedding customs have evolved over the centuries. And since there are so many distinct regions of Italy, wedding protocol varies depending on where you are; Southern Italian weddings are generally bigger, showier events than the intimate weddings to the North. But the following are a few customs that you'll still find alive and well in many parts of Italy:

- On either side of the door of the church, a small olive tree is placed for good luck during the ceremony.

- No purple! Italians believe purple brings bad luck.

- Italian brides used to have a trousseau, or hope chest, full of linens and silk nightgowns passed down through the women in the family. Though it's less common to have a hope chest today, middle-class families will often give their daughter all the linen belonging to her mother or her grandmother on her big day.

- It's still popular to dance the "Tarantella," a lively group dance.

- *"Viva gli sposi!"* or "Long live the couple!" is shouted throughout the day and is usually followed by a toast.

- Guests at an Italian wedding get a small gift, called a *bomboniere.* The bomboniere are placed in a basket, and the bride walks around the tables, greeting well-wishers and giving out the gifts before the cutting of the cake.

- The bride and groom rarely have a bridal party; instead, they choose a witness.

## You Are Going to Talk About the Food, Right?

Maybe one of the biggest advantages of getting married Italian style is that you get to enjoy the food. Italian cuisine is known worldwide for being extraordinary—and always plentiful.

Appetizers, breads, pastas, soups, meat dishes, salads, fruits, and desserts will be in abundance at an Italian wedding. It's not unheard of to enjoy 12 or more courses during the reception. Coffee, espresso, sweet liqueurs for the women and harder stuff for the men, and, of course, wine flows freely and everyone is encouraged to eat, drink, and make merry in the name of the happy couple. Plates of fried dough, twisted into bow-tie shapes and covered with powdered sugar, are often served for luck.

Many people have enjoyed Italian wedding cake, a decadent white cake filled with coconut and topped with cream cheese frosting. This cake is so good, it's actually on the menu at some restaurants—one more example of just how influential the Italian wedding has become.

# A Walk Down the Aisle

*This ancient ritual still has a modern (but different) meaning.*

## Getting Paid to Give Her Away

How many heads of cattle do you think you're worth? How about chickens? What about acres of land? Fortunately, American women don't have to speculate about their personal value in terms of commodities, but there are many cultures where that is still the case when it comes to wedding planning. Marriages were once based on social and economic pragmatism rather than love or compatibility, and for centuries, a groom's family was expected to pay a "bride's price" before a wedding could take place. In this scenario, the groom's family was essentially reimbursing the bride's family for her lost labor. Their daughter would no longer be available to work and help support the family, and they required compensation for this. On the wedding day, the father of the bride would present his daughter to the groom and give her away, verbally acknowledging their compensatory agreement had been fulfilled and that her family of origin had no further claim to her.

From a contemporary point of view, it's hard to believe there was ever a time when a woman had so few rights and privileges that she didn't have the choice of whom to marry. Of course, the age-old tradition of "giving away" the bride is still popular—although no longer as a conveyance of property from father to husband.

## Making It Modern

While some progressive-thinking brides feel a father escorting his daughter down the aisle is a remnant of a patriarchal system that failed to recognize women as the equals of men, it doesn't have to be interpreted literally (or historically). Some brides may chafe at the "giving away" ritual as an artifact of arranged marriages, but modern brides can put their own spin on the idea.

Christian brides, for example, sometimes prefer to interpret the ritual as an expression of the Bible verse that describes how a man and woman will leave their families and "become one." The subtext in this case is that the bride and groom are giving up their old support systems—and their identities with their original families—in exchange for new ones.

Usually, the way this plays out is that the father of the bride walks his daughter down the aisle of the church or ceremony site. Once the bride and her father have arrived at the front of the room, he may lift up her veil and give her a kiss or hug. At this time, the father may take the groom's hand and place it with the bride's hand or simply step back, allowing the bride and groom to stand as a couple. For a modern twist, some brides have their mother accompany them down the aisle as well.

### "Who Gives this Woman to Be Married?"

Nowadays, it's not uncommon to hear a father respond to the above, '"Her mother and I do" or "We do." He may even reply, "She gives herself freely, with her family's blessing." Or, the parents may reply in unison. Some couples have taken the evolution further by having the question posed to both the bride's parents and the groom's, for a more egalitarian touch.

Although the origins of some traditional wedding practices may seem archaic and out of touch, remember: They can be adapted to fit your modern sensibilities and, most importantly, help define your new life as a couple. Having the father and/or mother "give the bride away" has come to mean something few brides would turn away from: That the people who raised her embrace her future husband and approve of the marriage. Just a little tinkering with the language, and any self-respecting bride can confidently start her wedding off with a traditional expression of her parents' support—and be ensured a tear-jerker moment!

# Wedding Announcements

*These married names say more than the sum of their parts.*

Many factors are taken into consideration as couples decide whether to keep, blend, or hyphenate their surnames: preservation of a family name, political beliefs, feminist values, professional identities, and more. But no matter how well intended, some name combinations are not a match made in heaven. Having one of the following odd-ball combos could doom you to a lifetime of constantly having to spell, explain, and put up with "Are you serious?" looks from colleagues, neighbors—and even your own family.

- Badde-Mann
- Beebe-Makar
- Berger-King
- Best-Freund
- Betten-Kind
- Bichen-Carr
- Bird-Hunter
- Bogg-Downe
- Brake-Fast
- Brick-Laer
- Bumm-Diehl
- Bumm-Rapp
- Crabb-Appel
- Darling-Valentine
- Dills-Pickle
- Dollor-Bett
- Doll-Fase
- Dudley-Downer
- Ferris-Wheeler
- Fisher-Mann
- Flower-Garton
- Flower-Mill
- Fuller-Bottom
- Gold-Fisch
- Gott-Milk
- Hare-Kutter
- Hotze-Duff
- Hunt-Peck
- Lacy-Bumm
- Lemon-Dropp
- Lyon-Heartt
- Macon-Bacon
- Mann-Slaughter
- Mash-Schupp
- Near-Farr
- Nutt-Endouin
- Pancake-Stack
- Pan-Frye
- Papa-Baer
- Picken-Finger
- Poore-Mies
- Poore-Yu
- Rose-Bloom
- Schlapp-Bottom
- Stock-Potts
- Storey-Ours
- Uder-Panak
- Wonder-Barr
- Wynnen-Hand

# Fun with Photo Booths

*With more and more couples looking to personalize their big day and create a greater interaction with their guests, photo booths have started springing up all over bridal radars and have no intention of bleeping out any time soon!*

## A Top Trend

Both trendy and unique, these picture staging arenas—ranging from the big and formal studio and employees to jimmy-rigged backdrops and Polaroid cameras—follow the contemporary notion that wedding trends are just as important as more formal traditions.

Because they double as a place to create everlasting memories as well as provide couples an outlet to add their own individual flare, photo booths don't have to follow any certain rules; hence, their mass appeal. They can be big or small; inside or outside; propped with costume supplies and white boards to write advice or nothing at all. They can be as formal as London during a Royal Wedding or as informal as tailgating on game day. Heck, photo booths don't even have to be booths at all. They can be the brick wall outside the church and Auntie Mildred with her digital glam cam. (Ha ha, good ol' Auntie Mildred!)

## The Booth for You Is Out There

It's up to the couple to decide, and with the wedding industry busting at the seams with different ideas, they won't have a hard time finding just what they're looking for. All it takes is one Google search or blog inquiry to find thousands of sources on this hot topic.

It's so hot, in fact, the mere discussion of providing a photo booth may just melt the dairy right out of all those "say cheese" smiles...and if that's not worth signing up for, what is?

# Weddings the Wiccan Way

*A Wiccan wedding, while not the norm, could be to your liking.*

Weddings are steeped in time-honored tradition—and yet there are few other events in life with so many opportunities for self-expression. For some brides and grooms, this self-expression goes deeper than matching the color of the bridesmaids' dresses to the flowers. These couples personalize their ceremony by adopting a theme that expresses their spiritual beliefs and values. In this case, a Wiccan wedding.

## Set the Scene Naturally

So how exactly does one throw a Wiccan or pagan wedding? Let's start with the basics: Nature is highly revered in the Wiccan and pagan religions, so ceremonies are often held outside, and pagan couples usually decorate the ritual area with an assortment and abundance of flowers. The altar should be arranged with two white candles, flower-scented incense, and a willow wand. (The willow tree, which frequently appears in folklore and mythology, is considered the tree of enchantment. It is sacred to poets and significant in the life cycles of birth and death. It takes its place on the altar as a sacred object just as a cross might be displayed at a Christian wedding.) Additionally, cakes and wine may be displayed on the altar to be shared at some point during the ritual.

The witnesses are usually arranged in a circle, either sitting or standing, depending on how long the ceremony will last. The priest or priestess may want to call attention to the symbolism of the circle as an object without beginning or end.

Some couples wear traditional, formal wedding garb (a long white dress and veil for the bride; tuxedo or suit for the groom), and other couples dress in Celtic attire. Fortunately, there are no rigorous rules governing dress code for a pagan or Wiccan wedding, so couples may dress as their tastes and climate dictates.

# The Ties that Bind

The priest or priestess invokes the beings of air, fire, water, and earth and directs the couple to remember the qualities their union should possess. (Scripts for a Wiccan service are easily found on various Web sites.) The couple may light a unity candle, as is done in traditional weddings, or incorporate other elements of non-pagan weddings if they choose.

Finally, the bride and groom cross arms and join hands, creating the infinity symbol. The clergyperson loosely wraps the couple's hands with a cord or ribbon, and they state their vows. Most of us are familiar with the symbolism of wedding rings, but in a pagan or Wiccan ceremony, a rope or cord is the primary symbol of unity. In the ceremony known as *handfasting,* the ritual of tying the bride's and groom's hands together, is the culminating act—on par with the exchanging of wedding rings. Handfasting can occur either as a marriage ceremony or as betrothal. Either way, this is where the phrases "tying the knot" and "the ties that bind" come from, as the bride and groom literally have their hands fastened together, signifying their formal contract to be husband and wife.

Centuries ago, handfasting was customary in Great Britain—especially in rural areas where weeks or months could pass before a clergyman happened to travel through your village. So, eager couples bypassed the need for clergy by clasping hands, publicly declaring themselves married, and consummating their bond. It was the ancient equivalent of today's common-law marriages. In modern Wiccan ceremonies, the cord is knotted, the union is blessed, and the couple is publicly presented to their family and friends. You will still need to obtain a marriage license for the ceremony to be considered legally binding. But some couples consider the public performance of the ceremonial act to be sufficient. Legalities aside, the pagan/Wiccan handfasting ceremony can be a beautiful and memorable way to literally and metaphorically tie the knot!

# Index

# Contributing Writers

**Laurie L. Dove** is a multiple-award-winning journalist and published author who writes about topics ranging from celebrity weddings to archaeological discoveries. A former publishing executive, Dove resides in Valley Center, Kansas, with her husband and four children—who never pass up an opportunity to dance at a wedding reception. Learn more at LaurieDove.com.

**Mary Fons-Misetic** is a Chicago-based professional freelance writer and performer. Her popular blog, PaperGirl, can be read at www.maryfons.com.

**Mary Kidwell,** a graduate of Indiana University, currently resides in Indiana where she makes a home close to family and friends. As the Internet Marketing Manager for an online bridal company, she had the lucky fortune of inside-track information while planning her 2009 wedding. She feels blessed to be married to the love of her life and surrounded by friends and family, who make every day a better one.

**Erika Cornstuble Koff** is a freelance writer who has worn many hats, from stand-up comic to public relations executive to copy editor. Originally from Lafayette, Indiana, Erika holds a BS in Speech from Northwestern University and an MA in Writing from DePaul University. She currently resides in suburban Chicago with her husband, Ben.

**Nina Konrad** earned a BA in Journalism at the University of Wisconsin-Milwaukee and was also a contributing writer on *Armchair Reader™: Packin' It in Wisconsin.* In her free time, Nina loves to host get-togethers and is a cutthroat party-gamer. Recently, she has developed an obsession with the TV program *Supernatural*—her dream gig would be to write for that show.

**Sue Sveum** is a Madison area author and freelance writer. A graduate of the University of Wisconsin-Madison, Sue still lives in Wisconsin with her husband, two children, and their golden retriever. This is the third *Armchair Reader™* that she has worked on.

With a hyperactive mind, a short attention span, and an insatiable curiosity, **Kelly Wingard** finds writing for *Armchair Reader™* to be a natural fit. While writing for this wedding-themed tome, she simultaneously was involved in nuptial plans for two of her adult children. Wingard lives in Decatur, Illinois, with her husband, Ken, a hand-me-down dog, and part-time-resident granddaughter, Ella.

**Kelly Wittmann** is the author or coauthor of eight nonfiction books for both adults and children. She lives in Chicago.